BLENDI FEVZIU is a journalist, based in Tirana. He was a co-founder of the *RD* (Democratic Renaissance) newspaper and presents the popular TV talk show *Opinion*. He has written several books in Albanian.

ROBERT ELSIE is an expert in the field of Albanian studies. He is the author of over ninety books, including *Albanian Literature: A Short History* and *A Biographical Dictionary of Albanian History* (both published by I.B.Tauris and the Centre for Albanian Studies).

MAJLINDA NISHKU is a London-based translator who taught English at the University of Tirana. Since 2000 she has been working as a freelance conference interpreter and translator for various international organisations.

'To understand Albania requires knowing the man who dominated the country with cruelty and charm for 41 years, the omnipotent "Uncle Enver". Here Blendi Fevziu brings the dictator's dramatic tale to life: his rise to power, his paranoid purges, and the impoverished country he left behind.'

Fred Abrahams, author of *Modern Albania: From Dictatorship to Democracy*

'Blendi Fevziu's work is extraordinary. Written like a crime novel, based on unparalleled access to once closed Albanian archives, the book is a must read for anyone who wants to understand communist Europe and how dictatorships get set up and eventually survive. Fevziu succeeds brilliantly in capturing the horrors of Hoxha's 41 years in power and brings to life many of the voices he silenced. Not only that, given the Hoxha legacy, Fevziu helps us better understand why... Albania's path to democracy is so difficult. This biography is a major achievement.'

Robert C. Austin, Munk School of Global Affairs, University of Toronto

'Blendi Fevziu's exhaustively researched and path-breaking book demolishes many myths surrounding Albanian dictator Enver Hoxha and offers insights into how Hoxha gained and consolidated power, and then abused his power to impose on his nation one of the most repressive and dictatorial communist regimes Europe had ever seen. The book offers a lucid examination of Hoxha's long tyrannical rule and contains dramatic details of the regime's brutality. Based on exhaustive research and recently declassified archival sources, Fevziu, a dispassionate chronicler, describes in great detail the terror and violence that Hoxha employed to maintain power, resorting to periodic purges of senior communist officials that had done so much to buttress his regime. This is a very useful book, especially in view of Albania's inability to come to terms with its traumatic, communist past and recent attempt to reappraise Hoxha's role, advancing an alternative narrative that extols Hoxha's World War II record and recasts him as a great leader. A superb and masterfully written book, Fevziu's *Enver Hoxha* is required reading for anyone interested in Albania's post-World War II troubled history and Hoxha's legacies.'

Elez Biberaj, author of *Albania in Transition: The Rocky Road to Democracy*

'Based on archival, oral, and published sources, Blendi Fevziu's *Enver Hoxha* provides a fascinating, compelling and realistic account of the life and times of Albania's unremittingly Stalinist dictator and the country he ruled with an iron hand for four decades. This book is a masterful combination of biography and history.'

Nicholas C. Pano, Professor Emeritus of History, Western Illinois University

Blendi Fevziu

ENVER HOXHA
THE IRON FIST OF ALBANIA

Edited and introduced by Robert Elsie

Translated by Majlinda Nishku

I.B.TAURIS
LONDON · NEW YORK

Published in 2016 by
I.B.Tauris & Co. Ltd
London • New York
www.ibtauris.com

Copyright © 2016 Blendi Fevziu
Copyright, editorial and Foreword © 2016 Robert Elsie
English translation copyright © Majlinda Nishku

ISBN: 978 1 78453 485 1
eISBN: 978 0 85772 908 8

A full CIP record for this book is available from the British Library
A full CIP record is available from the Library of Congress

Library of Congress Catalog Card Number: available

Text designed and typeset by Tetragon, London
Printed and bound in Sweden by ScandBook

Contents

List of Illustrations

1. The communist leaders arrive in Tirana on 28 November 1944 (Archives of the Centre for Albanian Studies, London).
2. Congress of the Democratic Front on 5 August 1945 (Archives of the Centre for Albanian Studies, London).
3. Portrait of Enver Hoxha, ca. 1945 (Archives of the Centre for Albanian Studies, London).
4. Enver Hoxha and jubilating party members, 1972 (Archives of the Centre for Albanian Studies, London).
5. Stalin and Enver Hoxha in Moscow (Archives of the Centre for Albanian Studies, London).
6. Enver Hoxha and the mostly aged members of the Politburo, on the occasion of the 7th Party Congress in November 1976 (Archives of the Centre for Albanian Studies, London).

Foreword

S talinism, that particularly sombre phase of Eastern European communism, came to an end in most of Eastern Europe with the death of Josef Stalin in 1953, or at least with the Khrushchev reforms that began in the Soviet Union in 1956. However, in one country – Albania – Stalinism survived unscathed until 1990.

The regime that the Albanian dictator Enver Hoxha (pronounced *hodja*) led from the time of the communist takeover in November 1944 until his death in April 1985, and that continued unabated under his successor Ramiz Alia until 1990, was severe indeed. Such was the reign of terror that no audible voice of opposition or dissent ever arose in the little Balkan state, a European country that was as isolated from the rest of the planet as North Korea is today.

When the Albanian communist system finally imploded and multi-party democracy was introduced in 1990–1, it left behind a weary population, frightened and confused after decades of purges and political terror. It also left behind a land with a sub-Saharan economy, a country where extreme poverty was the norm.

It has been over two decades since the communist regime in Albania came to an end. The people of Albania, who woke up to find themselves at the bottom of the barrel in European terms, have been struggling since that time to keep pace with the new world around them. In their struggle, they have not had much time to look back dispassionately and reflect on the man who dominated their lives for almost half a century. Yet the spectre of Enver Hoxha looms heavy over the land and most observers would agree that the

Albanians are still coping in one way or another with the after-effects of his regime.

Few Albanians today will have a good word to say about the man who was once their god, but what do they actually know about him? Some still have recollections of the public image, created by official propaganda at the time, of their supreme leader as a benevolent 'father Enver', and imagine that, in his isolation in the Bllok with no one daring to contradict him, he may perhaps not have known how dire the situation at the grass roots really was. Others curse him as the devil incarnate who was directly responsible for all of the regime's failings, yet they, too, have no precise idea of the role he played in the calamities that beset the nation during communism. Who was Enver Hoxha? Or are people still too frightened to ask? It is curious amidst all the speculation associated with his name that in the 25 years since the fall of the dictatorship, not one serious book has been published about Enver Hoxha. Until now.

In the early years of the new millennium, Tirana journalist and TV personality Blendi Fevziu began broadcasting a series of programmes on the communist dictatorship and on the life of Enver Hoxha, based on previously unpublished archival material and unseen film footage – revelations that shocked the nation. He also conducted exclusive interviews with leading personalities of the communist period who had known Enver Hoxha personally and who were now willing to talk. Investigative journalism at its best.

The material compiled by Fevziu for TV has now been transformed into the first biography of Enver Hoxha since the fall of the communist regime. The original, Albanian-language version of this book appeared on the market in October 2011 when it was presented with great success at the annual book fair in Tirana. It is safe to say that no book in the history of Albanian publishing has had such success. Everyone suddenly wanted to know who Enver Hoxha really was. Within the space of a few weeks, the biography went through five or six editions and the publishers could barely keep up with demand. Such was public reaction that the book was even burned at public protests in four or five Albanian cities. These protest meetings were organised by the few ageing supporters of the old regime or, more often than not, by confused nationalist circles in Kosovo and Albania who regarded an attack on Enver Hoxha as an attack on the Albanian nation.

This book, based on archival sources and on interviews with people who knew the dictator, traces the life of a man who ruled a European nation with an iron fist for 40 years, and whose cruelty cannot be justified by a lack of knowledge or by any legitimate requirements of the state.

After the success of the Albanian-language edition, it is now a pleasure to present the biography of Enver Hoxha to the international public. To assist the general reader, a brief chronology of Hoxha's life, a glossary of the principal figures mentioned in the book and a bibliography have been appended to the English edition. Whether copies of this volume will be burned in public, too, remains to be seen.

ROBERT ELSIE
BERLIN
NOVEMBER 2015

List of Abbreviations

CPA   Communist Party of Albania (from 1948 the Party of Labour of Albania)

CPSU Communist Party of the Soviet Union

CPY   Communist Party of Yugoslavia

NLA   National Liberation Army

PLA   Party of Labour of Albania (until 1948 the Communist Party of Albania)

UDBA Yugoslav secret service (Uprava državne bezbednosti armije)

Death Comes Knocking

8 April 1985. The nurse sprang to his feet at the insistent sound of the buzzer. It was only a short flight of stairs up to the room where the Albanian communist leader, Enver Hoxha, was sleeping, a rather unassuming chamber adjacent to his extensive library. Nexhmije Hoxha was standing there waiting for him, calm and composed, though with a certain alarm in her glance. A feeling of unease had been with her from the day her husband took to bed, when he was no longer able to leave the mansion in the exclusive quarter of town reserved for the members of the Politburo, the so-called Bllok (Block). Enver Hoxha sat there in the room, slumped in his armchair, his eyes – the only part of his body that still gave any sign of life – scanning his surroundings inquisitively. 'Comrade Enver wishes to go out into the garden.' Such, more or less, must have been the instructions she gave with a sense of urgency. Her relief was understandable.

It was the first time in many weeks that Enver Hoxha had asked to be taken out to the garden. Unable to walk, too exhausted to utter more than a few words at a time, and in a perpetual state of drowsiness, he had spent the long and unusually harsh winter housebound. On 11 January 1985, for the first time in many years, Tirana had woken up to a blanket of snow which had lingered in the empty streets of the capital for a whole week. The weather then turned much milder and, on that day, the radiant flowers and cheap gypsum statues of the garden were bathed in the warm rays of sunlight.

The nurse must have hastened to get the dictator ready for his outing, while Nexhmije went off to fetch a large pair of dark glasses to help protect his eyes from the glare of the sun. Exposure to daylight after spending such a long time indoors could damage his eyes. Not that his eyesight had been much good in the last few years. The world around him appeared blurry and faint, while the faces of his friends and family were nothing but silhouettes.

Sulo Gradeci, his loyal bodyguard, hovered around the small party, camera in hand. It was a Western camera that had just replaced an older one made in East Germany. Contrary to usual practice in the communist regime, the old camera, bought in 1962 complete with processing equipment, stemmed from a private individual, a certain Ismail Kadare, who had just returned from Moscow after graduating there. No one knew why Gradeci had long been reluctant to replace it with a more modern Western model – in all likelihood, ease of use and familiarity must have played an important role. From 1963 onwards, he filmed all the events in the life of the dictator and his close family. There were long sequences in which Hoxha appeared quite relaxed, with none of the carefully staged pomp that oozed from the official documentaries shown in cinemas and on TV. It was by pure coincidence that the recording made on the last day of Hoxha's life was not lost like many others. It was discovered 24 years later in the archives of the Communist Party of Albania (CPA), later called the Party of Labour of Albania (PLA). Studying this film after so many years makes the task of reconstructing Hoxha's last moments on 8 April 1985 even more mysterious.

Forty-one years from the day he came to power, Enver Hoxha was still at the top of the Albanian communist pyramid. In all these years he had never been more powerful, yet, at the same time, he had never been feebler or physically more vulnerable. Placed in a wheelchair and unable to walk on his own, he was being shown the garden of the mansion in the Bllok where he had lived since November 1944, from the day when he led his partisan forces into Tirana to form the new government.

He was now as pale as death itself and dishevelled strands of hair stuck out around his black beret. Death was at hand and Hoxha seemed to have sensed its presence. There was no doubt about it. Neither the regime he consolidated nor the adulation he demanded of others could save him. He was not the first tyrant to die and would not be the last. Death was the only tyrant he could not overcome. The Grim Reaper alone, indifferent to communism and capitalism, would not submit to the laws of his Marxism. In Malaparte's words: 'death reserved the same fate for Stalin as it did for Churchill and Roosevelt: a gravestone to rest under.'

Did Hoxha ever read Malaparte? Did he know that his own fantastic powers, which allowed him to keep the lives of 3.5 million people under tight control, were now effectively gone? Death was indifferent to him and would not do his bidding. He had no power to lock it up in one of the cells of the 39 prisons he had built in Albania, or to intern it in one of the 70 camps where people he believed to be his opponents spent their lives in isolation and misery.

Death was hovering behind him, breathing down his neck. Anyone watching these newly discovered film sequences will ask the obvious question: 'What is going through his mind at this moment?'

No one will ever know the answer. Not even Enver Hoxha himself. His ailments prevented him from uttering more than a few words at a time and from explaining himself. Or perhaps he simply refused to do so. Enver Hoxha departed from this world without leaving any final words, a single clear utterance.

Deep within his empty gaze lay the dilemmas and paranoia that had plagued him for 40-odd years. None of his old comrades were with him, none of the men with whom he had waged his initial political battles. Not one of them survived the four decades of his rule. Some of them had died natural deaths, but most of them he had killed. They do not even have marked graves. Some minor figures were in fact still rotting in prison cells or internment camps. He did not even know where they were. Nor would he be able to find out whether they would outlive him. The thought must have tormented him. No doubt he knew that things were different now.

Enver Hoxha had no equals; he was the Alpha and the Omega; he was a man who imposed his own version of history. The 13 thick volumes of memoirs he published in the last seven years of his life were a testament to everything he did. They were written while he was still at the zenith of his power and were not subject to any revision whatsoever. They were to be accepted with unquestioned faith. These books paint the portrait of a man, but not of a real person, not what he was really like. They portray the man he would like to have been. He more than anyone else understood Wilde's words: 'No one is rich enough to buy back his past.' He was not a man of infinite wealth, but he was unquestionably powerful. Wealth was of no importance to him; it was power that gave him everything he needed. By deleting mistakes, erasing moments of weakness, airbrushing unwanted shadows and justifying executions as legitimate responses to hypothetical acts of high treason, these memoirs allowed him to be remembered as he wished to be. He appears strong, courageous and challenging in them. Yet the thousands of pages he left behind exude derision and sarcasm. And no one will ever have an opportunity to contradict him. His end is unlike that of any other dictator. No other tyrant took such care to preserve his legacy; no one ever wrote such memoirs. He was the first and, no doubt, will be the last. He was surely the only one to pen 7,000 pages dedicated to a single protagonist – himself.

Albania was in total isolation when he died. It was the third-poorest country in the world. After an insane age of extreme collectivisation, it suffered equally extreme poverty. The political class was out of touch with reality and had become totally incompetent. Virtually no one in the Politburo had ever had a higher education. Indeed it was something of a tradition in the CPA/PLA, a custom adhered to faithfully from 1944 to the end, that none of its leaders had a proper education. No one could boast a modest college diploma, not even Hoxha himself. In this, Albania was number one in the world. But he was not interested in such things. He did not live for the future, he lived for the past. He lived for what he believed was his era, an age he was now abandoning as a cripple in a wheelchair, half dead, yet stronger and more repressive than ever. He left behind a void, over which remain two vexing questions:

Who was the man who ruled Albania for half of its existence as an independent state?

What inspired him to become one of the most notorious dictators on earth, and to isolate his people from the rest of the planet?

History has not provided us with any answers to these questions, but the version of history that he tried to impose has fortunately not survived. It has vanished into thin air and been replaced by another story. This story thus begins with a man at the height of his power, an old man being called over into the kingdom of death on the sunny afternoon of 8 April 1985.

2

28 November 1944

A convoy of 12 cars and three trucks carrying Albania's new Provisional Government from Berat to Tirana left Elbasan in the early hours of the morning. Dawn had not yet broken, but a bright glow in the morning sky promised a beautiful autumn day. The weather had been glorious throughout the second half of November of 1944. A crowd of people had been waiting for hours in front of the curiously named Hotel Moderno, where the government had settled in for the night. Enthusiastic supporters, curious onlookers and activists had come there for one reason only – to get a glimpse of Albania's new 36-year-old prime minister. Presently the man himself appeared on the balcony and gave a euphoric speech. The crowd cheered and there was thunderous applause.

The government had set off from Berat on 27 November. At the head and tail of the convoy, a mix of vehicles of assorted makes and sizes, were two large trucks. They were carrying partisans from the special battalion in charge of providing security for the General Staff, a sort of improvised national guard that had been accompanying the government everywhere. Liri Belishova, the government envoy who had arrived in Tirana three days earlier, ensured that every metre of the route from Berat to Elbasan was secured by partisan forces.

Enver Hoxha was travelling in the fourth car – a Ford that had recently been confiscated from its one-time owner in Korça. In the car with him was Omer Nishani, chairman of the Anti-Fascist National Liberation Council. They did not pause anywhere en route except for a forced stop on the banks of the Shkumbin, near Rrogozhina. The old bridge there had been blown up and the prime minister and ministers of the Provisional Government had to use a raft to get across the river. To save time, a new convoy of cars awaited them on the other side. Enver Hoxha made himself comfortable in a Mercedes-Benz, which, but a few hours earlier, had been property of Ibrahim Biçakçiu, the outgoing prime minister of the collaborationist government and Hoxha's benefactor in the early years of the war.

The convoy did not use the shorter route which would have taken them to Kavaja, Durrës and then ultimately Tirana. Reportedly, they had received intelligence that the road was mined. There was, however, another reason the government was in no great hurry to get to Tirana. The plan was to make a grand entry in the capital on 28 November precisely, Albania's Independence Day. With this in mind, they turned towards Elbasan and spent the night at Hotel Moderno, the main hotel in town. It was the first time that armed guards of partisans had ever been placed at the main entrance and at the door of the room where the prime minister was to spend the night.

The next leg of the journey, from Elbasan to Tirana, took little more than two hours. The capital had been liberated. With the retreat of German forces 11 days earlier, a new Provisional Government had come to power and had delegated the task of running the capital to military commander Mehmet Shehu. The 31-year-old partisan commander had been educated at the American Vocational School in Tirana (also known as the Harry Fultz School) and had subsequently been expelled from a military academy in Naples for being a communist rowdy. He had taken an active part in the Spanish Civil War, where he had risen through the ranks to become commander of an international battalion of volunteers, consisting mostly of Italians.

As they were nearing Tirana, four motorcyclists of the National Liberation Army (NLA) joined the motorcade as a guard of honour in military parade formation. Shehu came out to greet the government at the roundabout near Sauk, a village on the outskirts of town. Right in the centre of the roundabout, a bullet-riddled and barely legible road sign pointed the way into the city.

Mehmet Shehu stood to attention and the guard of honour gave a shoulder-length salute to the new head of government, a tall and handsome young man all buttoned up in a fine dress uniform that bore the insignia of a colonel general. Contrary to what had been the partisan custom of the past three years, the prime minister did not embrace Mehmet Shehu, the commander whose forces had liberated Tirana, or any of the other senior figures who had come out to greet him. He simply acknowledged their presence with a clenched fist, saluted the guards and returned to his car. The convoy then set off towards the Royal Palace on the Sauk Hills, where the partisans had set up their General Staff.

Hoxha spent but a few minutes in the palace built by Francesco Jacomoni, the former Italian viceroy. It was his first visit to the opulent building but he did not seem particularly impressed. In fact, in his 41 years as supreme ruler of Albania he never spent a single night in the sumptuous and elegant edifice.

The convoy then continued towards Skanderbeg Square (named after Albania's national hero) and down the new boulevard that ran from the town centre to the rolling hills to the south of the capital. The boulevard was lined with ministerial buildings and somewhere near the halfway point was Hotel Dajti, a luxurious hotel built by the Italians. A podium for the parade had been erected on the road across from the hotel. At the southern end of the boulevard, near the Dopolavoro building, formations of partisan units had already fallen in, ready for the ceremony. They looked splendid with their shiny weapons and brand-new British uniforms. These men had emerged victorious from the war and were now eager to see who their commander was. Most of them had never had a chance to see him in person and only a few were able to recognise him from the photo on the pamphlets that had been distributed in August of that year.

The cars did not stop in front of Hotel Dajti but somewhere near the Italian legation, which a few days earlier had been the seat of the Regency. It is not known why they chose to stop there. They got out of the cars and continued on foot to the statue of General Tellini, then along Kaceli Street towards Skanderbeg Square. Hoxha instinctively stopped in front of the damaged minaret of the Et'hem Bey Mosque, allowing the feverishly clicking cameras to capture the moment. The propaganda chiefs had made sure that the government's grand entrance would be properly caught on photograph and film.

The party then continued towards Hotel Dajti. In the middle of the group and slightly ahead of the others walked Enver Hoxha, the man who had been elected head of government in the Congress of Përmet earlier in May. Although holding the rank of colonel general and chief of the General

Staff of the NLA, Hoxha was still relatively unknown. As a young politician with no ties to the old political class, he had not been in politics for long and, to many, his name did not mean anything. Throughout the war he had remained largely unknown, operating under nicknames such as 'Taras' (after Taras Bulba, the Russian protagonist of a very popular British film that played in Albania in the 1930s, starring Harry Baur, whom Hoxha was said to resemble) or 'Shpati' (after a mountainous area in central Albania where he went into hiding from the Germans). For a period of time he had been in hiding in Tirana, in the house of his sister and her husband, Bahri Omari. Only a handful of people could remember him from earlier times, when he worked at the Flora liquor and tobacco store owned by Ibrahim Biçakçiu, the collaborationist prime minister who had recently resigned and been thrown in jail. Hoxha and his friend Esat Dishnica, nephew of millionaire Biçakçiu, were relatively well-known characters in some circles in Korça, but in the capital things were different. Those who knew or had befriended this young man before the war had never noticed any particular propensity for politics in him. No one could explain what happened in the next three years, which metamorphosed the disinterested, dandy-like shopkeeper into a communist militant and political leader.

Of course, very few people were aware then that this young man of no obvious talents had already discovered his passion in life: politics. In less than three years this new-found ardour, coupled with an almost demonic quest for power and dominance, propelled him to the head of the Albanian communists and of the National Liberation Movement. He was to hold on to the reins of power and steer Albania through stormy seas for the next 41 years.

For most people used to prime ministers from influential families with long-standing political traditions, his name bore no weight whatsoever. With no university diploma to his name, with an inglorious career as a one-time substitute teacher at the *lycée* of Korça, and as the son of an average family from Gjirokastra whose only claim to fame was their close relations with Bahri Omari – an MP and staunch opponent of King Zog – Enver Hoxha was a complete nonentity.

In postwar Tirana, few people were inclined to take the new government seriously. In the last few months of the war, Albania had seen a number of prime ministers, some of whom had held the post for less than a day. But Hoxha had other plans – he was there to stay. He had groomed himself to become an imposing figure, leaving nothing to chance. Upon arrival in Tirana, the new prime minister clenched his fist to salute the commander of the partisan forces that had just liberated the town – no more hugs between comrades-in-arms – and proceeded straight to the centre of town. After an absence of about two years, he was now making a comeback as the most powerful man in the land.

Where did this new political leader come from? What sort of background did the man who was destined to run the country have? He was the figure who had led the so-called National Liberation War and had methodically eliminated all of his rivals and opponents, one by one, but what did he really stand for? What sort of abilities and talents would he, the 'man of hope', bring to the service of Albania's postwar recovery efforts?

For decades that followed, Enver Hoxha imposed his own terms on history. He unashamedly manipulated historical accounts and brushed aside or physically eliminated political rivals and witnesses to ensure his dominance as the one and only protagonist of Albanian history. Unlike other dictators, these calculated manipulations and eliminations were a feature of his leadership from the very start of his career as head of the nascent CPA, when he was still operating underground and did not yet enjoy the consolidated position of power he would later hold.

In the 1990s, several attempts were made to tell the story of Enver Hoxha's rise to power, but the authors were unable to do so without exaggeration, unjustified denigration and bias. Their aim was to topple Hoxha from every possible pedestal by questioning the basic facts: had he ever really been a communist? Was he genuinely a key figure in the party or did he simply usurp the leadership? Nearly all of them failed to understand that these things were of little or no significance. Whether Hoxha was the first, second or tenth person to join the communist movement was meaningless scorekeeping. Enver Hoxha proved that he knew how to keep one step ahead of the movement. He used internal strife to his own advantage, manoeuvred skilfully among the various communist leaders, gained their trust, imposed himself on them, rose to the top and eventually got rid of them, one by one.

3

From Gjirokastra to Korça

E nver Hoxha's story began in the early years of the twentieth century. Son of a modest family, it is generally held he was born on 16 October 1908, in the Palorto quarter of Gjirokastra, to Halil and Gjyle Hoxha. Although his official birthday was celebrated on this date, records are inconclusive as to his true date of birth. No fewer than five different dates are to be found in the Central State Archives alone. According to the Gjirokastra civil register, Enver Hoxha was born on 12 May 1908. The same record contains the names of his parents as Halil (father) and Gjylo (mother). An additional two dates are found in the records at the *lycée* in Korça: 17 June and 3 October (from the 1929 and 1930 records respectively). In France, his date of birth was recorded as 3 October, while a trade union newspaper, *Bashkimi* (Unity), gave his date of birth as 3 September. 16 October, the day marked by Hoxha himself, was first made public in *Bashkimi* on 16 October 1947.

Enver Hoxha spent his childhood and teenage years in Gjirokastra and Korça, two towns at the southern and south-eastern tips of the country. In later years, while at the zenith of power and especially towards the end of his life, Hoxha attempted to build an image of himself as a scion of a large and influential family from the stone city of Gjirokastra. This sounds rather unusual considering that communists normally went to great lengths to prove their humble origins and close ties with ordinary people – the working class and peasantry – and dissociated themselves from anything remotely regarded as 'aristocratic remnants'. It seems Hoxha had stopped bothering about proving himself to the working masses, but the idea of a 'noble' descent never really took off. The modest house that his family once inhabited was burned down in 1914, never to serve as a family home again. It was then rebuilt in the early 1960s in the style of a grand Ottoman saray, as if to make up for the lack of social status.

Ismail Kadare, the best-known Albanian writer of modern times, a Gjirokastrite born and bred whose family used to live opposite Hoxha's in the curiously named Sokaku i të Marrëve (Mad Men's Alley), described how the communist chief's family and residence were never regarded as part of the town's prominent circle – a tightly knit clique extremely proud of their roots, traceable back to medieval times. In a 2003 interview, Kadare spoke about his relatives' memories of Hoxha's family:

> The Hoxhas were relatively new in town; the surname itself is telling – it is not one of the traditional family names. There were some really old families in Gjirokastra whose surnames never changed over the centuries. A surname was the basis for social recognition. My family and other old families on the street had a tendency 'not to notice' the more recently established households like the Hoxhas.[1]

Probably because of some inferiority complex, or for other reasons much more difficult to fathom, Hoxha's father, Halil, is rarely mentioned in his memoirs. Conversely, he had a lot more to say about his uncle, Hysen Hoxha, or 'Baba Çeni', a character with a certain standing in the small town. Hysen was a member of the Gjirokastra delegation to Albania's declaration of independence in Vlora in November 1912, but only arrived well after the event had taken place. This did not, however, prevent the making of a movie in 1982 entitled *Nëntori i dytë* (The second November), in which Hysen Hoxha is shown greeting Ismail Qemali as the latter entered Vlora.

A resourceful and well-connected man, Baba Çeni served for some time as Gjirokastra's *belediye başkanı*, a sort of appointed town mayor. It is not unlikely that Hoxha, who was very close to Baba Çeni, got his first taste of politics from the dinners and meetings held by his uncle at their home in the turbulent years between 1913 and 1930. This was the time when the Greeks were feverishly campaigning for the annexation of Gjirokastra.

Hysen Hoxha became young Enver's patron and role model. He is ubiquitous and warmly remembered throughout Hoxha's memoirs. However, the same warm feelings did not extend to some other of Baba Çeni's relatives: Abaz Omari, Baba Çeni's grandson and Hoxha's childhood friend and classmate, was executed in Berat in 1945 on Enver Hoxha's orders, on charges of joining nationalist ranks against the communists.[2] His decapitated body was found in 1993.

It is curious that Hoxha's own father did not receive the same kind of attention in the memoirs. Halil was admittedly a timid man, devoid of any ambition or aspiration. Although he continued to live with his son for many years after the latter became leader of the country, he remained unassuming and shy to the end. Halil was a deeply religious man who had served as an imam up until a few years after Albania's independence. Later on he worked as a market weigh master in Gjirokastra. He was reportedly unable to comprehend why communism and religion had to be so much at odds with each other and did not approve of his son's fierce antagonism to religion from the early years of his rise to power.

In his memoirs about 1927, the year of his transfer to Korça, Hoxha described how his 'uncle' could not afford to pay for his education and applied for a scholarship on his behalf. It is a detail that has given rise to considerable confusion, but the truth is that Enver Hoxha never called Halil Hoxha his 'father'. Halil was always 'uncle' to him. The habit probably came from the time when the families of Hysen and Halil Hoxha lived together under one roof, and Hysen's children, older than Enver, called Halil 'uncle'. As the youngest in the household, Enver, too, became accustomed to calling his own father 'uncle', a habit which remained with him till the end of his life. In his memoirs Hoxha relates how, as he was preparing to leave for Korça, his uncle got him a black coat and a pair of heavy boots for the winter:

> I once asked uncle for some money to buy a thick pullover and a pair of winter boots. It was not easy for him, but uncle managed somehow to send me some extra money to have a suit made. I was extremely happy. I went and chose the fabric, light beige, and then had it made by a tailor at 'Pallas'.[3]

From 1927 to 1930 Halil Hoxha was still working as a market weigh master in Gjirokastra and his earnings could hardly cover his son's expenses. A few years earlier he had travelled as a migrant to America, together with his eldest son, Beqir. They had been away during the most decisive years of the young boy's upbringing. Young Hoxha remained at home with his three sisters, and it seems Baba Çeni, who did not have a male child, was very fond of him and raised him like his own son. Halil returned to Albania five years later. Beqir, Hoxha's eldest brother, never had a chance to create a family of his own. He died from tuberculosis at 27, leaving behind Enver and the three sisters.

Very little is known about Hoxha's childhood and early youth in Gjirokastra. What we know today comes primarily from a single source – Hoxha's own writings. Making allowances for some embellishments which no one dared to challenge at the time, they sound nonetheless sincere: his was an ordinary childhood, with the usual difficulties and aspirations for a good education.

According to the memoirs, Hoxha received his elementary education in a *mektep*, a Muslim faith school where he learned to read and write both Turkish and Albanian. In 1917 he transferred to the first ever Albanian school in Gjirokastra and was, in his own words, 'a hardworking pupil'. In the early 1920s he attended the French *lycée* that had just opened in Gjirokastra, where he began to learn French and became acquainted with French literature. His first teachers were mostly Swiss and Belgian. He always remembered them with fondness in his later years.

Seventy years later, in his memoirs, Hoxha mentioned all his childhood friends by name, despite the fact that some of them later became opponents of his regime and were eventually jailed or executed. The usual practice until then was that, once declared enemies of the people and eliminated, these people were never mentioned, as if they had never existed. Hoxha described them as 'problem' children, most likely a hindsight opinion reflecting the ideological divide between them in later years.

As a teenager Hoxha was not known for any special talents. Neither his contemporaries nor Hoxha himself ever mentioned anything out of the ordinary, if one ignores his involvement in a drama club and the small part he played in a production of Albanian playwright Sami Frashëri's *Besa*, put on stage by the first-year students at the *lycée*. He was not known to be a particularly charismatic young man or a leader among his peers. He had little interest in literature – a fashionable pursuit at the time – but he could recite verse by Albanian authors, especially Andon Zako Çajupi, by heart.

Gjirokastra's influence on the upbringing of young Hoxha was negligible; Korça was to play a far more decisive role. He transferred to Korça after finishing his second year at the *lycée* in Gjirokastra (which only offered a two-year course of studies). Apparently the Hoxhas were determined that their only surviving son would continue his education at the *lycée* in Korça, arguably the best school in the country. In his childhood memoirs Hoxha explained how his uncle applied for a government scholarship as he could not afford the tuition and accommodation fees in Korça. He wrote to the Ministry of Education, which accorded Enver Hoxha a grant to study at the *lycée*. This was only the first of several scholarships accorded to Hoxha by the Kingdom of Albania. All of them were secured through the intervention of the Libohovas, one of the most influential families in the country.

The 19-year-old Hoxha, all dressed up in his new uniform and school cap fresh from Janina, arrived at the south-eastern town one autumn day in 1927. He was also wearing a black overcoat given to him by Baba Çeni and carried a leather suitcase in which his deceased brother, Beqir, had brought back his belongings from America. The trip to Korça took the better part of two days. The road was in terrible condition, but the magnificent views of the woods around Përmet, the small town where he spent the night, more than made up for the strenuous journey. After Përmet, the route passed through Erseka, then continued on a stretch of Greek territory, before finally reaching Korça.

The new town must have fascinated him; it was completely different from his native Gjirokastra, which was built of stone on very steep slopes. Korça was built on a flat plain 800 metres above sea level, at the foot of Mount Morava. In contrast with imperial Gjirokastra, with its Ottoman feel and old-school officials, Korça was a modern town that owed its splendour to a new class of worldly and forward-thinking Christian merchants. It was a pleasant place with a wide boulevard lined with fine villas on both sides, a town where the rising bourgeoisie – the merchants, lawyers and doctors of Korça – lived. The orderly wrought-iron fences, the front yards blooming with flowers and the belle époque style of the houses must have made quite an impression on him.

Enver Hoxha lodged at the *lycée's internat*, a sort of dormitory providing accommodation for about 150 students from all over Albania. Alongside the Malet Tona Dormitory in Shkodra, the American Vocational School in Tirana and the Commercial School in Vlora, Korça's *internat* was a cradle of a rising Albanian elite.

Korça was much more modern, more spacious than Gjirokastra, and played a key role in Hoxha's upbringing. Surprisingly, his memoirs barely touch upon the years he spent there as a student and focus almost exclusively on the time later when he worked there as a substitute teacher, between 1937 and 1939.

Enver Hoxha was in the same class as many of his childhood friends from Gjirokastra. One of them was Hamit Kokalari, whom Hoxha mentioned in his memoirs. Author of *Kosova, djepi i shqiptarizmit* (Kosovo, the cradle of Albanianism), published in 1943, Kokalari was the only one of Hoxha's friends with a good education and relatively prominent career who did not suffer personally later on. Two of his brothers were executed summarily in 1944 while his sister, Musine Kokalari, Albania's first female writer and one of the most attractive and best-educated women in the country, spent 18 years in jail and died in internal exile.

Abaz Omari, Baba Çeni's grandson by his daughter, went to the same school as Hoxha and both of them would spend time together in France in later years. In his *Kur u hodhën themelet e Shqipërisë së re* (published in English as *Laying the Foundations of a New Albania*), Hoxha made some scathing remarks about his cousin. Hoxha never forgave Omari for siding with the nationalists instead of with the communists, and apparently deemed this reason enough to order his execution.

Sabiha Kasimati, the only female student at the *lycée* and Hoxha's classmate, who was born in Turkey and transferred to Gjirokastra with her family after independence, did not fare any better. According to stories that circulated after 1990, although they were both from the same town and probably even distant relatives, Sabiha would often make fun of him at school. Contemporaneous photos of Kasimati show a very attractive young woman. She graduated from the University of Turin in Italy and become one of the first women scientists in Albania. Although never involved in politics, she was arrested after the bomb incident at the Soviet embassy in 1951 and summarily shot by firing squad – the only woman among the 22 intellectuals, all graduates from European universities, who were executed. The sole witness to the execution, a local shepherd, told the court in 1994 that the bullets fired by the firing squad and the prosecutor failed to hit her, so the order was given to finish her off with rifle butts. Eight days after their execution as 'authors of the bomb incident', the real culprit, who had thrown the Molotov cocktail, was apprehended. As it later transpired, the Politburo of the PLA had issued the execution order four days after they were shot. The mass grave where Kasimati and the 21 men were buried was only discovered in 1994. As identifying the remains proved an impossible task, the relatives decided to rebury them all in a common grave, this time at the Cemetery of the Martyrs of the Nation. In his memoirs about his years at the *lycée*, written many years after the execution, Hoxha does not mention Kasimati by name, but he devotes a couple of paragraphs to 'the only girl at the *lycée*'. In lines more suited to a teenager's diary than the memoirs of a revolutionary leader, he described how vivacious she was, how she made fun of everybody, how the boys would try to chat her up, which boy was most in love with her and whom she had taken a fancy to. Hoxha's bitterness towards this young woman is revealed by Vedat Kokona, a former student at the *lycée*, who knew Enver Hoxha very well. What he writes may provide a glimpse into the reasons for Hoxha's bitterness: 'Enver was in the same class as my brother, Nedin, Enver Zazani, Hamit Kokalari, Selami Xhaxhiu, Kiço Karajani and Sabiha Kasimati, who often made fun of him.'[4]

Sabiha Kasimati, who apparently used to laugh at Hoxha or ignore him, was not the only one to meet a tragic end. Other former friends suffered equally tragic fates. Isuf Hysenbegasi, Nedin Kokona and many others were arrested and convicted after the war when Hoxha had made himself the country's prime minister. Vedat Kokona was one of the very few who survived. After reading law at the Sorbonne, Kokona abandoned his dream of becoming a writer and turned to translation, becoming one of the master translators of world literature into Albanian. He outlived the dictator and in 1990 published his own memoirs, presenting a completely different version of events from that found in Hoxha's memoirs: 'Enver was the most mischievous and clownish of them all; he teased everyone and was teased in return; he would always play tricks on the others. His friends had nicknamed him *"gazhel"* [which meant] a donkey.'[5]

Some memoirs written by people after the dictator's death claim that he was a mediocre student and was abrasive and brutal with his friends. These alleged traits have not been corroborated by any subsequent scholarly publications; but, equally, no one has ever held that he was a bright student or that he stood out in any other way. The marks on a 1929 school report found in Hoxha's own archives are for the most part 'passable', with few 'mediocres' in between.

In the three years he spent at the French *lycée*, Hoxha did not distinguish himself in any way: he never excelled in any sports, literature or music, or in his studies, as many of his friends did. Those who knew him at the time describe him as mediocre, a young man with no particular talents or gifts. But they all failed to see the obvious. Enver Hoxha was a man who did not stand out in his youth and who did not seem to have any specific calling or ability. He was thus universally underestimated and often disparaged. But Hoxha was gifted in one way – he had political talent and a strong penchant for power. One could describe him as a sort of political magician, a force to be reckoned with, a man who thrived on power struggles, but also as a man whose talent was sad, pitiful, violent and often macabre. It was this talent that kept him in power for 41 years, that made him the longest-serving dictator of his time. He dominated 41 of the 73 years of Albania's existence as an independent state.

In the summer of 1930 Hoxha finished his studies at the *lycée* and moved to Tirana. It was his first time in the capital. On his way there he stopped briefly at the house of Shyqyri Çuçi, a wealthy maternal uncle, who had always been there for Hoxha's family in times of need. While in the capital, he shared a room with three other people at Hotel Durrës. He was a man on a mission: he was there to meet Eqrem Libohova, who had supported him in the past.[6]

In his memoirs, Hoxha wrote that he did not like Tirana because that was the place where the royal family lived, but this sounds too contrived to be true. One thing is, however, certain: he now had to make his own way in life; he had to become somebody. Of course, as he roamed the streets of Tirana, it would never have occurred to him that 15 years later he would come to the capital as prime minister of the country.

Although he was a mediocre student, Enver Hoxha managed to obtain a scholarship offered to him by the Kingdom of Albania. He set off to study botany in Montpellier in southern France. It has recently transpired that Hoxha had the support of Eqrem Libohova, Albanian foreign minister at the time. Libohova was an influential man, a benefactor of the Hoxhas and a friend of Bahri Omari, Enver Hoxha's brother-in-law. Mufit Libohova, Eqrem's brother, was interior minister in the first government of independent Albania in 1912. Eqrem Libohova himself had served as Prince Wied's adjutant and later first adjutant and foreign minister in several of King Zog's governments. Securing a scholarship for Hoxha in 1930 was only the first of several interventions he made on Hoxha's behalf. People say that Hoxha had waited for days outside the minister's door to beg him for this favour.[7]

4

From France to Belgium: The Dropout

With his old leather suitcase in hand – the only memento from his late brother's journey to the United States – Enver Hoxha set off for France one August morning in 1930. As part of a group of students from Gjirokastra, he took the ferry from Durrës to Brindisi, then the train to Ventimiglia, and from there carried on to the French Riviera. Hoxha eventually arrived at Montpellier where he was to study at the School of Biology and where he would spend the next three years of his life.

On the way to France the young man stopped to spend a few days with his elder sister Fahrije and her family, who had been living in Bari since 1924. Fahrije's husband, Bahri Omari, a democrat and anti-monarchist, had been a deputy in the first Albanian parliament. He had left Albania together with Fan Noli following a failed coup d'état, Noli's failed attempt to hold elections and Zog's subsequent return to Albania. A leading opposition politician in exile and a man with good connections, Omari was in all likelihood on the payroll of both the Yugoslavs and the Italians, who thought he might be useful in the future if and when relations with Zog turned sour.

In his memoirs Hoxha dedicates many pages to Omari and the alleged differences between the two of them. Omari was no doubt the man who introduced Hoxha to the big world of politics and created opportunities for him to rub shoulders with prominent Albanian politicians. His brother-in-law would take young Hoxha to Caffè Stoppani on a central Bari street, to meet some of the politicians who had played a crucial role in the movement for independence and the building of the new Albanian state. Caffè Stoppani was a popular meeting place for Albanian and Croatian émigrés and Hoxha recalls the atmosphere there with fondness. Discussions focused on news of King Zog's failing health or on his imminent overthrow. Hoxha would frequent the café twice a year when he travelled back and forth from France to Albania. It is not known what effect, if any, those meetings had on him; in his memoirs Hoxha played them down as if he had never taken them too seriously. It is ironic that the same political émigrés whom Hoxha met at the café and who would complain about King Zog's evil government and their life in exile, would be forced ten years later to flee Albania again, this time to escape persecution at the hands of a government led by the very young man they had befriended at Caffè Stoppani. This time around they were never to see their homeland again: they all died in exile, none the wiser about what it was that propelled the quiet young man to the top.

France would make a lasting impression on Hoxha. Towards the end of his life he was wont to reminisce about his years in France. He had not set foot outside Albania since 1961 and every time his children returned from a trip to Paris, he would question them in great detail about the places, streets and people they had seen. France was the only country he maintained normal relations with; it was where he ordered his suits and books every year.

Enver Hoxha arrived in France at a time when political passions were running high, though still not as high as after the start of the Spanish Civil War and the rise of the Nazis. The 22-year-old was hardly interested in political developments; indeed, he had not shown any apparent interest in politics at all. At least this was what his classmates and roommates in Montpellier thought.

The young Hoxha did not seem very keen on his studies either – he would spend his time in coffee shops, with pastimes and adventures of his own, rather than concentrating on his books and lectures. In his memoirs he explained that he was not remotely interested in botany. He did not pass any exams in his first year; in fact it was only in his third year at the University of Montpellier that he passed some of his first-year exams. Consequently, on 6 February 1934, Mirash Ivanaj, the then Albanian minister of education, cut off Hoxha's scholarship. This meant that Hoxha had to go back to Albania and refund to the government three years' worth of scholarship money, as stipulated in the terms and conditions of his scholarship. He never did, nor was he penalised for it in any way. Ten years later, by then prime minister of Albania, he invited Mirash Ivanaj for coffee. The latter had just returned to Albania from Egypt, where he had spent the years of the Italian occupation. A well-known figure of the Albanian National Awakening, known as the 'Rilindja' (Revival) period, and a popular author of textbooks, Ivanaj sincerely congratulated the new prime minister on his appointment. From what he tells us himself, Hoxha interrupted Ivanaj and jested: 'Professor, you once signed a paper to cut my scholarship off.' The old man responded calmly: 'If I did so, it means you deserved it; you were not exactly the academic type.'[1]

A few years after this conversation took place, Mirash Ivanaj was arrested, charged with being an 'anti-Yugoslav' and sent to prison. He died in his prison cell years after Hoxha broke off relations with Tito, when he was playing the 'anti-Yugoslav' card himself.

Though his scholarship was revoked, Hoxha decided not to go back home. One evening in May 1933 he instead took the train from Montpellier to Paris and arrived at the Gare de Lyon the next morning. He had no job, no scholarship money and no other means of making a living, only a promise from a childhood friend studying there that a solution would be found. The childhood friend had spoken to Hasan Jero – a well-to-do student also from Gjirokastra – who agreed to take Hoxha in and pay for two of his daily meals. Enver Hoxha thus moved into a modest student hostel with his friends Babameto and Jero, in rue Monsieur-le-Prince, close to the Latin Quarter, and waited for his luck to change. Hasan Jero paid dearly for the good turn he did for a friend in need. Upon returning from France, he joined the partisan movement and fought the occupiers for two years. Immediately after Enver Hoxha's rise to power, however, he was arrested, charged with 'spying for France' and sentenced to 35 years in prison. He served 25 of them and was one of the few who lived to tell the tale.

In 1994, Hasan Jero returned to Paris and told journalists there about the episode that had inadvertently led to the years of trauma he was to experience. In an interview with a journalist from the TV channel France 2, he described how he had shared a room with Enver Hoxha for nearly a year. He stated that Hoxha was a peculiar character who slept in till noon, stayed up late at night and had no particular interests. Jero also stated that Enver Hoxha's claims about writing articles for *l'Humanité* and meeting Paul Vaillant-Couturier were simply made up.

Jero was not the only one unlucky enough to cross paths with Hoxha in his youth. Most of the people who knew him at the time, be they close friends or mere acquaintances, would end up in prison or be executed after the war. Only a handful survived, and these were usually too scared to speak or they preferred to endorse Hoxha's version of his years in France. After his death, some of those who were still alive published their own memoirs. One of them was Vedat Kokona, a well-known writer, translator and lexicographer, whose memoirs were published posthumously in 1998. His portrayal of Hoxha is believable and very realistic.

In his memoirs, Hoxha describes himself as a communist militant who wrote articles for *l'Humanité* in which he lambasted King Zog's 'bloody regime'. He also claims that he was involved in the French Communist Party:

> Then I went to the reading room of the French Communist Party and asked the person in charge whether I could see comrade Paul Vaillant-Couturier as I needed to tell him something. He told me to come back the next day for a response [...] I did, and fortunately, Valliant himself received me. We shook hands and he asked me to take a seat. I briefly explained my story to him.
>
> 'There is one thing I'd like to ask you about,' I continued. 'I am a communist in both heart and soul. The party, your press and the sufferings of my people have turned me into a communist. If I receive any news from my country in the future, can I write a short article or two for *l'Humanité*, to denounce Zog's feudal regime?'
>
> Vaillant looked at me warmly and said: 'Of course you can, comrade. We will be happy to publish them [...] you speak good French so I assume you write it well, too. Please sign all your articles with a pseudonym. We will know that all articles coming from Brussels concerning Albania are yours, comrade Hoxha.'
>
> When we parted, Vaillant added: 'Cherish communism and fight for it.'
> 'I will fight for it until the day I die,' I replied.[2]

It is not known whether this conversation really ever happened. What is known is that, in 1987, a team of researchers sent by the Central Committee of the PLA to investigate Hoxha's communist activities in France and Belgium did not manage to trace anything. The search for the purported articles produced nothing. A team member explained later how he had leafed through entire collections of *l'Humanité* from 1932 to 1936 but could not find a single article in Hoxha's real name or his pseudonym, or any other piece of writing that could be attributed to Hoxha in any way.

Hoxha's version of his life in Paris and especially of his involvement in the communist movement were vigorously contested after the 1990s; indeed, the possibility of his being involved in the movement was more or less flatly rejected by his contemporaries and associates. However, some information to this effect does exist. One of the most interesting details is contained in a statement by Anastas (Nastas) Plasari.

A professional journalist and a prominent communist in the country in the 1920s and 1930s, Plasari met Hoxha in 1943, after an invitation from the latter to a 'working meeting' in an unoccupied region of Albania. The letter of invitation, addressed with a 'Dear comrade', is preserved at the archives of the Central Committee of the CPA/PLA.[3] They had not known each other from before and it seems this was the first time they met face to face. Plasari had heard some 'anecdotes' (as he calls them) about Hoxha from friends of his like Llazar Fundo and Tajar Zavalani, and had received some more information from Dhimitër Canco, another representative of the left-wing movement in Albania, who was the owner of Cinema Gloria and the Argus Bookshop in Tirana. This is how Plasari describes Enver Hoxha:

> This was the first time I met Enver. Until then he had only been a nodding acquaintance; I had seen him on occasion in Tirana with Esat Dishnica, a mutual friend before he went underground. I had a certain idea about his involvement in the left-wing movement based on anecdotal accounts exchanged between Fundo and Zavalani at the end of 1938 or the beginning of 1939, and on some interesting details provided by Argus [the pseudonym of Canco].
>
> According to them, Enver Hoxha had joined the left-wing movement

while in Paris, where he had ostensibly gone to study; in fact his stay there
was linked to his political and ideological interests. Like other comrades, he
was probably in contact with the one-time Berlin Office, which had been
moved to Paris in 1932. However, it must have been an indirect contact,
unlike the involvement of Fundo, Zavalani and Malëshova later on. Enver
became acquainted with left-wing, pro-Soviet and pro-Stalinist figures
in Paris through an eccentric character and Parisian dandy, publisher of
fashion magazines and avant-garde literary journals, by the name of Lucien
Vogel. Lucien Vogel's Parisian cell was in fact run by comrade Münzenberg.
Vogel's famous fashion magazine *Vu* and the avant-garde journal *Lu* were
sold at Dhimitër Canco's Argus Bookshop in Tirana. Vogel had business
dealings and ideological affinities with Hachette, whose representative
in Tirana was Argus, until the fascists banned both publications because
of their openly anti-fascist stance. According to Argus, they were Enver
Hoxha's favourite magazines, and Canco would often insert *l'Humanité*,
which he continued to smuggle into Albania, between their pages.

According to Argus, Fundo and Zavalani, in Paris Enver used to frequent
a famous villa just outside town, on the edge of the forest of Saint-Germain.
Canco described it as 'a mansion fit for the Count of Monte Cristo' and
admitted that he had also been there. It was there that the crème de la
crème of left-wing Paris intelligentsia rubbed shoulders with all sorts of
socialist activists, trade unionists, communists, social democrats, exiles,
avant-garde artists and even 'pro-revolutionary White Russians'; Lucien
Vogel welcomed them all. The house teemed with people and buzzed with
political and ideological discussions. According to both Canco and Fundo,
Enver was close to Lucien Vogel's daughter, called Marie or something,
who was engaged to Paul Vaillant-Couturier. This explains how Hoxha got
to know Vaillant-Couturier himself, the leader of the French communists
and mayor of a Paris arrondissement, and possibly met other comrades like
Maurice Thorez, Marcel Cachin, etc., who also frequented Lucien Vogel's
circle. Argus also spoke about Enver Hoxha's attempt to enrol in the Karl
Marx school, founded by Vaillant-Couturier in Paris in 1933, but by then
Enver had been forced to return home. I was never able to ascertain the
truth of such information, but I never considered it was my duty to do so.[4]

Some interesting information about the characters mentioned in the above description and their respective social circles is to be found in general encyclopedias.

Willi Münzenberg was head of the Paris Office of the Third Communist International (also known as the Comintern) for Western Europe, and was known as a very effective recruiter of the European intelligentsia and of prominent figures from the fields of culture, art and literature into the left-wing, pro-communist movement. His propaganda machine was credited with the organisation of the 'Counter-Trial' after the Reichstag fire, the campaign in support of the anarchists Nicola Sacco and Bartolomeo Vanzetti (who were wrongly convicted of murder in Massachusetts in 1920 and executed seven years later), and the establishment of pro-Soviet intelligence networks in Great Britain (such as by infiltrating the Bloomsbury circle). Stéphane Courtois and Marc Lazar's *Histoire du Parti communiste français* (History of the French Communist Party) corroborates the claim of Hoxha's involvement in the Comintern bodies. Referring to the writings of Münzenberg, they state that one of the French Communist Party's contributions to the world communist movement was the assistance it provided to the communist movement in Albania:

> [w]ork in Albania, which, according to Paris, helped set up a communist movement [there] under the leadership of Enver Hoxha, a student at the Sorbonne and future dictator of communist Albania.[5]

Hoxha's failure to mention Münzenberg in his memoirs is rather conspicuous, but has a simple explanation: Münzenberg is rumoured to have been purged by Stalin in 1940 after the two men had a major falling out. Hoxha never mentioned Lucien Vogel either, although he was well acquainted with the life of French 'party intellectuals' inspired by the bohemian spirit of Montparnasse, and places like the Closerie des Lilas, the Pavillon de Flore and the Bateau-Lavoir, which produced, in his words, 'the Aragons, the Elsa Triolets, and many other friends of the Lazarevs, Tristan Tzaras, the Dadaists, the cubists, and a multitude of other schools of decadent art and literature'.[6] Similarly, there was no mention of Marie-Claude, although, according to Fundo and

Canco, she was Hoxha's girlfriend. It is likely that Hoxha had something to do with the subsequent involvement of 'comrade' Marie-Claude in the French Communist Party and with her becoming an MP representing that party for several decades. After the death of her first husband, Paul Vaillant-Couturier, she married Paul Villon, another important French communist politician. There is no indication that Marie-Claude herself ever mentioned Hoxha till the day she died in Paris in 1996. Her father, Lucien Vogel, the Parisian dandy, died in 1954, leaving his mark on Parisian avant-garde art.

According to his biographers, Lucien Vogel's soirées were often frequented by people of open sexual orientation, free of any complexes, including many gay people. This was a known and accepted dimension of that environment. The fact that Hoxha also frequented these circles at the time could provide a basis for the very hushed rumours that circulated for years in Albania that he had been gay in his youth. Indeed, in anti-communist émigré circles, such allegations were made openly.

In 1990, on the eve of the collapse of the communist regime in Albania, Arshi Pipa, one of the most active opponents of communism in exile, published a book entitled *Albanian Stalinism*, a comprehensive compilation of his work, mainly pamphlets against the communist regime in Tirana. At the end of the book, he included a poem about Hoxha, written many years earlier:

> *O bandill të lumtë bitha,*
> *Ajo i shpjegon të gjitha!*
> *Ç'duhen dituri e mend*
> *Kur njeriu ka fatin tënd!*

> [Glory to your ass, oh dandy,
> This is what explains it all,
> Who's in need of brains or knowledge
> When he's got your lucky call.][7]

These lines were probably written in a bout of rage. About 20 years earlier, Pipa had published a pamphlet in which he remarked on Hoxha's uninhibited sex life and his homosexual orientation. It circulated among the émigré circles and eventually made its way to the Ministry of the Interior in Albania. It is possible that this document played a role in Mehmet Shehu's elimination in 1981.

This was the sort of rumour that could lead to one's execution if it reached the ears of the state security service, the Sigurimi. However, with the fall of the regime in 1991, people began to speak about it openly. The names of some well-known gay men from Tirana circulated, whose *dylber* (lover) Hoxha was said to have been. However, no one has been able to prove this allegation: none of his one-time friends who had survived were able to say anything about this side of his life. It is likely that this was just a label that stuck to him because of his association with Lucien Vogel's circles in Paris in the mid-1930s, where the gay element was quite prominent. In fact, it was because of this and other publicly made allegations that were turning into scandals that the Comintern decided to cut off the group's funding.

At this time, the young Hoxha started to get involved in politics, mostly with anti-Zogist opposition circles in Paris. Without the support of a scholarship, he began to approach well-known Albanians in exile and took part in the activities of their organisations. According to Hana Klissura, the daughter of Ali Këlcyra, a staunch anti-Zogist activist living in Paris at the time, Hoxha met her father on a number of occasions. While, according to Hoxha, they only met once, when Hoxha delivered a letter from Bahri Omari, his description of Ali Këlcyra is bitter and insulting: 'I saw the back of the man and never saw him again, either in France or in Albania.'[8] In fact, it was because of Hoxha that Këlcyra had to flee Albania again in 1944: this time for good. Today his remains lie in the Non-Catholic Cemetery, next to the Pyramid of Cestius in Rome. Këlcyra never returned to his native land, alive or dead. According to Hana Klissura, Bahri Omari had asked her father to find Hoxha a part-time job in Paris, which he did. A few months later Eqrem Libohova, foreign minister of the Kingdom of Albania, came to Hoxha's rescue again. He recommended him to the honorary consul of Albania in the Kingdom of Belgium, suggesting that he could be employed as a consular secretary.[9]

In 1935, nearly 11 months after his arrival in the French capital, Hoxha boarded a train from the Gare du Nord for Brussels. For about a year he worked as secretary to Georges Marothy, Albania's honorary consul in Belgium. Very little information exists about his time in Brussels. Records

show that in the academic year 1934–5 he was enrolled to study law at the
Law School on avenue Franklin Roosevelt, but there is nothing else in his
student records, which must mean that he did not take any exams. Hoxha
did not say much about his time in Brussels, although, according to other
people, his stay there was quite eventful. Stories circulated about an incident
in which he was allegedly apprehended in a Brussels brothel; in another he
was said to have shown up at a reception at the Royal Palace posing as the
heir to the Albanian throne. It is not unlikely that all of these stories were
the fruit of his opponents' imagination, as there is no proof to show that the
incidents really happened. What is known is that, while he was working at the
Honorary Consulate, its coffers were broken into and Hoxha was subsequently
fired. Hana Klissura relates Eqrem Libohova's interpretation of the incident:

> Then an incident happened, that the contents of the consulate's coffers
> were pilfered, no one knows by whom, but he was the one in charge. They
> said he took the money for himself, but this has remained an unsolved
> mystery.[10]

It is equally a mystery why Hoxha did not return to Paris or go to stay with
his sister in Bari in southern Italy, as he had initially planned. It is likely that
he chose instead to return to Albania after being promised secure employ-
ment. Eqrem Libohova intervened on his behalf once again and the Albanian
minister of education offered him a job as a substitute teacher at the Tirana
Secondary School, and later at the *lycée* in Korça.

Unlike the other patrons who helped and supported Hoxha over the years,
Eqrem Libohova did not linger around to feel the full force of his protégé's
wrath. After serving as prime minister of the collaborationist government in
Albania, Libohova fled to Rome in 1943 and died there in 1948. Towards the
end of his life, Libohova was reportedly in disbelief that the former problem
student, who never managed to graduate and whom he had helped with
finding jobs, had become the prime minister and leader of Albania. At the
time of his death, Libohova was number seven on the list of 'war criminals'
sentenced to death *in absentia* and a request had been sent to Italy for his
extradition to Albania.

5

Teacher of Moral Education

On the morning of 29 July 1936 Hasan Dosti was feeling quite poorly. He had travelled to Shkodra as part of a larger delegation of young men from Gjirokastra to collect the remains of Çerçiz Topulli and Muço Qulli, who had been killed in an ambush by the Montenegrins in 1916 and buried at Shtoj near Shkodra. The mission of the delegation was to carry the remains of the two fallen heroes back to their native Gjirokastra, and Dosti had been asked to give a speech on behalf of the delegation. It was to be a solemn ceremony, with a number of other speeches by local dignitaries and people who had known the heroes personally. A recent graduate from a French law school and quite well known in Albania at the time, Dosti had prepared a short address on behalf of the young generation, pledging to uphold and further the cause of the martyred patriots. Unfortunately he was too ill to speak to the crowd from the balcony of the town hall. Under the circumstances, he decided to give his speech to another member of the delegation, a young man just back from France: Enver Hoxha. Personally invited by Jonuz Topulli – brother of one of the heroes – and by Dosti himself, Hoxha had some obvious advantages: he was good-looking and, more importantly, he had a deep, melodious voice.

Hoxha appeared on the balcony of the town hall at noon and gave the speech which was subsequently published in *Demokratia*, a widely read newspaper in Gjirokastra. Just back from Brussels and his five years in France, this was his first important public appearance. For him, this was a fortuitous rise to prominence at a ceremony of great national significance.

Both commemorative ceremonies in Shkodra and Gjirokastra were very impressive. It was at the rally in Shkodra that the first ever photo of Hoxha, then 28, was taken, by Marubi, the famous photographer. In addition to being a nice memento, it is also the only photo of him as a young man at a public event of such major significance. As with many photographic and other records from his past, the image was unashamedly doctored after Hoxha's rise to power. The original disappeared and was replaced with a heavily retouched version, in which Hoxha appears on the balcony entirely on his own. The same happened to a second group photo, in which Hoxha originally appeared in the second row, behind Javer Hurshiti, Father Anton Harapi and Ernest Koliqi, renowned personalities of the time. Nine years later, in the wake of Hoxha's rise to power, Father Harapi and Javer Hurshiti were executed by firing squad, while Koliqi died in exile in Rome in 1973. Hasan Dosti, the man whose speech Hoxha read from the balcony, became one of the leaders of Balli Kombëtar (the National Front). He fled Albania in 1944. Hoxha had him tried as a 'war criminal' and pursued him till the end; Dosti died in Los Angeles in 1991.

In the autumn of 1936 Enver Hoxha returned to the French *lycée* in Korça. This time he reported not to the registrar's office to enrol as a student, but to the headmaster's office. The latter had received a recommendation from the Ministry of Education to hire Hoxha as a substitute teacher. In the spring of the same year he had worked for three months at the Tirana Secondary School, where he had not made any lasting impression. Five years earlier, when he left Korça and the *lycée* as a new graduate, it would never have occurred to him that the same *lycée* and the same town would again become such an important part of his life. It is not unlikely that, quite apart from Eqrem Libohova's recommendation, he was hired because of his fluent French from the years spent in France and Belgium. As Hoxha had no particular speciality, he was assigned to teach 'Moral Education' and put in charge of the school library. It is somewhat ironic that the brightest and the best young men in the country, Albania's future elite, would be taught morals by an unqualified 'professor' who had squandered all the scholarship money awarded to him by the government.

Enver Hoxha rented a room at the house of a widow called Polikseni, which included a bed, a desk and a brazier. For a brief period, he shared the room with Vedat Kokona, an old friend from his years in France, who had also been appointed as a teacher at the *lycée* there. Hoxha's presence in town did not go unnoticed. He was a frequent patron of the town's cafés: a handsome, 28-year-old bachelor, who, according to his friends, had quite a penchant for the women. However, none of his contemporaries ever came up with any concrete names of women he courted or was romantically interested in. As with all the other high-ranking communist officials of Eastern Europe at the time, Hoxha's erotic interests, if they existed at all, remained completely unknown. Hoxha himself did not reveal anything of significance about his relations with women during his life as a student at the *lycée*:

> The boys at the *lycée* would call dibs on a girl, which usually amounted to nothing. We would go, as a group, to the street where she lived; she would stand at the door and, after getting used to our presence, she would sometimes even smile at us. But we could not tell who exactly she was smiling at; we never really knew, because there were so many of us. The addressee of the smile had to be established. For this, each boy had to go by himself and stand outside her gate, and many did give it a try.[1]

In his memoirs, Vedat Kokona described an episode from the first morning he woke up in the room he shared with Hoxha in 1940:

> In the morning, when I got up, I saw Enver standing at the window, smoothing his hair with the palm of his hand. I rose up onto my elbows and followed his gaze. On the balcony of the house opposite, amidst the pots of flowers, was a young lady, her face radiant in the glorious morning sun. 'Quite curvy, isn't she?' he said. 'She's my student.'[2]

Abaz Ermenji, a Sorbonne graduate and history teacher at the *lycée*, also remembered the time when Hoxha arrived in Korça to teach Moral Education:

> I first got to know Enver Hoxha in the autumn of 1938, when I was appointed as a teacher at the *lycée* in Korça. Enver Hoxha was a non-tenured teacher, in other words he did not have a full status and a set monthly salary. He taught French to the lower classes and was paid by the hour.[3]

Beqir Ajazi was the student in charge of the school library when he learned of the arrival of Enver Hoxha, the new teacher who would be responsible for the library from then on. Ajazi met Hoxha on the same day, and for three consecutive years they would meet every Saturday afternoon and spend hours among the books, as Ajazi relates:

> Enver Hoxha was a tall man with straight hair, a bit on the chubby side. He had a capote, a big grey overcoat, and was very tolerant. He was just like the son of an imam, as the saying goes […] I thought well of Enver and was very fond of him. For three whole years I spent every Saturday with him; sometimes we would also meet on weekday evenings and talk about things.[4]

Ajazi, like many of Hoxha's former friends, joined the monarchist forces under Abaz Kupi, known as the Legaliteti (Legalists). He has left detailed memoirs about his time with Hoxha at the *lycée*. Some of his stories seem somewhat tainted by the way events unfolded later and by the fact that, in Ajazi's eyes, Hoxha was the main culprit responsible for the misfortunes that befell the country and him personally (Ajazi served a long prison term; his father was executed; his son was also imprisoned), but his account is surprisingly frank in places. He describes how Hoxha often spoke about patriotism and political developments in Albania:

> He spoke about Albania, different events in the country's history, the Congress of Vlora, the Congress of Lushnja […] He was different from other teachers in one thing: he did not keep his distance from the students. For instance, it would be quite unusual for me to talk to a French teacher or Albanian teacher. Not to him, he was not aloof. He was open to everyone. I remember one occasion when we went to Mborje during a break between classes. Near the school gate there was a footbridge and a café. On our way back to school, Aleks Buda and Enver Hoxha were having coffee there. Enver Hoxha was very open-minded. He invited us to sit down and have coffee with them. Someone snitched to the headmaster, as this was not allowed, but he [Enver Hoxha] stood up for us, saying: I invited them.[5]

As a young man used to life in Montpellier, Paris and Brussels, life in his country must not have been a very pleasant and welcome change. Hoxha reportedly frequented left-wing circles in town (in his memoirs he called Korça the 'cradle' of the communist movement), but there is testimony which seems to contradict this. Many of those who knew him at the time claim he was never a communist or active member of the Korça Communist Group, whose membership consisted mainly of workers and craftsmen. Ajazi, for instance, said that in the three years that the two were close, Hoxha never mentioned anything about being a communist. Vedat Kokona, who knew Hoxha from his *lycée* years in Korça and Paris, and who continued to be a close friend in Albania, seemed to be of the same opinion. This is how Kokona remembered the moment when he learned that Enver Hoxha was the 'chief of the communists':

> I was the first to sneer and laugh at the suggestion that Enver, whom I knew so well and who had never ever mentioned anything about communism until 1940, had now become the first secretary of the Communist Party! I laughed it off; little did I know how bitter that laughter would turn out to be.[6]

It is likely that his friends at the time had just overlooked this aspect of his life, or were simply unaware of it. According to his memoirs and some photos published before the 1990s, Hoxha did sometimes frequent the Puna, a trade-unionist and left-wing association. Abaz Ermenji, a former colleague who would later become one of his staunchest political opponents, testifies to this: 'I knew that Enver Hoxha was a communist and I had no interest in talking to him about politics.'[7]

Quite apart from all the arguments for or against his involvement – anyone with a sudden career advancement is bound to attract all sorts of comments – Hoxha was never a staunch communist militant, but he was not a man devoid of political interests either. Korça was his main link to the communist movement; after the Italian occupation he became leader of that movement and, indeed, leader of the entire country for 41 years.

It seems Hoxha had no intention of settling in Korça definitively. A letter written by him in October 1938 to a certain Talat Shehu from Gjirokastra, living in New Jersey and apparently quite well off, contained a request for a loan to pay for his fare to America. In the letter he explained that he had arranged to get an immigration visa and wanted to try his luck abroad, like his father and late brother had done years earlier, albeit with little success. It is not known what the addressee's response was, or indeed whether the letter, which was published in the press in the 1990s, was a genuine one. Similarly, we do not know whether it was because of his friend's refusal to lend him the money, or because Hoxha himself eventually changed his mind about going, but in 1939, at any rate, he was still in Korça and his dream of going to America, if it still existed, never took off.

The Italian occupation found Hoxha in the same town in south-eastern Albania. He was not an active participant in the mass demonstrations in which people demanded weapons to defend their homeland, something he himself admitted in his memoirs 40 years later. In his book *Kur lindi Partia* (When the party was born), Hoxha described how communists in Korça, himself included, were determined to defend the town from the Italians and organised demonstrations. A representative delegation was sent to the prefect, who, incidentally, was found dead in his hotel room on the first night after his arrival in town. Some sources have claimed recently that Hoxha never participated in any of those demonstrations and was not active in any way during those days. He was convinced that the occupation was a bad thing but did nothing to oppose it. For instance, he did not join the group of young protesters who had decided to barricade the road King Zog was expected to take in fleeing Albania. Nor did he join the volunteer battalion formed by students and young teachers at the *lycée*, who mobilised to defend the town and trained on the surrounding hills every afternoon. Many of the battalion members recalled later how Hoxha had refused to join, although, admittedly, they did not get a chance to fire a single shot.

Enver Hoxha's reaction to these dramatic events was little more than detached indifference. He just stood in front of the wrought-iron fences of the main boulevard in Korça and watched King Zog as he left the country, never to return. At that time he couldn't have known that he would be the man to ban King Zog from returning to Albania for life, in his capacity as colonel general and prime minister of the Provisional Government that arose from the Congress of Përmet in May 1944. At that time, in April 1939, he was not politically active and there was no indication that he would ever be. Indeed, he seemed to have no clear ideas or plans for the future.

Many of those who knew Hoxha at the time remember him as a carefree young man, who was ready to embark on new adventures, rarely took things seriously and showed no particular interest in politics. Contrary to his own account in *Kur lindi Partia*, during the first months of the Italian occupation Hoxha was not a political activist, nor was he involved in the anti-Italian resistance in any way. Here is how Abaz Ermenji remembered his last meeting with Hoxha:

> My last meeting with Hoxha was in December 1939. On 28 November we had staged a powerful demonstration against the Italian occupation. Of course, I was one of the main organisers of the rally, as I was well respected by my students and young people in Korça generally. Twenty days later, we were summoned by the fascist police and some of us were arrested and later sent to prison in Italy. Not Enver Hoxha. He left Korça, went to Tirana to open a tobacco shop, and that's where he was all the time while I was serving time at Ventotene, Italy.[8]

Upon his return from Ventotene, Ermenji found Enver Hoxha was already the leader of the Albanian communists. It did not come as a surprise to him:

> His rise to the head of the Albanian communists did not surprise me much because those who lead revolutions are generally Enver Hoxha's type. At the *lycée* I never thought Enver Hoxha would amount to anything, but I eventually came to realise that people like him could actually pull it off.[9]

Ermenji, who was Hoxha's junior by three years, returned to Albania after serving three years of internment on the island of Ventotene in Italy. In 1943, he became one of the leaders of the nationalist Balli Kombëtar and commander-in-chief of its armed wing. After Balli's defeat by the communist-led National Liberation Movement, he was driven out of Albania by Hoxha's forces in 1946. He settled in Paris and for many years served as the leader

in exile of Balli Kombëtar, a party in opposition to the CPA/PLA, and of
the Free Albania (Shqypnija e Lirë) Committee. After the war, his name
was second on the list of wanted war criminals, despite the fact that he had
fought against the German occupiers. Ermenji lived to see the collapse of 50
years of communism. In 1993 he returned to Albania, resumed the leadership
of Balli Kombëtar and even stood in the first multi-party elections in the
country. He died in 2003.

6

The Founding of the Communist Party

In June 1939 the French *lycée* was shut down, only to reopen a few months later as an Italian-language school with an Italian curriculum. Enver Hoxha was dismissed and once again found himself without a job. Without a secure income or a university diploma to help him get a public-sector job, he began to explore other options. The only option he had left under the circumstances was to start a private business. He and Esat Dishnica managed to convince Dishnica's maternal uncle, Ibrahim Biçakçiu, one of the richest men in Albania and owner of the Flora cigarette factory, to lend them some money as start-up capital for a new business in Tirana. Biçakçiu agreed; he rented a shop in the centre of the capital with the same name as his factory. The Flora, managed by Esat Dishnica and Enver Hoxha, was frequented by many an extravagant character in the capital.

By now 32 years old, tall and handsome as ever, a fluent speaker of French and with a cursory knowledge of the philosophers and politicians of the time, Enver Hoxha moved to Tirana, where his brother-in-law, Bahri Omari, had also returned after 15 years in exile. Beqir Ajazi, who also moved to Tirana after the *lycée* was shut down, recalled how he often went to the shop in the centre of Tirana to meet up with his former teacher. Although they would discuss politics sometimes, he was not aware that Hoxha was a communist:

> I would go to Flora quite often, to see him. He sold his cigarettes and we talked. Once he asked, 'How are things going at the *lycée*? How many approve of fascism; are there others who don't?' I told him straight away that I didn't. 'No one likes fascism at school. I think almost all hate it,

except for those whose fathers are prefects and ministers, they don't say anything.' That was true; they did not want to commit themselves one way or the other. He said, 'Boycott them!' I did not know what 'boycott' meant at the time. I looked it up as soon as I got home.[1]

Hoxha never disclosed to Ajazi the fact that he was a communist, not even in their last meeting together. Other people who frequented the Flora seem to have been aware of his involvement in the movement. According to Fadil Hoxha, a Kosovar immigrant and former student at the Shkodra secondary school who had joined the communist group there, Enver Hoxha was a communist and his shop was used by the Korça Group as a base for their meetings. In an interview 60 years later, Fadil Hoxha described Hoxha's political commitment, although, admittedly, he was not particularly close to Hoxha at the time:

> Enver Hoxha had a shop where he sold revolutionary literature. All left-wing journals that came out in French, English or German could be found at Hoxha's shop. I think I went there a couple of times to ask whether they had any Italian journals. I could speak and read Italian. I did not find any, but I could see that there were journals from France, Spain, England, America, from all over. Enver's shop became a sort of meeting point for the Korça Group in Tirana. As to how many followers they had, who of them were the leaders of the Korça Group... that I don't know.[2]

It is unclear how Hoxha managed to penetrate into the heart of the Albanian communist movement; neither contemporaneous sources nor more recent memoirs have been able to shed light on how that came about. Who or what persuaded him to get involved and what was his role in the movement?

It is not unlikely that Hoxha already knew most of the communist activists of the time, or at least those who came from Korça. He had also shown some interest in the left-wing press, and was of course familiar with communist literature. The majority of the Korça Group members were blue-collar workers, and Hoxha, a former *lycée* teacher, must have stood out. Still, nothing is known about him between the spring of 1940 and the autumn of 1941, except for the three weeks he spent at a spa in Italy for a leg condition.

According to Kristo Frashëri, Hoxha's former student at the Tirana Secondary School, one-time Youth Group member and a founding member of the CPA, no one was aware that Hoxha was a communist:

> He kept to himself. I wouldn't say he was a militant, in the sense we used the word then. He was just a supporter and I have no idea why he was reluctant to tell anyone. His colleagues did not know either. Later we asked our former teachers and they said, 'He never told us anything.' Maybe some biographer will eventually be able to shed some light on it.[3]

According to Frashëri, Hoxha was not known to be profoundly communist in his convictions: 'He was not a left-wing militant, you know, one that would roll up his sleeves and do things. He admitted himself that he was just a supporter.'[4]

At the Berat plenary meeting of November 1944, Hoxha became the target of heavy criticism from members of the Politburo and the Yugoslav envoys to Albania, whose aim was to remove him from the party leadership. In his speech at the meeting, a four-page statement of self-criticism, he described his involvement in the communist movement and the Korça Group:

> At the time I became involved with the movement as part of the Korça Group we used to work underground. I was close to the comrades and to Koço Tashko. The others thought I was one of the group leaders, but the fact is that I was just a supporter, not a full member.[5]

In those turbulent times, Hoxha must have kept his options open. One October day in 1941, Beqir Ajazi went to the Flora to say goodbye to his friend before leaving for the 'free world'. Ajazi had had an altercation with an Italian officer and feared he would be arrested and sent to prison in Italy. This was the last time Ajazi saw his former teacher and friend from the *lycée*. The two never met face to face again; the closest he would get to Hoxha later was watching him on TV in prison:

I told Enver Hoxha I had decided to leave the country, to avoid being arrested and sent to Italy. As a graduate from the *lycée* I thought it would not be too difficult to find a job as a French teacher in Tunisia, Algeria or Morocco. He said, 'Don't leave just yet. We shall leave together.' This is actually what he said. Eventually I decided I could not wait any longer and sought to meet him. I went to the shop but he was never there. 'Esat Bey, can I see professor Hoxha?' I would ask. The answer always was: 'He's gone to Gjirokastra; his sister is ill.' He gave me the same answer for several weeks. Until the day we learned.[6]

It is not known whether Hoxha really intended to leave Albania, or whether this was just a show of support for his former student and library colleague. Towards the end of 1940, Hoxha spent nearly three weeks at a spa near Salsomaggiore Terme, Italy, for a leg condition, but never attempted to leave for France or somewhere else subsequently. It is not known whether he had made up his mind by then. The fact is that Beqir Ajazi never met him again. By late October of that year Enver Hoxha had gone underground. He was wanted for arrest for punching an Italian captain of the *carabinieri* at a demonstration on 20 November 1941. Ramiz Alia, Hoxha's successor 44 years later, then a student at the secondary school and communist supporter, witnessed the incident:

I saw him with my own eyes as he was fighting with the commander of the *carabinieri* at the demonstration in Skanderbeg Square. This was the first time I ever saw Enver Hoxha, albeit from a certain distance and just for a brief moment.[7]

This participation in the Tirana anti-fascist demonstration and the subsequent inclusion of his name on the wanted list may have been the turning point in Hoxha's life and career. The path Hoxha chose in 1941 defied all expectations of those who knew him. In all likelihood, his closeness to Koço Tashko, former Comintern envoy to Albania and head of the Korça Group, must have influenced his choice. Little did Tashko know that by introducing Hoxha to the Albanian communist movement and promoting his career, he would condemn himself to a lifetime of persecution. Early in 1961, Tashko was sentenced to 18 years in prison. His family was banished to an internment camp, while Tashko himself, after serving the full sentence, died a lonely death in a village near Laç, northern Albania.

Thus, in the autumn of 1941 Enver Hoxha appeared, rather unexpectedly, at the founding meeting of the CPA, organised under the auspices of two Yugoslav envoys, Miladin Popović and Dušan Mugoša. It was the opening chapter to one of the most intriguing mysteries in the history of the communist movement in Albania.

Nearly all the participants at the CPA founding meeting who survived to tell the tale explained later that Enver Hoxha had not been on the original list of participants, but somehow ended up coming to the meeting. In his *Kur lindi Partia* Hoxha claimed he was both organiser and chair of the meeting. This was patently untrue, as was the imaginary speech he quotes in his book:

> I stood up. 'Comrades,' I said, 'it is a great honour for me and the Korça Group to be the first to take the floor [...] Comrades, on behalf of the membership of our respective groups whom we represent here, I propose to proceed with the founding of the Communist Party of Albania. Upon approval of this motion, we can solemnly and unanimously declare the Communist Party founded.[8]

And further on:

> Rather excited, I stood up and said, 'Comrades, after the proposal advanced by the Korça Group and the opinions expressed by all present here, I am putting the following draft resolution to the vote: Today, on this eighth day of November 1941, representatives of the three communist groups of Korça, Shkodra and the Youth Group, after constructive discussions in the communist spirit in a plenary meeting and as representatives of the will of other comrades from their respective groups, founded the Communist Party of Albania [...]' All those present raised their hands [...] Then I announced, 'I hereby declare the Communist Party of Albania founded by unanimous decision! Long live the Communist Party of Albania!'[9]

Was this really how the events unfolded at the meeting that led to the founding of the CPA? How did it happen that the least active and the least known of them all became such a central figure at the meeting? While there is general agreement that Hoxha was certainly not the one who read out the founding statement, opinions on his involvement in other aspects of the meeting are widely divergent.

Years later, while serving his jail sentence, Koço Tashko, who had been a key figure at the founding meeting and the person who had liaised with the Yugoslavs, told his prison mates that it was he who took Hoxha along to the meeting. The delegation from Korça was one member short, and Hoxha was asked to fill in. But Tashko's account was only half the story. Whether because of his fear of Hoxha, or because he was reluctant to cast a shadow on the history of the CPA, Tashko never really fully explained why he asked Hoxha to attend the meeting. According to Kristo Frashëri, Miladin Popović and Dušan Mugoša had demanded that the Korça Group have a Muslim member in their delegation. This explanation seems quite plausible. The Korça delegation was initially composed of five members, all of them of the Christian Orthodox faith, so the addition of a Muslim would be perfect to ensure that the largest religious community in the country was represented. But if being a sympathiser and Muslim was all that was needed, why choose Hoxha, and not, say, Ymer Dishnica? Or Mustafa Gjinishi? Koço Tashko reportedly explained what happened to his prison mates in Burrel:

> After the decision to hold the meeting had been made, it occurred to me that I could take Enver Hoxha along as part of our group. I had helped him get a job at the tobacco shop of my friend Esat Dishnica. Enver was known as an intellectual: he had taught at the Korça *lycée* and studied in France for some time. In addition, he was known as a good speaker and writer, and on top of that, he was good-looking. The main reason I took Enver along was that he was of the Muslim faith; the rest of us were all Orthodox. It had to be done, there had to be someone to represent the Muslim majority in Albania.[10]

It seems that Hoxha played no great role in preparations for the CPA founding meeting. While there is some evidence of his involvement in the communist movement in the late 1930s, albeit sporadic, there is nothing to show that he was one of the organisers or, indeed, the person who set the tone for the meeting. Fadil Hoxha, member of the Shkodra Group and a senior communist leader in Kosovo and former Yugoslavia for several decades, has left valuable testimony about the founding of the CPA. According to him, after Nazi Germany attacked the Soviet Union, the communist parties in Europe received instructions to start organising the resistance movement. The Communist Party of Yugoslavia (CPY) decided to step in and put an end to the squabbles among the Albanian communist groups and help them form a communist party, which would be in charge of organising the anti-fascist resistance there. Dušan Mugoša, a Serb member of the CPY who spoke very good Albanian, and Xhevdet Doda, a Kosovar Albanian and member of the Shkodra Group, set off to meet with the heads of the Albanian communist groups. Mugoša held talks with members of the Shkodra Group and the Youth Group, including a very open discussion with Qemal Stafa, but the Korça Group refused to see him. They demanded to see some sort of Comintern credentials or mandate that authorised him to hold talks with the communist groups in Albania. Mugoša was annoyed, sent the Korça Group a message that could be called a threat, and left the country. Whether because of Mugoša's message, or for some other reason, the Korça communists were prompted to action. Elhami Nimani went to Kosovo to carry the message that Koço Tashko wanted to meet with members of the Central Committee of the CPY. According to Fadil Hoxha, who was present at the meeting held in Prizren, Tashko confirmed that the Korça Group was in agreement regarding the founding of an Albanian communist party, but had reservations about the other group leaders and their political line. In 2000, Fadil Hoxha recalled:

> The meeting was chaired by Borko Boro Vukmirović, the provincial organi-
> sational secretary, or Boro, as we called him. He had replaced Miladin,
> who had been interned in Albania. Koço Tashko started speaking and
> his presentation was extremely interesting. We were very happy with it.
> He told us how he had returned from the Soviet Union, how some of

them had studied and had become party members in the Soviet Union and were now continuing their activity in Shkodra, Albania. The core of the group was in Korça. The group's members were mostly workers, but they had also tried to draw other people in the movement, and so on.[11]

Fadil Hoxha explained the main purpose of Koço Tashko's visit to Prizren and the objectives of the CPY:

> Koço Tashko said: 'We are all in favour of having a party; it is not we who are standing in the way, but the disagreements between the groups.' Boro tried to pacify the situation: 'We are ready to help with whatever we can or know. But the situation there, as you describe it, seems to be very serious. This is all the group leaders' doing – according to them, their own group is the party. Your groups are not parties, they are just groups. They must come together [...] all the senior leaders must come together and found the party. I would suggest that none of the present heads of groups be elected to the Politburo, because it was they who created this climate of tension and distrust in the first place.'[12]

As Koço Tashko returned to Albania, Boro Vukmirović debriefed the Central Committee of the CPY and the Shkodra and Youth groups. The CPY leader, Josip Broz Tito, ordered Boro to go to Albania together with an Albanian comrade. Vukmirović was preparing for the trip when the news arrived that Miladin Popović had been freed from his internment by Albanian communists and taken to a secure base in Tirana. Popović, a 31-year-old Montenegrin and leader of the CPY Provincial Committee, was well known in the region. He spoke rudimentary Italian and French and did not have a university degree, but what he lacked in education he more than made up for with his charisma. After the fascist occupation of Montenegro, he was among a number of Montenegrin and Serb communists and nationalists who were arrested and interned in Albania. They lived together in an abandoned school on the outskirts of Peqin, with a duty to report to the *carabinieri* twice a day.

Miladin Popović's release and arrival in Tirana (which Hoxha never mentioned in his memoirs, most likely because he did not play any role in it) was the work of Mustafa Gjinishi. Contrary to what some people think, Gjinishi did not carry out an armed attack; he just pulled a few strings with the government in Tirana. With Popović already in Tirana, the plans changed. Boro Vukmirović was instructed to remain in Kosovo, while Miladin Popović was instructed by the CPY to help with the founding of the CPA. It was hoped that the presence of a foreigner, uninvolved in the internal squabbles among the groups, would help accelerate the founding of the party. The initial plan was that Ali Shukria, an ethnic Albanian communist from Kosovo, would also attend. For some reason, he was ordered at the last moment not to go and Dušan Mugoša went in his place. This was the same man who had failed to bring the Albanian communist groups together a few months earlier. Here is what Fadil Hoxha recalls:

> As Miladin was already [in Albania], the Provincial Committee decided that he should stay for the meeting while another comrade would join him to help with translation between Albanian and Serbian. Miladin did not speak Albanian. First they told Ali Shukria to go. He went to Mitrovica to receive instructions. But then something happened at the Provincial Committee, I don't know what exactly. Ali was ordered not to go and Dušan went in his place. Dušan spoke Albanian – he was the only Serb that could speak Albanian. Elhami Nimani was also present at the meeting in Tirana.[13]

Dušan Mugoša's instructions were to help form the party at any cost, try to prevent the troublesome group leaders from becoming leaders of the new party, and find someone new for the top position who would lead the party in the armed struggle to follow. The founding meeting did not come up with a leader, but Miladin Popović seemed to have made his choice: Enver Hoxha was the least involved in the power struggles among the groups, hence he was the best candidate to become leader of the new party. During the three years that he remained in Albania, Popović kept copious notes on the relations among Albanian communists, as well as their relations with the Yugoslav envoys. His notes were never published: they were used later by authors like Vladimir Dedijer (1949) and Milan Komatina (1995), in a rather biased and incomplete way. A copy of the notes, handwritten in Cyrillic, was sent to the Central State Archives in Albania in 1968, by a 'Kosovar comrade'. They remain there, but have never been translated.

Forty years later, when the relations between Albania and Yugoslavia were extremely tense and the two sides were hurling accusations against each other publicly, the Yugoslavs reminded Hoxha that the CPA had been formed under their auspices. Hoxha responded by publishing a 400-page book, *Kur lindi Partia* (When the party was born), in which he only recognises the contribution of one Yugoslav man, Miladin Popović. There were two reasons for this recognition: firstly, Miladin was the man who had propelled him to the top and Hoxha was grateful to him for that; secondly, Miladin was not alive – he had died 35 years earlier, gunned down by a Kosovar Albanian.

There were several reasons why Enver Hoxha became one of the key leaders of the newly founded party. First and most important, he had not been involved in the internal disputes, which made him a candidate who was acceptable to all. Secondly, he was seen as the least threatening candidate – he had not shown any leadership ambitions until then. The others must have regarded him as a temporary compromise, a pushover who could easily be thrown aside as soon as one of the existing leaders won the race. Thirdly, Hoxha was 33 years old, more mature in years than, say, Qemal Stafa, the most prominent communist figure of the time, who had only just turned 21. Lastly, in the words of Kristo Frashëri, Hoxha was an intellectual who 'could talk the talk':

> On each break between sessions, Anastas Lulo would come and tell us what they had been doing. He said Enver Hoxha was always against his ideas. Enver was a good speaker, he used his logic. He was not one to speak just for the sake of speaking. He had logic. That was what made him rise to the top, like the one-eyed in the kingdom of the blind – this was the first reason. The second, he had the support of Miladin Popović.[14]

When the Central State Archives were opened to the public in 1991, documents were discovered in which Enver Hoxha himself spoke of Miladin's support. In November 1944, in his auto-critique at the plenary meeting in Berat, Hoxha said: 'I seemed to be Ali's [Miladin Popović's] favourite. He had great trust in me. I trusted him too [...] Ali trusted no one, except for me.'[15]

7

A Leader with an Iron Fist

Kristo Frashëri met Enver Hoxha, recently elected to the Central Committee, at a base on the outskirts of Tirana nine days after the foundation of the party, on 17 November 1941. Seventy years later, the face-to-face encounter with the man who would have such an impact on his life and career was still fresh in his mind. The 21-year old Frashëri had reason to be excited about meeting Hoxha, 12 years his senior. He regarded the new leader as a breath of fresh air in the party and saw in him an end to the infighting among the communist groups:

> When I first met him, he seemed quite reserved. In the beginning, he would listen more and say little. He wanted to get to know us. He did not bring up anything unpleasant, he just said, 'This is the beginning of a new era; we must leave the past behind us.' We were impressed. At times he would use French terms, or quote famous sayings from French philosophers, which we found very impressive. The others, the likes of Koçi Xoxe and Vasil Shanto, were more run-of-the-mill. They would say things like, 'Let's kill the enemy; let's destroy them and win.' That was the extent of their oratory. They were completely uncouth, whereas he [Enver] spoke like an intellectual. He was a well-read man. He adored Diderot and quoted him often.[1]

Frashëri stayed at the same base as Hoxha and Popović for about a month. He came to know the leader well and began to have his first reservations. Seventy years later, Frashëri published his first book on the history of the

Albanian left-wing movement and the foundation of the CPA, based on numerous sources and personal contemporaneous notes.

In November 1981, when Enver Hoxha published his memoirs about the founding of the CPA, none of those who attended the first meeting was able to challenge his account of events. Qemal Stafa and Vasil Shanto were killed during the war. Anastas Lulo also died during the war – he was executed by a partisan firing squad on Hoxha's orders, for being a member of the Xhelal Staravecka unit. Koçi Xoxe was executed in 1949. Koço Tashko, Sotir Vullkani, Kristo Themelko and Tuk Jakova had been expelled from the party, dismissed from their government positions or interned as 'enemies' of the party they had themselves founded, or they had died in prison. Dušan Mugoša died, while Miladin Popović was killed in Kosovo soon after the war. By 1981, only four of the original participants were still alive. Of those, two were still in Albania: Pilo Peristeri, the only founding member not executed or punished as an 'enemy', worked as the managing director of a tractor plant. The second, Ramadan Çitaku, led the life of a recluse away from the eyes of the world. The third, Sadik Premtja, emigrated to Paris and was constantly looking over his shoulder, fearing liquidation by the Sigurimi. The fourth, Elhami Nimani, a Kosovar Albanian, who had kept the minutes of the founding meeting, chose to keep his mouth firmly shut. He lived in Belgrade and served as a Yugoslav ambassador to various countries of key importance for Tito's government and policies. Hoxha never mentioned Nimani by name in his memoirs; he was just 'a Kosovar comrade'. There seems to have been a silent pact between the two men. To his death in 1998, Nimani never mentioned the founding meeting, and Hoxha never used Nimani's name in public.

Enver Hoxha was not elected first secretary of the CPA at that meeting. Like Qemal Stafa and Vasil Shanto, he supported Miladin Popović's proposal that none of the former group leaders, who were now locked in a bitter power struggle with each other, should be nominated for party leader, and that no leader should be elected until the next meeting. A seven-member committee, composed of Qemal Stafa, Koçi Xoxe, Ramadan Çitaku, Gjin Marku, Tuk Jakova, Kristo Themelko and Enver Hoxha, was to serve as a collective leadership until the next meeting. Hoxha was in charge of finances and logistics.

His name was put forward by Koço Tashko, as Hoxha himself would admit in 1944: 'At the founding meeting, Koço proposed me for membership in the Central Committee.'[2]

Out of the seven original members of the Central Committee of the CPA, only Ramadan Çitaku died at home in bed. The rest were either killed or jailed, almost all of them on Hoxha's orders.

Although it was conceived as a committee of equals, Hoxha soon began to assume the role of leader and to encroach on the powers of others, in contravention of what the founding meeting had decided. This raises a number of questions about the Albanian communist movement. Why did Hoxha gain prominence, in spite of the declared parity between the committee members? What role did Popović have in all this and why was Enver Hoxha his 'chosen one'? Hoxha himself shed some light on this, in the auto-critique he submitted to the plenary session in Berat, in November 1944. Under attack from all the other Politburo members, who seemed intent on removing him from his post as first secretary, Hoxha gave his own account of events in this document, explaining his rise through the ranks to the top position in the CPA and responding to any criticism of him.

On 18 March 1943, he explained to the party conference at Labinot how he came to be elected to the top position in the CPA:

How did it happen that I became close to Ali [Miladin Popović]? I don't know. The fact is that I did. We went to the national conference together. I seemed to be Ali's favourite there. He had great confidence in me. I trusted him, too. How the conference was organised is another matter. As with all other party events, Ali was present all the time. But the key person at the conference was Blazo. When Blazo arrived with instructions from the Comintern, it was like God descending among us [...] I would like to emphasise my election as a political secretary. Ali trusted no one but me. I don't know about any decisions made in this respect; all I know is that Ali was in favour of me becoming a political secretary.[3]

In fact, from the moment he was elected to the Central Committee on 8 November 1941, Enver Hoxha and Miladin Popović, or Ali, as he was known among the communists, were almost inseparable. After spending time together at a number of bases in Tirana, they left together in 1942, to join the General Staff of the NLA in Labinot near Elbasan. Miladin Popović spoke rudimentary French, so for a long time he relied heavily on Hoxha to communicate with the Albanian communists. Hoxha interpreted at the meetings and translated his orders. In the absence of an elected first secretary, Miladin Popović was the de facto leader of the CPA from 8 November 1941 to 18 March 1943. It was he who chaired meetings and gave the opening and closing speeches. Popović was also responsible for the decisions made at the time, including orders to spread violence and terror. All this was explained by Hoxha in his auto-critique at the plenary session in Berat.

In spring 1943 Popović received a dispatch from Tito instructing him that it was time the CPA was led by a local communist, one of the members of the Central Committee. Popović had already made his choice. Enver Hoxha had shown he was able to manage difficult situations and quell political passions that often flared at the meetings. At the meeting of 18 March in Labinot, Ymer Dishnica moved to propose Enver Hoxha for the post of 'political secretary', or first secretary of the CPA. Miladin Popović endorsed the proposal. No minutes of that meeting exist, which makes it difficult to reconstruct the scene. Hoxha himself did not leave any notes about that meeting in any of the 71 books he wrote about everything related to the history of the party. Whatever the background of his election, from that day on, Hoxha single-handedly dominated the CPA and the Albanian political scene until 9 April 1985 when he went into a coma. He was succeeded by Ramiz Alia, a week after his death, on 18 April 1985.

From the early days, the leader of the CPA used purges and ostracism as means to impose discipline and absolute obedience. Expulsions and ostracism started immediately after the founding of the party, but became a more prominent feature of the CPA's political philosophy after Hoxha's official election as its leader on 18 March 1943. Hoxha's career was characterised by the systematic elimination of all 'rival' fellow communists. It is a sad tale, one familiar to all communist countries, but only in Albania was the tactic used in the manner of the great purges that Stalin conducted in the 29 years of his rule. Enver Hoxha introduced new methods into politics, which Kristo

Frashëri, the first one to be expelled from the party, in early 1942, described as follows:

> As soon as he took the reins of the party, he devoted himself exclusively to his work. Throughout the war he was a man of steely determination. I did not particularly like him, though I did appreciate what he achieved during that time. After the war he became a totally different person. He would still have the same pleasant smile on his face, but his methods, borrowed from Miladin, were deadly: 'Purges were the way to strengthen the party. If there are no enemies, you come up with some anyway.'⁴

Frashëri was sent off to the Peza military unit for 're-education'. In his pocket was a handwritten note in a sealed envelope, which he handed to the political commissar of his unit, unopened. Sixty years later, the note was found in the Central State Archives. It read: 'Dangerous individual, keep an eye on him; at the least sign of wavering, execute him! Enver.'⁵

Had he searched further into the papers of Enver Hoxha and Miladin Popović, the historian Frashëri would have discovered another note with a list of instructions sent to Nako Spiru in March 1944:

> Watch out for splinter groups. We have sent so many letters to Gogo [Nushi] about them. I also wrote to Delikatja [codename for Nexhmije Xhuglini, future wife of Enver Hoxha] when I was in Martanesh. Kristo Frashëri was there while he was preparing to leave for Tirana. Kristo Frashëri told Isuf Keçi to go and meet Old Nezi and probably Xhepi, too […] These groups concentrate in towns as they find it difficult to operate within our units. There they organise and hatch their plans; our comrades must be vigilant, keep a close watch on them and put them down. This is not a time for Gogo and the others to be soft-hearted. No great harm will come to the party if some damage is done; one has to take the rough with the smooth. It's not the end of the world, they should not be afraid.⁶

Kristo Frashëri was not the only one to become a target. Enver Hoxha was ruthless to anyone who did not do his bidding or stood in his way, or those whose personality and charisma would potentially upstage him. Notes and orders dictated by Hoxha to his adjutants during the war, now preserved in the Central State Archives, reveal a stern and cynical man, devoid of any human feelings. The following order given to the North Division on 21 September 1944 concerns Llazar Fundo, one of the first Albanian communists, personally known to Hoxha from their time in Korça:

> Torture Zai Fundo to the brink of death and then execute him. Ask him questions about the following: why did he go to Kosovo? Who sent him there and what instructions had he received? What are Gani [Kryeziu] and the English aiming to do? He must be held to account for his former activities and his treason. Send us his deposition with a trusted person. Then have Zai killed on the spot. Enver[7]

Apparently Hoxha had been looking for Llazar Fundo for quite some time, as seen in a couple of other documents found in the Central State Archives: in August and September he demanded that NLA forces in the north of the country gather intelligence about Fundo's whereabouts and activities, and if they got hold of him, 'not to treat him as just any other hostage'. Hoxha had learned that Fundo had some leverage with the British mission, had joined the Kryeziu brothers in the fight against the Germans, and had nothing to do with the collaborationists. But Hoxha resented the fact that Fundo had received training as a communist in Moscow and had been a Comintern envoy to many countries of the world. Vedat Kokona, who knew Fundo both from Paris and Korça, wrote the following in his memoirs, published 60 years later:

> [Fundo] was tall and blonde, with the facial features of a Scandinavian. He stood out among other Albanians in cafés, not only because of his looks and appearance, but also because of his comportment and broad knowledge [...] I have rarely met an Albanian as cultivated as he was.[8]

From the scathing remarks in Hoxha's memoirs, written 40 years after Fundo was killed, it is clear that the two were not on the best of terms even much earlier, when both of them were still in Korça. It is likely that Enver Hoxha bore a grudge against Fundo because the latter used to make fun of him and often dismissed him as a 'scoundrel'. But Hoxha's hatred of Fundo could also have been instigated by the Yugoslavs. A dispatch sent by Tito to the CPA on 22 September 1942 described Fundo as an 'enemy'. This was the second time Tito had complained about Fundo: in 1939 he had sent Miladin Popović to Shkodra to persuade the members of the Shkodra Communist Group not to fall under Fundo's sway. Tito's letter, cited in Vladimir Dedijer's book on Yugoslav–Albanian relations in 1939–48, stipulated:

> Trotskyite Fundo and his collaborators must be denounced publicly in front of the entire membership of the CPA; he must be treated as the dangerous enemy of the Communist International and the Communist Party that he is, and divested of all powers in the party.[9]

Llazar Fundo was indeed executed after undergoing horrendous torture. In fact, there was no need to take him to the firing squad – he expired under torture by his captors. His death was witnessed by a horrified radio operator of the British mission and by Said Kryeziu, both of whom were captured at the same time. The partisan fighters handed the British radio operator over to the British mission attached to Hoxha's staff. Said Kryeziu managed to flee thanks to vigorous British intervention. After leaving the country he went initially to Britain and then to the United States, where he died in 1993.

Archival documents show how, towards the end of the war, when victory and power were almost within reach, Hoxha attempted to eliminate some individuals who were publicly recognised as founders of the Albanian communist movement. It is not known whether they were targeted simply because of their more prominent roles in the movement, or because of their fractious and impulsive natures, which would sometimes cause trouble in the party. Of course, such behaviour must have caused Hoxha many a headache. Keeping the party united and under control was no easy task. Ruling with an iron fist was necessary, not only to win the war, but also to ensure a hold on power once the war was over. But the methods he used to achieve these aims were often blood-curdling. In the 1990s numerous documents were found in the archives of the CPA, containing orders similar to the above. Some of them were carried out; others, fortunately, were not.

One such diabolical document in Hoxha's handwriting, now preserved at the Central State Archives in Tirana, refers to the elimination of Anastas (Nastas) Plasari, another prominent figure in the Albanian left-wing movement. In his book *Historia e lëvizjes së majtë në Shqipëri* (History of the left-wing movement in Albania), Kristo Frashëri provided the following biographical sketch of Plasari:

> A. Plasari was born in Korça in 1903; emigrated to Romania in 1913; became a member of the Socialist Youth of Romania in 1918 and member of the Communist Party of Romania in 1922. That same year he attended the Marxist school where Ana Pauker taught. For a period he was an activist of the Communist Party there. He was arrested several times for his activities, until his expulsion from Romania in January 1925. Upon returning to Korça, Plasari was involved in the organisation of workers' associations. He was detained in April, released two months later for lack of evidence, and was subsequently sent to Vlora where he served three years in internment.[10]

Given his prominence in the Albanian communist movement of the 1920s and 1930s, it is a bit of a mystery why Plasari, and other equally well-known communists like Hasan Reçi and Xhevdet Doda, were not present at the 1941 founding meeting. Frashëri thinks they were 'deliberately left out because they had renounced the Bolshevik line and defected to social democracy'.[11] In spite of the ideological differences, Plasari agreed to recognise the authority of the CPA in 1942. On 8 June 1943 Enver Hoxha sent Plasari a note, addressed to 'Dear Comrade Nastas', with the following invitation:

> You need to come here for four or five days to meet and talk to the comrades who are not properly informed. You can explain the issues to them and we can then continue with our work. In addition, I would like to discuss an issue regarding Hysni Lepenica; I went to Vlora to meet him

[...] When you get here, go to the Çekani pharmacy and ask for Raqi Kërënxhi. He will tell you where to meet us and then we can speak to the other comrades. Tell Raqi Kërënxhi: 'I am here to meet Dunaveci.' Looking forward to seeing you. Regards.[12]

The same courier delivered a second note to Gogo Nushi, CPA leader for Tirana, in which Hoxha had written the following: 'We never asked Anastas Plasari to come here; your order was to get rid of him *sans bruit et sans trompettes*. Do not ask about this again [...] Taras.'[13]

After consultation with the other members of the Tirana leadership, Nako Spiru and Ymer Dishnica, Gogo Nushi decided not to execute the order he had received. Anastas Plasari did indeed go to Korça to meet comrade Enver. In a letter she sent to her fiancé on 14 October 1943, Nexhmije Xhuglini (Delikatja) explained why the order for Plasari's elimination was not carried out:

> In relation to the purging of certain individuals – I did communicate your instructions to the comrades. As Deti [Nako Spiru] wrote, they do not agree with what we decided there. They are not convinced that I reported the issue of Anastas Plasari and the others properly. They are dithering for fear of acting unjustly. I'm loath to respond to minor allegations, but you should know that it was not my decision to have Anastas Plasari sent there [...] Delikatja[14]

It is unknown who the 'others' mentioned in the letter of the 22-year-old Xhuglini were, or whether or not they were killed. But it is likely that Gogo Nushi, Nako Spiru and Ymer Dishnica sent Plasari into the lion's den so that Hoxha could carry out the elimination himself if he wanted. Feeling awkward at Plasari's presence, Hoxha sent another scathing note to Nako Spiru on 29 September 1943: 'We never asked you to send Anastas Plasari to us. A bullet is all he deserves.'[15]

As a one-time follower of the Marxist activist Max Wexler and aware of the methods used by Stalinist communism, Plasari must have already sensed something was amiss. He probably realised that he was a target from the time of the first CPA conference in Labinot, where Enver Hoxha was elected leader. In his memoirs, Plasari wrote:

> The conference issued directives for an 'all out war' against the enemies of the party, who were now being called 'Trotskyites', 'traitors', 'agents', etc. In addition to Andrea Zisi [...] other names were mentioned, including Dhimitër Fallo, Aristidh Qendro and Llazar Fundo. Denouncing people like them – that was something I was prepared to accept – I had been long enough in the movement to know how things worked. But two comrades who came from Labinot said that there was talk of physical elimination. At first we refused to believe it, but then it transpired that it was true. After the conference, Anastas Lulo, [Hoxha's] friend and a founding member of the CPA, was executed in April 1943. I discussed the matter with some trusted friends and concluded that we needed to be extremely cautious and protect ourselves. It was not to be excluded that each of us was in real danger.[16]

Even later on, Enver Hoxha was unable to rid himself of his 'Plasari complex'. He feared that some other authoritative figure would rise to lead a new left-wing party. He reveals his concern in his letter of October 1943 to Gogo Nushi:

> Regarding the famous A. P., you'd better give the matter some serious thought. When Deti [Nako Spiru] said the social democrats would attempt to form another communist party, he did not mean under Xhepi, but by winning over some other 'comrades'. This is not just a rumour, it is based on the information you gave us. You said he was a bad influence, and now you seem to have changed your mind. We stand by our opinion. God forbid that you get your way [...] Taras[17]

Anastas Plasari survived by being very cautious and because of the authority he enjoyed among other communists who refused to carry out Hoxha's orders for his liquidation. He worked in the agitprop department of the NLA led by Sejfullah Malëshova and was often in close proximity to Enver Hoxha – a virtual hostage situation, as he described it in his memoirs. After

1944 he served in various positions, including director of the Albanian Film Agency and of the Tirana Theatre, which was later known as 'The People's Theatre'. He was arrested on 23 March 1946 – the day after Enver Hoxha was sworn in as prime minister of the first government of the People's Republic of Albania (22 March–1 October 1948) – and expelled from the CPA for 'anti-Yugoslav agitation'. He was initially charged with embezzlement and being a British agent, but was pardoned in 1949 after the fall of Koçi Xoxe and his associates. After his release he worked at the Ministry of Agriculture in a position similar to the one he had held at the Ministry of National Economy under King Zog and the Italian occupation. According to Plasari, he was saved thanks to the energetic intervention of his friend and teacher, comrade Ana Pauker, then known as the 'iron lady' of the communist East. After Ana Pauker's fall from grace because of her differences with Stalin, and her house arrest at the end of 1952, Plasari was forced to leave his job as a civil servant for good. In spite of the medals of honour he received for his participation in the National Liberation War, he was now an 'undesirable element', which, among other things, meant that he also lost his food stamps. He spent the rest of his life well away from the political scene, working as a manual labourer. Plasari died in Tirana in the mid-1980s. He left an unpublished manuscript of memoirs which, together with his personal file at the Ministry of the Interior, constitute an important source of information not only about his life, but also about the history of the left-wing movement in Albania.

Asked in 2007 how he managed to survive Hoxha's purges, while his close friend Anastas Lulo ended up being shot by firing squad, Kristo Frashëri responded:

> I was saved by 250 leks. Remember those Tutius padlocks they used to sell for 250 leks? I bought one of them and locked my mouth shut. I abandoned politics, never to return to it again. I never spoke about anything political at all.[18]

Plasari, for his part, did not have it as easy, perhaps because of the choice he made not to 'padlock' his mouth. His Sigurimi file contains a report dated

27 February 1959, in which an informant recounts a conversation Plasari had with a friend:

> They met [with Anastas Plasari] on the evening of 24 March 1959 and I overheard Anastas tell him the following: 'On the fifteenth anniversary of the liberation of Albania, four people will be decorated as "pioneers of the communist movement". These are: Enver Hoxha, Ali Kelmendi, Halim Xhelo and Qemal Stafa. Now, all of them, except for Enver, are being decorated posthumously. Had they been alive, Halim Xhelo and Ali Kelmendi would probably be in prison now. As for Enver, it is true that he led the party, both during the war and after, but he was actually not a pioneer. Enver started his revolutionary activity quite late.'[19]

Zef Mala, one of the founders of the Albanian communist movement and leader of the Shkodra Group, was also targeted, but he managed to survive the war. In a letter to Nako Spiru on 4 April 1944, Enver Hoxha instructed: 'Zef Mala must not go to Kosovo. Decorate him with a bullet in the head. He is not a good man and must be liquidated. Find a way to keep it quiet, but it has to be done.'[20]

Whether it was an act of defiance or soft-heartedness, the fact is that Nako Spiru and Ymer Dishnica refused to carry out the order to kill Zef Mala – they only stopped him from going to Kosovo. After the war Mala worked briefly as director of the Central State Archives, but was soon arrested and convicted, and died in prison while serving his 27-year sentence. His only crime was that he was one of the few remaining people who could belie Hoxha's version of history about the latter's involvement in the communist movement.

In fact, Hoxha's rancour against people like Plasari and Mala was clearly fuelled by his jealousy as a young and as yet politically inexperienced communist leader. Plasari and Mala were prominent militants who had contributed to the left-wing movement in Albania since the mid-1920s. By eliminating them, Hoxha practically eliminated the entire history of communism in Albania prior to his appearance on the scene.

Another important figure of the Albanian communist movement and its most important ideologist, Sejfullah Malëshova, was purged in 1946. He was a left-wing activist of almost mythical status. After graduating from the College of San Demetrio Corone, founded by Girolamo De Rada in southern Italy, he went on to study medicine in Rome but cut his studies short and returned to Albania at a difficult moment in the country's history. In 1924, at 23 years of age, he was personal secretary to prime minister Fan Noli, one of the most renowned figures in the history of the Albanian state. After the fall of Noli's government and Ahmet Zogu's return to Tirana, Malëshova fled the country, but did not return to Italy to resume his studies in medicine. Instead, he went to Moscow where he studied philosophy and worked as a manual labourer in the Caucasus after the purges of the 1930s. He was later active at Lomonosov University as a professor of philosophy. A member of the Communist (Bolshevik) Party of the Soviet Union (CPSU) and a Comintern activist, Malëshova returned to Albania in June 1943 and immediately made a name for himself as the most prominent communist ideologist in the country. A renowned poet, philosopher and translator, he rose against Hoxha by initially denouncing the CPA as 'a party with terrorist tendencies' that exercised terror on the 'former ruling classes', carried out mass and large-scale nationalisations and established relations with the East at the expense of the West. Labelled an 'opportunist', he was gradually removed from the political scene. He was first divested of his functions and then banished to Fier, where he worked as storehouse manager until his death in 1971. His death was as lonely as his life – he was avoided by everyone in town, except for those who worked with him. Hoxha's memoirs are full of scathing remarks about him. After the 1990s, those who had known Malëshova personally spoke well about him, including Hoxha's widow. In her memoirs published in 1998 she subtly observed that had Malëshova been alive, he would have become a member of the Democratic Party, the Socialist Party or the Social Democratic Party, but he was far too soft to be a member and leader of the CPA.[21]

Purges and disappearances were common occurrences in the CPA from the first months of its existence. Qemal Stafa, the best known of the young communists and Hoxha's strongest rival within the party, was eliminated in suspicious circumstances on 5 May 1942. His death is one of the unsolved mysteries of the Albanian communist movement. It was alleged that Hoxha had something to do with it and rumours continue about this to the present day. The allegations are supported by a simple detail: in his 1981 memoirs Hoxha lied when he said that he had been with Qemal Stafa the night before he died. This is how he described the death of the communist activist in his book *Kur lindi Partia*:

> I last saw Qemal on 4 May. We met at base 66, on Shëngjergj Street, in Hysen Dashi's house. We were in the house all day, working. The old man brought us something to eat. I was preparing a lecture on the Red Army; Qemal was getting ready for his trip to Vlora the next day. We slept beside each other, on a sofa, wrapped in blankets. In the morning we hugged and parted. He set off for Vlora; I had a meeting with the comrades. With pistols tucked in our belts and grenades in our pockets, we could meet death at any street corner any time we went out, but we tried not to think about it. It never occurred to me that that was the last time I would hug Qemal Stafa, one of the best comrades in the party, my dear friend and comrade-in-arms. Someone came around to where I was staying and told me with tears in his eyes, 'The enemy has killed Qemal Stafa.' I hid my face in my hands and could not help crying. 'Where did they kill him?' I asked. 'In Tirana,' he replied, 'in a house on the riverbank.' I stood up and said, hoping against hope, 'It can't be true, Qemal left for Vlora this morning. I am sure about this. Don't believe rumours, the enemy plants them!' 'Alas,' he countered, 'it is true. Qemal was killed in the fight, he fell heroically covering the retreat of other comrades who managed to escape. He used up the entire ammunition he had on him.' This is the story he told me, the one that you will now find in any history book.[22]

In fact, the story of Qemal Stafa's killing, told after 1990 by his fiancée at the time, Drita Kosturi, is completely different. The account she gave to the weekly *Klan* in April 1998 is unequivocal as to how he died:

> Qemal Stafa, leader of the Albanian Communist Youth and one of the key party leaders, arrived at the Tirana base on the afternoon of 4 May 1942. This was a one-storey house composed of two buildings. The owner lived

in one of them; the other had been rented out to a communist militant, Beqir Minxhozi. Qemal Stafa was not the only undercover activist in the house. His fiancée, Drita Kosturi, had also arrived there a week earlier. Drita and two other young female communists, Maria Lezha and Gjystina Sata, whose previous base had been discovered [by the authorities], had been ordered to transfer to that base. On the evening of 4 May all three were there, as were Qemal and Beqir Minxhozi. Qemal had received orders to go to the south and was to leave the next morning. The couple stayed up all night recalling their years of study in Italy. It was one of those long nights that made one lose any sense of time, until the first break of dawn put things into real perspective.

The morning of 5 May found them up already. They were all awake when Kristo Themelko and Isuf Keçi arrived at the base. Drita Kosturi finds it difficult to remember why they arrived there. She just remembers that Beqir Minxhozi went out to buy some groceries and Isuf Keçi left to get some salt. Beqir and Isuf tarried longer than usual. Drita and Qemal were in the front room, while Kristo and the other two young women were in the back room. Qemal was reading some poetry by Manzoni, when he noticed armed civilians close to the house. 'We are surrounded!' he shouted and jumped to his feet. The besiegers did not notice the commotion in the house. Confident that there was no way anyone could escape, they were taking their time. The young women grabbed some documents and started chewing and swallowing them. Kristo Themelko burned some others and then he broke the bathroom window and they all climbed out. Behind the house there was a wide, barren field so it was not easy to escape unnoticed. 'Follow me,' Qemal shouted and hastened to the right. Maria and Gjystina followed him. Kristo ran to the left, so that the pursuers would have to follow them in different directions. He threw a Breda hand grenade, the only offensive ammunition available to them at that moment. The pursuers stopped following Kristo and focused on Qemal, who was lagging behind. The three young women could not run as fast as he could and, a few metres further on, they fell into the hands of the police. Kristo Themelko escaped by doing something counter-intuitive: he walked towards the centre of town. Qemal fled in the opposite direction, towards the river. This is

where the whole story gets really complicated and neither the owner of
the house, nor the rest of the people involved, can explain what happened.
The only witness to the tragic moment was a man who requested to remain
anonymous. His presence at the scene was officially confirmed only much
later. Y. B., a farmer from the Tirana area, was going into town by following a shortcut. On the riverbank he came face to face with a young man
with a pistol in his hand. The enemy was close, their presence could be
felt. Qemal had been wounded. He could not walk any further. He had a
Smithson with two rounds of ammunition left in it. The farmer realised
that the young man was a member of the resistance and offered to swap
clothes with him, but the latter declined. Qemal Stafa fired his last shot
into his own chest, without any explanation or last words.[23]

It seems that Qemal Stafa's encounter with the militia was an unfortunate
accident. A report on the operation filed with the Italian police, now in the
Central State Archives, does not say anything about a tip-off; it only states
that Beqir Minxhozi, who had been stopped earlier that day, was searched and
that two home addresses were found in his pocket. This had raised suspicions,
which led the Italians to the base where Qemal Stafa was staying. In fact the
Italian police did not recount the operation as anything of significance and
Qemal Stafa was merely described as a 'former student'.

The fate of Drita Kosturi, Qemal Stafa's fiancée and close friend of
Nexhmije Xhuglini (Hoxha) and Fiqirete Sanxhaktari (Shehu), was no less
tragic. A member of the underground resistance movement, she later joined
the NLA. Her elder brother was killed by the Germans. She survived the
war, but her future was bleak, as described in a 1998 interview:

> My future was to be even bleaker. I was arrested in 1946 and charged with
> being an English agent. I was sentenced to death and for the next three
> months I was kept in handcuffs 24 hours a day as I awaited execution.
> In 1948 I was pardoned. I then served 13 years in prison, with two good
> friends of mine, Musine Kokalari and Frida Sadedini. After my release I
> was interned in Shtyllëz near Fier. I lived there until 1988, when I returned
> to Tirana.[24]

Drita Kosturi did not know it then, but she was witness to an event that marked a turning point in the CPA. Wounded and unable to flee, Qemal Stafa had killed himself, thus eliminating Enver Hoxha's main competitor in the party. This opened the way to Hoxha's election as first secretary of the Central Committee of the CPA, on 18 March 1943, nearly one year after Qemal Stafa's death and the purging of Anastas Lulo, Sadik Premtja and others.

Anastas Lulo had been expelled from the party as a 'deviationist'. Just like his close friend and comrade-in-arms Kristo Frashëri, he had been sent to a partisan unit and remained there until 1943, but was not able to escape elimination, like some of his luckier friends. As with Fundo, Hoxha gave orders for him to be killed, but only after interrogation under torture, so that he would disclose the names of his associates in the CPA and what they had discussed about Hoxha and Miladin Popović.

Sadik Premtja, nicknamed 'Xhepi', managed to escape death thanks to a fortuitous coincidence. After receiving information that Premtja had been stirring up feelings against him, Hoxha ordered Vlora partisan forces to ambush and capture him. Someone told Premtja about the plan and he decided to flee Albania. He settled in France where he lived for 47 years, working as a manual labourer and living daily in fear of being liquidated by the Albanian Sigurimi. A document preserved in the archives of the Ministry of the Interior reveals that Llambi Peçini once tried to kill him in Paris. The same file contains dispatches sent to Albanian agents in Paris, instructing them to provide detailed information on Premtja's whereabouts, his activities, and his friends and associates in exile. Sadik Premtja died in 1991, six months after the collapse of communism in Albania. He was found lifeless in his bed on the morning he was supposed to travel to Albania to meet a daughter he had not seen in 48 years, and a handful of remaining friends. On the night table was his flight ticket, bought with money borrowed from another Albanian émigré in Paris, and a letter his daughter had sent him in 1990.

At the plenary meeting held in Berat in November 1944, Enver Hoxha was directly accused of eliminating CPA members. In his auto-critique, he explained that he had acted on orders from Miladin Popović and Dušan Mugoša:

The terrorist line was mostly championed by Dušan, Ali [Popović] and Liri. I was more of a reflection of Ali in this. When someone arrived from the front and reported that so-and-so was acting improperly, a decision was made to execute that person. There were no clear rules. If Gogo sent us a report about Sotir Kondi, we would tell [Gogo] to execute him. If there was a report about Anastas Plasari and Zef Mala, we would give orders for them to be killed.[25]

On 18 March 1943 there was no one to stand in the way of Hoxha's becoming the supreme leader of the CPA. He had risen to the top with the help of Miladin Popović, who was still calling the shots in the party. Miladin had complete trust in Hoxha and supported him without reservation, as Hoxha himself admitted in his speech in Berat:

In order to do our work and discharge our responsibilities we had to rely constantly on Miladin and Dušan. We were like pupils who asked their teacher for advice about everything, seeking their approval and guidance. Everything we did had to have Miladin's seal of approval. To all intents and purposes, Miladin was the Central Committee; there was no Central Committee outside him.[26]

A new Politburo emerged from the meeting of 18 March 1943, composed of Enver Hoxha, Koçi Xoxe, Nako Spiru, Liri Gega, Ymer Dishnica, Ramadan Çitaku, Gjin Marku and Kristo Themelko. Forty years later, only Enver Hoxha was still a member of the Central Committee: Koçi Xoxe and Liri Gega had been executed by firing squad; Nako Spiru had committed suicide; Gjin Marku and Kristo Themelko were languishing in prison, and Ymer Dishnica and Ramadan Çitaku had long been expelled from the party.

8

Nationalists and Communists

Now a leader of the CPA – which came to life only a few months after Hitler's Germany attacked the Soviet Union, but was already commanding authority among the various resistance groupings led by Myslim Peza, Haxhi Lleshi and Abaz Kupi – Enver Hoxha embarked upon a strategy for winning the war and, more importantly, for maintaining his grip on power once the war was over.

Documents that have come to light recently have revealed that Hoxha was convinced that an Allied victory was just a matter of time. He focused his efforts on strengthening his position as leader and removing any impediments to his postwar rise to power. Hoxha knew this was not going to be easy: Albanians tended to be very conservative; they had a deep-seated dislike of Russia and the Slavs generally, as well as an equally profound distrust of anything related to communism or communists. The advice he had been given by the Yugoslavs (following Comintern instructions to all communist parties in Eastern Europe) was to avoid publicly referring to the CPA as the leader of the Albanian resistance movement. Instead, Hoxha would usually speak of 'a patriotic resistance movement', in which the communists had a role to play, albeit not a central one.

On 16 September 1942 a meeting was convened in Peza, near Tirana, which came to be known in history as the Peza Conference. Among the delegates to the meeting were numerous nationalists, prominent figures, armed fighters and so on, who had come together to found an organisation that would mobilise people in the fight against the enemy and provide leadership to them. Hoxha later claimed that the Peza Conference was his brainchild – which he had convened in an attempt to unite all forces, be they communist or anti-communist, in the fight against fascism. This claim, which appears in his book *Kur u hodhën themelet e Shqipërisë së re* (*Laying the Foundations of a New Albania*), directly contradicts what Hoxha himself stated at the plenary meeting held in Berat on 26 November 1944, where his claims were much more modest:

> I won't go into details about how we worked with the nationalists later; I will only focus on what I knew about the Peza Conference at the time it was being organised. This, too, had to do with Ali [Miladin Popović]. He was there in Peza; I stayed behind in Tirana. We had discussed the matter earlier, but only briefly. I received a note asking me to send out invitations for people to attend the meeting. When I eventually arrived in Peza, the comrades were already squabbling over who was going to give what speech.[1]

Hoxha appears to be telling the truth here – at that time the CPA did not yet have a confirmed leader and Miladin Popović was the one who made all the decisions on behalf of its leadership. According to Ymer Dishnica's memoirs, the task of organising the conference was given to him and to Mustafa Gjinishi, both of whom held some sway among the nationalists.

The conference, which was attended by numerous non-communist anti-fascist activists, elected a National Liberation Council headed by Ndoc Çoba, himself not a communist. The council brought together a mix of influential Albanians but the communists pulled all the strings. Abaz Kupi was elected deputy chairman. From that time until August 1944 all anti-fascist propaganda in the country was conducted in the name of the National Liberation Council rather than the CPA, which kept a low profile until 1950. The Albanian constitution of 1950 then sanctioned the creation of a one-party state under the rule of the Party of Labour of Albania (PLA) – the new name assumed by the CPA about a year earlier.

The 34-year-old Hoxha knew that there were two potential threats to his hold on power. One of them was the exiled King Zog and his numerous followers in the country; the other was Balli Kombëtar, a nationalist movement which became a political party in 1942.

King Zog had been living in England since 1940. In truth, he did not hold much sway over Albania. Hoxha's position was undoubtedly helped by the fact that Zog was not afforded the same reception in London as other dethroned or banished monarchs. His government in exile was not recognised by the British; the exiled king was not considered an ally in the war against the Axis powers and was not officially received at No. 10 Downing Street. Because of pressure brought to bear by the Greeks, who considered him an obstacle to their territorial claims, Zog was sidelined to all intents and purposes – to the point that the British were even annoyed by news of pro-Zog propaganda that came from Albania. On 5 November 1943 Major Tilman of the British mission, seconded to the General Staff of the NLA, received a telegram from London, which he officially transmitted to Enver Hoxha. The message said:

> NO, repeat NO truth in the story of a meeting with Zog! Churchill did NOT, repeat, did NOT, talk to him and has no intention of doing so.[2]

Balli Kombëtar, on the other hand, was much more of a real threat. As a chaotic and eclectic political organisation, it boasted membership of some of the most prominent figures in Albanian politics from the time of independence onwards, mostly opponents of King Zog and proponents of a republic. As the son of Abdyl Frashëri and nephew of Naim Frashëri, two much-loved figures of the Albanian 'Rilindja' (Revival), Mid'hat Frashëri was held in great esteem by young people in Albania at the time. A scholar of Albanian language and literature, as well as a publisher and writer under the pen name Lumo Skëndo, Frashëri also had a distinguished political career. He was one of the signatories of the declaration of independence in 1912 and minister in the first Albanian government under Ismail Qemali. Mid'hat Frashëri and his cousin Mehdi Frashëri, who at the time was living in exile in Italy, were considered two of the most prominent figures of public and political life in Albania.

If we are to believe Hoxha's memoirs published 40 years later, he and Mid'hat Frashëri met at least once. In his book, Hoxha recognised the fact that the scion of the influential Frashëri family was very popular among the young generation, which makes his account of their meeting in a corner of the Lumo Skëndo bookstore on Rruga Mbretnore sound unconvincing. In his version of events, Hoxha spoke to Mid'hat Frashëri sternly and chided him for speaking ill of the communists, and then left the bookstore thinking that Frashëri was a hopeless case. When Hoxha's memoirs were published, Mid'hat Frashëri could not possibly rebut them, as, by then, he had been lying in his American grave for 32 years. Frashëri did not leave any memoirs to enable a comparison with Hoxha's. While he was alive, he never mentioned having met the communist leader.

However, the personal relations between the two leaders were of no great importance. It was clear that the nationalists and the communists would not be able to fight side by side against the Italian and German occupiers. Their approaches to the anti-fascist resistance and the war were totally at odds with each other.

The communists showed that they were more determined to fight and much better organised than the nationalists. They operated under a single command structure that managed to impose a level of discipline until then unknown in Albanian politics. Their determination to fight the foreign occupier ensured the support of the British and American Allies, whose primary concern at the time was ensuring victory over the Germans, rather than postwar power politics.

Balli Kombëtar was a rather disorderly organisation led by fractious local beys turned politicians whose 40 years of bickering made it difficult to take a unified and consequential stance. The Ballists set up several fighting units but only a handful of them ever took part in any real military action against the occupiers. In fact the various factions within the organisation often ignored Mid'hat Frashëri's leadership and authority. Hoxha wrote of his disdain of Balli and the Ballists from an early stage, when he had contacts with anti-monarchist émigrés in France and Italy. He would describe them as a bunch of self-styled leaders and commanders, and 'generals without soldiers'. Hoxha was right. With their Ottoman-style, old-school way of doing politics, the Balli leaders were no match for the up-and-coming young communists and their dynamic political style. To the end of their lives, the Ballists could not quite comprehend how it happened that World

War II brought not just a change of government, but a total revolution in the way politics were done in Albania. The new communist wave that 'came down from the mountains' swept away the entire political class of the post-Albanian-independence years.

The two major political forces kept their distance from one other, thus maintaining a certain détente until August 1943. The idea of a united front was launched and relaunched several times, urged and supported by the British. An earnest attempt to bring the two sides together was made at a meeting in Mukja, a village near Tirana, in August 1943. It became known in Albanian history as the Mukja meeting or the Mukja Agreement.

On 1 and 2 August 1943, delegations from the National Liberation Council and Balli Kombëtar gathered at the house of Ihsan Toptani, a young Albanian scholar who had studied in Austria and had just returned to Albania. Son of Abdyl Toptani, a signatory to the declaration of independence and a well-known patriot, Ihsan enjoyed the trust of both parties. He used his father's renown to get the representatives of the anti-fascist resistance together in his house in Tapiza, a few kilometres from Tirana. But the gathering of so many armed men in a place so near Tirana raised the suspicions of the Italian authorities and it seems the two delegations were warned not to go. The meeting was then transferred to a small hamlet a few kilometres further north, closer to Kruja, where the delegates would be much safer. It seems that both parties attached considerable importance to the meeting. Balli Kombëtar was represented by Mid'hat Frashëri, head of the delegation, and members Hasan Dosti, Thoma Orollogaj, Skënder Muço, Hysni Lepenica, Jusuf Luzaj, Kadri Cakrani, Major Raif Fratari, Nexhat Peshkëpija, Halil Mëniku, Ismail Petrela and Vasil Andoni. The National Liberation delegation was headed by Ymer Dishnica and Mustafa Gjinishi, both communists, and among its members were a number of prominent partisan fighters and well-known nationalists, including Lieutenant Jahja Çaçi, Myslim Peza, Abaz Kupi, Omer Nishani, Sulo Bogdo, Shefqet Beja, Medar Shtylla, Haki Stërmilli and Gogo Nushi.

It is not known what instructions the National Liberation delegation had received about the negotiations. According to Enver Hoxha, their mission was to convince Balli Kombëtar to join the National Liberation Movement,

recognise its authority, and join forces in the fight against the occupiers. No
one knows how true this claim is. So far no written documents have been
found that contain any instructions to that effect. What is known is that a
week prior to the meeting, the delegations had met and agreed in principle
on the following points:

I. Establish a Joint Committee for the Salvation of Albania with the
   following programme:
   1. Engage in immediate war with the occupiers for the liberation of
      Albania.
   2. Achieve the full independence of the country within the borders
      set in 1913 and unite all Albanian-inhabited territories, pursuant
      to the general principle of national self-determination, universally
      recognised and guaranteed by the Atlantic Charter.
   3. Build a free, independent and truly democratic Albania.
   4. The form of the regime shall be determined by the people through
      a constituent assembly elected by universal suffrage.[3]

On 1 and 2 August, the parties returned to sign the agreement after consultations held at their respective headquarters. The minutes of the meeting were
made public only 60 years later. The statement issued by the representatives
of the two parties, also made public about 50 years later, contained a solemn
appeal to the Albanian people. This is the text:

DECLARATION
   Albanian People!
   It has been nearly five years now that Fascist Italy has occupied our
beloved country, sowing suffering and misery everywhere.
   Their barbarism knows no bounds. They have recently burned and
destroyed villages and towns, killed and impaled men and women of all
ages with unprecedented bloody voracity; even elderly people and infants
have not been spared. The Committee for the Salvation of Albania,
which has the mandate to represent the nation, presents the following
programme:

1. Joint and immediate action, alongside our great allies – England, the USA, the Soviet Union and the oppressed people – to fight against the barbaric occupier.
2. Fight for an independent and ethnic Albania pursuant to the globally recognised principle of self-determination guaranteed under the Atlantic Charter.
3. Fight for a free and democratic Albania; an Albania for the Albanian people.

Albanians!

There is no time to wait! The occupier has usurped our homes.

The time has come for all of us, young and old, men and women, intellectuals, patriots from towns and villages, to take up arms and expel the foreign occupiers from our sacred Albanian lands as swiftly as possible.

Therefore, rise to action! Make a solemn pledge around the flag of Skanderbeg; unite around the Committee for the Salvation of Albania and attack the enemy everywhere with weapons or whatever you can find! Break free from the chains of servitude and avenge the blood of our fallen heroes who lost their lives on the battlefields for the liberation of Albania! The day of salvation is nigh!

Down with the enemies and occupiers!

Long live Albania united as one in the war against the occupiers!

Long live our great allies – England, the United States and the Soviet Union!

Long live independent and democratic Albania!

Committee for the Salvation of Albania[4]

But the Committee for the Salvation of Albania was never constituted and aspirations of joint resistance and a Western-style democratic regime after the war were never realised. Enver Hoxha was in Vithkuq, near Korça, when he received news of the committee and the Mukja Agreement. He was reportedly very agitated, and sent an urgent letter to Dishnica asking for more information.

The information arrived at the General Staff field camp via the Korça communist cell on 8 August. It was a copy of the agreement reached between the communists and the Ballists. Enver Hoxha, Miladin Popović and others were extremely unhappy with its content. Eyewitnesses described how Hoxha banged his fist on the table and promptly dictated a letter, or circular, in which he repudiated the Mukja Agreement. A few days after it was signed by Mustafa Gjinishi and Ymer Dishnica, Hoxha denounced the agreement as an act of treason by the members of the National Liberation Movement. He held that the agreement had been signed without seeking authorisation from the CPA. On 8 August 1943 he sent the following circular, which was subsequently printed as a tract, to all party chapters in the regions:

CIRCULAR ON THE REPUDIATION OF THE MUKJA AGREEMENT
8 August 1943
Dear comrades,
    We have received information that a tract signed by the Committee for the Salvation of Albania, claiming an alleged fusion of the National Liberation Council and Balli Kombëtar, was sent to you for distribution. This tract is in contravention of the national liberation line and was not approved by the Central Committee of the party. Therefore, if you have not distributed it already, tear it up and forget it ever existed. If Balli demand an explanation, tell them that unity has to be achieved on your terms: tell them we will only reconsider it if they stop fighting against the National Liberation Movement, stop their anti-communist and anti-Communist Party propaganda, purge their ranks of criminals and fascist agents, publicly declare themselves anti-fascists, and act like such, as our English–USSR–US allies do. If the tract has already been distributed by you or Balli, then condemn it. Tell people that what is important is a genuine commitment to fight the occupiers for a democratic Albania, and not signing pieces of paper with promises that Balli never even meant to keep. Emphasise to the people that Balli sabotaged our war in the past and is continuing to do so at present. Both at meetings, and in your communiqués, make sure to expose Balli's acts of sabotage and treason. Make sure that this campaign does not sound like an all-out war; this is

an appeal to Balli to change their ways and stop committing fratricide. The goal is to expose Balli – especially its leaders – so that people can see for themselves who they really are; to urge the positive elements in Balli to distance themselves from the organisation, and more importantly, to separate Balli from the people.

Comrades, we need to understand that Balli's aim is to rise to power by fighting against us. Therefore we must take care to strengthen unity within our ranks, to mobilise the people around us and not to let reactionary forces attack and snatch the reins from our hands.

Our stance towards Balli has not changed. Unity cannot be achieved by paying lip service to it; that would only undermine unity. Any agreement between us can only be achieved if they revise their policies, repudiate their erroneous practices, and join our fight.

For this, comrades, you must mobilise the entire membership of the organisation; speak to our comrades, mobilise councils and friends. Our agitation work must be ten times more powerful than Balli's. Comrades, the situation is changing fast; we must not be caught daydreaming. To deal with this situation and emerge victorious, we need to strengthen our organisation [...]

Regards,

For the Central Committee of the CPA

Shpati[5]

Speculation was rife, both at the time and later, that Hoxha was fully aware of the agreement and that he was the one who had authorised Gjinishi and Dishnica to sign it. Most such sources emphasise that Hoxha decided to repudiate the agreement at the insistence of Miladin Popović, who was uncomfortable with the notion of an ethnic Albania which, in all likelihood, would include Kosovo. Although plausible, this can only be one of the explanations for the turnaround, and not necessarily the most important one. The two protagonists who signed the Mukja Agreement did not leave their version of events. Mustafa Gjinishi was liquidated one year after the meeting, while Ymer Dishnica kept total silence until the day he died in 1998. In his memoirs published after 1991, he condemned Hoxha's regime, but provided no explanations about Mukja. When asked by journalists whether he was ordered by Hoxha to sign the agreement, he either refused to answer or provided ambiguous answers, but never actually provided a straight 'yes' or 'no'.

It is likely that Dishnica signed the treaty without asking Hoxha first. He must have thought this was in line with CPA policies and would help the cause of the war. In a note sent to Hoxha before signing the joint statement, Dishnica wrote that the issue of Kosovo and ethnic Albania was leading the talks into an impasse. A contemporaneous letter Hoxha sent to Shafingo (Dishnica's codename) on 9 August 1943 confirms that he was aware of the problem:

Shafingo,
    You failed to inform us in advance about the tract sent by Hysen; we cannot understand this. You always put us before a fait accompli. You never told us anything about a tract being printed or its contents, nor did you consult us about an event of such historical significance. In Labinot, Tafari [Mustafa Gjinishi] and you were both told that your powers did not extend that far (I won't dwell on this at length; you know full well what powers you had and the fact is that no one ever tried to curtail your initiative, as long as it benefited the party and did not undermine it). Your task was to talk with Balli, urge them to join us in the fight. However this is not the kind of unity that can be reached around a table, but on the ground, on the battlefront. You were also given the points to discuss with them (see letter of 6.8.43). With this tract you totally endorse Balli's position: it speaks of an ethnic Albania but has nothing to say about the fight against fascism and our war. There is no mention of the Communist Party in the tract. Unity with them would mean parity between Balli, an organisation with limited membership, and the National Liberation Movement, which represents the people and their Anti-Fascist Front. With this tract you practically drew a curtain over Balli's abominable past and present and ushered their triumphant entry into history. That is why the Central Committee thinks it is in complete violation of our political line and condemns it.

You must understand that Balli and all the rest of the opportunists will do whatever they can to leave their past behind; you must understand that they are trying to jump on the bandwagon in order to succeed fascism, which is dying (but is far from dead yet, you tell Tafari!). Their plan is to seize power and relegate us from frontrunners, which we are today, to runners-up, so that they can rid themselves of us more easily tomorrow. Today, as the situation abroad is changing swiftly, you choose not to declare war on fascism but to declare independence and launch the thesis of an ethnic Albania advocated by fascist and reactionary elements.

For all of the above reasons, if the tract has not been distributed yet, do not send it out, because it is nothing but a total capitulation to Balli. With this tract you erase the national liberation councils, our staff and army, set up with so much blood and sacrifice. You erase the slogans that inspired our people's fight for freedom over the past two years. The very name of the Committee for the Salvation of Albania is totally wrong; both in content and form, and the four points outlined in your letter do not coincide with those in the tract. You besmirched our war with Balli's filthy deeds and had the audacity to put Balli's name before that of the council whose members laid down their lives, killed by the fascists and Balli themselves. By printing this tract, you created a difficult situation. Stop all the talks and, more importantly, do not enter into any more agreements. The party will soon send another delegate.

For the Central Committee of the party,

Enver Hoxha[6]

The above letter makes it clear that, rather than simply reflecting Yugoslav concerns over an ethnic Albania, Hoxha was quick to denounce the treaty because it opened the way to power-sharing with Balli Kombëtar. This was of course totally unacceptable to him, as Balli was manifestly much weaker and less organised than the communists were. Hoxha had one fear only, that of a potential British and American landing in the Balkans. If this did not materialise, his rise to power would be unhindered.

The two people responsible for Mukja were soon held accountable and punished. Ymer Dishnica lost his position in the party. A medical-school graduate educated in France, he was the only one with a university degree among the senior communist leadership in Albania. Although he was spared from going to jail, he spent the rest of his life working as a doctor in Berat under the close surveillance of the Sigurimi, as proven by his copious file in their archives. Dishnica received many an angry mention in Hoxha's works, although it must be said that the tone was not nearly as aggressive as one would have expected in such cases. Dishnica served briefly as head of the Association of Veterans of the Second World War until his death in 1998.

Mustafa Gjinishi's life was cut short just one year after the Mukja Agreement. He was killed in an ambush under mysterious circumstances while travelling in the north of Albania. He was the third most important communist leader, after Qemal Stafa and Vasil Shanto, to lose his life during the war. The CPA issued a tract on the 'loss' of Mustafa Gjinishi. On 26 August 1944, a daily order signed by Colonel General Enver Hoxha, general commander of the NLA, read as follows:

> Comrade Mustafa Gjinishi, lieutenant colonel, member of the Executive Committee of the National Liberation Council and of the General Staff, fell on the Maqellara front in Dibra. An indefatigable and fearless fighter, Lieutenant Colonel Mustafa Gjinishi laid down his life on the front line of the war for the liberation of our HOMELAND and the Albanian PEOPLE […] As a sign of mourning and in remembrance of comrade Mustafa Gjinishi, all the units of the National Liberation Army must place their flags at half-mast for three days starting from today.[7]

From the beginning, Mustafa Gjinishi's death was considered to be the work of the leaders of the CPA. Enver Hoxha was accused directly and publicly of being involved – not only by his opponents, but also by important members of the party, especially at the plenary meeting in Berat. Gjinishi's death was the first time that Hoxha openly admitted to a terrorist crime committed by the CPA, at the instigation of the Yugoslavs. In his auto-critique at the Berat meeting of 26 November 1944, he virtually admitted his direct involvement in the decision for Gjinishi's liquidation, but said he was unaware how it was carried out and sought to lay the blame at Miladin Popović's door:

In Mustafa Gjinishi's case, the matters stood differently. We thought it had to be done. I was the one who decided on the matter [...] We had planned to tell Mustafa that he was no longer considered trustworthy, but there was no decision to kill him. I don't know how that happened. Perhaps Miladin said something to Liri [Gega], I don't know. Then the telegram came, which had been worded in such a way that even Gogo would understand. It said: 'The job is done.' The next day we received news that Mustafa had been killed.[8]

Mustafa Gjinishi was proclaimed a 'hero', only to be denounced as an enemy later. His remains were unburied and moved several times, in accordance with Hoxha's mood. His ultimate condemnation, as an 'enemy' and 'British agent', appeared in Hoxha's book *Rreziku anglo-amerikan për Shqipërinë* (published in English as *The Anglo-American Threat to Albania*), as the following excerpt shows:

In August 1944 a British officer brought me a message that had just arrived from his general headquarters. It said: 'For General Hoxha. I regret to inform you that Mustafa Gjinishi was killed on the First Division front. Smith and [Gjinishi] were ambushed by a German patrol. Smith [is] well. A great loss to the Allied cause.' The British officer added: 'Mustafa Gjinishi was always our great friend.' It is clear from this document what a loss Mustafa Gjinishi's death was to the British. It was equally clear to us that he was constantly at Smith's side, an agent in the service of the British until the day he died.[9]

According to information that has come to light recently, Mustafa Gjinishi was executed by Liri Gega and Ndreko Rino. The former, who held the highest position ever attained by a woman in the PLA, was in turn arrested and executed on Hoxha's orders in the mid-1950s, together with her husband, General Dali Ndreu, a prominent figure of the National Liberation War. Liri Gega was executed with a bullet to her head only a few moments after the execution of her husband right before her eyes. She was said to be several months pregnant at the time. An officer who witnessed the executions described their last moments: General Dali Ndreu's last words had been about his children, while Liri Gega, still alive when her husband fell to the floor, told the officer who pointed the pistol at her: 'Everything is over. Hurry up, do what you have to do!'[10] After the fall of communism the couple's surviving children made several attempts to find their parents' burial place, but without success.

Sixty years after the Mukja Agreement, protagonists from the two opposing camps were still of the same opinion – it would not have worked in the long term anyway. Here is what Abaz Ermenji, a Balli commander and leader, said in an interview in 1998:

> I do not think that the Mukja Agreement would have had a long life –
> it could probably have held for a while, but not for long. By that time,
> communism was an international movement aspiring to achieve an
> unscrupulous goal, and did so without any human feeling and which
> gave the people no hope. They would have found something else to
> attack Balli for. The communists were supported by both the East and
> the West at the time. Even the British and the Americans aided them.
> Whether that was deliberate or not, whether they realised what they
> were doing or not... I don't know. As Atatürk said to an American
> journal about a year before he died: 'The West will never understand
> communism.'[11]

The repudiation of the agreement and the propaganda that went with it led to what came to be known as the 'civil war'. The clashes the communists had with the nationalists and Abaz Kupi's Legaliteti became increasingly violent, causing a great number of casualties. The fight against the German occupiers took second place. Documentary sources make it clear, however, that the communists were more determined to fight the Germans, while Balli and the Legaliteti movement, although officially at war with the Germans, rarely engaged seriously in any battles, with the exception of the forces of Gani Kryeziu in Kosovo and of Muharrem Bajraktari in Luma.

Liri Belishova, a former senior communist leader, had this to say about the repudiation of the agreement of Mukja, in an interview she gave in 2004:

The annulment of the agreement of Mukja caused the loss of many lives, and much burning and destruction in Albania. Had it not been annulled, these could have been avoided or minimised. After the annulment of the agreement, Balli Kombëtar was taken over by opportunistic elements caught in a life-or-death struggle with the communists that pushed them right into the arms of the Germans.[12]

In the wake of the revocation of the agreement, Balli Kombëtar came under attack by the partisan forces, something it was unable to withstand. The organisation split into several smaller factions that spent their time in fruitless discussions, thus losing any of the credit or influence they had enjoyed in the beginning. As champions of an obsolete kind of politics, unorganised and undisciplined, the Ballists and nationalists were inevitably doomed. Sixty-two years after the war, Hana Klissura, daughter of Ali Këlcyra, a key exponent of Balli Kombëtar, said this in a 2007 interview:

I am convinced that my father had some very good ideas, but he could not be successful because he did not have the courage to make the decisions that Enver Hoxha was able to make. Imagine, Hoxha had his own brother-in-law murdered![13]

9

Head of the Provisional Government

Early in 1944 Enver Hoxha realised that the moment was drawing close when the question of power would be decided. With this in mind, parallel to leading the national liberation effort, he worked hard to consolidate his position as leader of the CPA. The national liberation councils established in the occupied areas moved quickly to fill the power vacuum left by the retreating German forces. As they did, collaborators were arrested and executed, including leaders and well-known activists of Balli Kombëtar. The councils acted as administrators of justice and indeed claimed to deliver justice in the name of the people. They were not communist bodies, and whatever communist members they had did not advertise their political affiliation. In a letter to Dušan Mugoša, who had already left Albania by this time, Hoxha wrote that the war would be over in a matter of months. A communist-ruled postwar Albania was undoubtedly what he had in mind when he spoke of 'establishing the power of the people by fighting the reactionaries and their henchmen'.[1]

Hoxha was acutely aware of the importance of Tirana and its institutions. In September 1943, after the capitulation of Fascist Italy, he moved the General Staff to Arbana, a village on the outskirts of the capital. Contemporaneous letters and orders written by him reveal that numerous partisan forces were ready, concentrated in central Albania for an eventual attack on the capital. In his memoirs published 40 years later, Enver Hoxha explained that the General Staff were preparing to launch an assault for the liberation of Tirana. At that time, the communists, either on their own or in conjunction with Balli forces, controlled nearly all the towns of southern Albania. The attack was, however, aborted as the General Staff realised their forces would not be able to hold the town against an attack by German forces which had already begun entering Albania. The Albanians decided this was not the right moment for the attack and withdrew to their strongholds in the south.[2]

In May 1944 Enver Hoxha took a first step that would ensure his hold on power: a move to give the National Liberation Movement semi-official status and turn it into the only viable alternative in a future race for power. On 24 May 1944 he convened what came to be known as the Congress of Përmet.

The Congress of Përmet was proof that the communists were taking the question of postwar power very seriously and confirmed their superiority over their political opponents. The General Staff had already decided where the congress would be held, but the name of the town was kept secret. Delegates from both liberated and occupied areas were to gather at prearranged meeting points and were taken to Përmet in groups. They were not told where they were going or even when the congress would be held. In addition to the special battalion providing security for Enver Hoxha and the General Staff, four partisan brigades had taken up positions around Përmet. Prior to the arrival of the communist leaders, every corner of the town had been searched and strict security measures were taken. The congress hall, the decorations, the cafeteria and even the menu were thoroughly security checked.

It was in Përmet that the forces of the security brigades saw their commander for the first time in public. The country was still under German occupation, but it was clear that Hoxha was steadily climbing to the zenith of power. In fact, in May 1944 the forces of the NLA had more territory under their control than the Regency government in Tirana. In addition, Enver Hoxha was convinced that the war would not have any more surprises in store: it had already been won by Allied forces. To the Germans, Albania was now nothing more than a retreat route. Hoxha was now the only viable candidate for prime minister. Everything was just a matter of time.

It was around this time that an intensive public relations campaign began to make Hoxha known. In August 1944 the CPA issued an initial pamphlet with a biography and photo of the leader, entitled 'Enver Hoxha, general commander of the National Liberation Army'. The article was not signed, but it later transpired that the author of the tract was Liri Gega. The pamphlet sketched Hoxha's activities since 7 April 1939. The biography was also reproduced in the first issue of *Ylli çlirimtar* (Liberation star), the newsletter of the First Division of the NLA. It then disappeared from circulation after 1946, which could only have happened on Hoxha's orders. In the original pamphlet, Enver Hoxha's name was mentioned 47 times and he was given credit for everything achieved during the war, the victories of the partisan army and the political victories within the CPA. This pamphlet, which at first sight looked just like all the other pamphlets issued during those turbulent times, is probably the first official document that promoted Enver Hoxha's cult of personality, a cult that persisted for the next 41 years. Among other things, it said:

> The immense value and service of our shining leader can be seen in all the victories achieved by the National Liberation Army, in all the political successes of the National Liberation Movement, in which communists lay down their lives crying out: Long live the Communist Party!
>
> Prudent in his decisions, always patient and untiring in explaining matters to all those who need clarification, kind and smiling to everyone, but firm against any kind of opportunism and compromise, a staunch enemy to all those who want to take away the freedom of the people, Enver is the worthy leader of the Albanian masses seeking liberation.
>
> To the broad masses of workers, oppressed women, youth and intellectuals, to all those who hate oppression, Enver is a loyal champion and an unyielding fighter for their rights.
>
> The First Division and all the other partisan forces of the National Liberation Army are marching victorious because they are led by a leader like Enver, because they know that under his leadership they have gained so many victories, because they know that thanks to his leadership, the true victory of the people will finally become a reality.[3]

At the plenary meeting held in Berat (23–7 November 1944), there was an attempt to oppose what was openly called 'Enver Hoxha's cult of personality'. Nako Spiru and Sejfullah Malëshova were very critical of the Yugoslav-style line followed in popularising the figure of the leader, attributing everything that was achieved exclusively to him. In the words of Nako Spiru: 'At Panarit,

Dušan and Miladin introduced the idea that the movement should be linked to one leading figure. Until yesterday, no names were mentioned. Today one can't even find a menu that does not have Enver's name on it.'⁴ After a short interruption, the myth and cult of Enver Hoxha regained momentum after the war.

The Congress of Përmet laid the foundations of the future communist regime. As late as 1992, the emblem of the Republic of Albania still featured the date on which it had been held, 24 May 1944, under two spikes of wheat. The congress decreed the establishment of an Anti-Fascist National Liberation Council, a body that would serve as a sort of parliamentary assembly until the next elections; it banned King Zog from returning to Albania, and elected an Anti-Fascist Committee, with all the attributes of a provisional government, headed by Enver Hoxha. Enver Hoxha was also promoted to the rank of colonel general. In addition to the position of prime minister (or chairman of the Provisional Anti-Fascist National Liberation Council), he also held the posts of minister of the interior and chief of General Staff of the army. At that time, Albania had two governments, one that governed from Tirana, and Hoxha's parallel and mobile government in the south of the country.

On 26 June 1944, Enver Hoxha decided to deal a final blow to opposition forces, not only to the collaborationists and anyone who refused to acknowledge his authority. The First Division of the NLA, which included the First Assault Brigade created on 15 August 1943, received orders to cross the Shkumbin River. The order was clear: avoid clashes with the German forces retreating from the country, and destroy all forms of local opposition.

The First Division was a highly disciplined and dedicated military unit and was well equipped with British weapons and uniforms. Its march northwards produced much unease among nationalist leaders, who had strongly believed that communism would never take hold in the north. The dwindling nationalist forces were not able to stage any resistance, not least because the divided northern chieftains failed to unite their forces against the NLA. Enver Hoxha followed closely the First Division's cleansing operation in the north. For nearly a year he took personal interest in the liquidation of influential and popular figures, as seen in this telegram sent to the First Division command on 21 September 1944:

> Stop making appeals to Gani [Kryeziu] to surrender; mount a fierce attack
> and kill him. If Gani has already surrendered, let us know as soon as pos-
> sible. You need to act swiftly as the Kosovars may come to his rescue. Enver[5]

Gani Kryeziu had not collaborated with the Italians and the Germans. Scion
of one of the most influential clans from Gjakova, at the time he had become
head of his clan after the assassination in Prague of his elder brother, Ceno
bey Kryeziu, former Albanian interior minister and brother-in-law to King
Zog. Shortly after the occupation of Albania by Italy, Gani Kryeziu met up
in Belgrade with a young British officer by the name of Julian Amery. Amery
persuaded him to take up arms and begin a guerrilla war, together with his
brothers. Gani Kryeziu, his brothers Hasan and Said Kryeziu, Major Abaz
Kupi, a well-known Albanian officer, and Mustafa Gjinishi, a communist
militant, crossed the border in the spring of 1941. The British provided them
with weapons for their 300 fighters and several bags of gold coins.

Gani Kryeziu embarked upon armed resistance, and about a year later a
British mission was attached to his forces. The Kryezius fought independently
for several years and refused to join forces with either Tito's partisans or
the Albanian partisans. Gani Kryeziu responded negatively to a request to
place his forces under the command of the First Division, when the latter
approached Gjakova. He paid dearly for his refusal: one of his brothers,
Hasan, was killed by the partisans, while Said was arrested and tortured on
Hoxha's direct orders, and only managed to escape with his life after pressure
was brought to bear by the British at Allied headquarters in Bari. After the
war he emigrated to New York and lived there until his death in 1993. Gani
Kryeziu himself was captured by the forces of the First Assault Brigade of
the NLA and was turned over to the Yugoslav partisans. It seems Hoxha
bitterly regretted consenting to the handover. Forty years later he described
it as 'Yugoslav pressure we failed to stand up to'. He claimed he agreed
because, although Kryeziu had been fighting on the territory of Albania and
was of Albanian ethnicity, he was officially a Yugoslav citizen. Gani Kryeziu
was transferred to Belgrade and, after serving some time in prison, charged
with armed resistance against partisan forces, he was eventually released.
The last time anyone caught sight of him was as he was emerging from the

prison gate, after which he disappeared, never to be seen again. It is likely that he was liquidated by the Yugoslav secret police, who were waiting for him at the gate.

Other leaders and fighters like Muharrem Bajraktari in Luma and Abaz Kupi in central Albania managed to escape with their lives. But they lost everything else. The communists called on Muharrem Bajraktari to surrender and place his forces under the command of a young partisan commander called Shefqet Peçi. He refused and was treacherously attacked. Bajraktari, an experienced soldier, managed to break the siege and escape. He continued his endeavours to mount some resistance from the mountains for a couple more years before he crossed the border into Greece in 1946. He lived in Brussels as a war veteran until his death in 1989.

Abaz Kupi was undoubtedly the most important figure with whom Hoxha initially collaborated, and then clashed, during the war. His story has been told not only in a number of books published in Albania, but also in the memoirs of former members of the British mission to Albania. Born in a village near Kruja in 1892, Abaz Kupi very soon became a household name under the nickname 'Bazi i Canes' ('Baz of Cane' – 'Baz' is short for Abaz and 'Cane' was his mother's first name). A brave and charismatic man, also known as a bit of a brigand, he had an altercation with Haxhi Qamili in 1914. The tumultuous story of friendship and conflict between Kupi and Qamili came to an end when the latter was hanged by Esat Pasha Toptani and Kupi married his widow. In 1925, Ahmet Zogu, the new president of the Republic of Albania, invited him to join the gendarmerie. On 7 April 1939 Abaz Kupi, now a major and commander of the Durrës gendarmerie, put up impressive resistance to the Italian army that landed on the Albanian coastline. Eleven Italian military men and seven Albanian soldiers and volunteers lost their lives in the clashes. Abaz Kupi was wounded, but managed to retreat to safety and subsequently joined King Zog and his government in exile in Turkey. In 1940 he went to Yugoslavia from where it was easier to enter Albania. In Belgrade he met some of his old friends, most of them anti-monarchists and émigrés, including Myslim Peza, Mustafa Gjinishi, Xhemal Herri, Gani Kryeziu and others. It was around this time that the British got in touch with him. Julian Amery met Kupi and talked him into returning to Albania to fight alongside the Allies. Kupi entered Albania in 1941 together with Gani Kryeziu and 300 fighters. He went straight to Kruja, his birthplace, where he soon established a fighting unit. Abaz Kupi and Enver Hoxha first met at the Peza Conference, where Kupi was elected deputy chairman of the National Liberation Council. Getting Kupi to join their war was one of Hoxha's greatest victories. He was so excited about it in February 1943 that he wrote the following in the newspaper *Zëri i popullit* (the *People's Voice*):

> Abaz Kupi and Albania's young men fought in Durrës on 7 April 1939 [∴] Major Baz was ubiquitous; he urged his fighters on with his words: 'Come on sons, hit the centuries-long enemy without mercy; this is what our Homeland asks of us!' [...] The enemy used its cannons and aeroplanes, but Bazi i Canes did not budge from his position [...] Bazi eventually retreated, but he was not defeated, he was not beaten; his heart was full of love for his country and hatred for the occupiers [...] He crossed the snow-capped mountains of the north to enter Albania, where duty called him [...] Bazi i Canes fought the fascists without mercy [...] Bazi i Canes fights for the sacred goal of the liberation of the country [...] Bazi of Durrës, Bazi of Kruja, Bazi of Peza will not stop fighting until the ultimate victory over the occupiers.[6]

A version of this article, with all references to Abaz Kupi heavily redacted, was later reprinted in Enver Hoxha's works.[7]

Abaz Kupi fought side by side with the communists up until September 1943, when Enver Hoxha denounced the Mukja Agreement and rejected Kupi's request for King Zog's return to Albania. In November 1943 he founded a political organisation called the Legaliteti (Legalists). Kupi and his followers believed King Zog was the only one who had a legitimate right to govern Albania after it regained its independence, which was the reason he engaged in fighting the Germans as well. A British mission was attached to his headquarters. With the start of their irrevocable falling out, a few months after the panegyric article quoted above, Enver Hoxha published another article in *Zëri i popullit*, in which he wrote:

The shots fired in Durrës [were exploited for a different purpose than what was intended by those who laid down their lives]. Bazi i Canes, Zog's henchman, used the revolt of young men like Mujo Ulqinaku to cover up his master's shameful flight [...] When our movement had gained impetus, Abaz Kupi, Zog's gendarme, returned to Albania, though not to fight, as he had in the past, but to commit an act of betrayal [...] Sent to Albania by his master, Abaz Kupi never intended to fight the occupiers [...] He never fired a single shot against the Italian occupiers, in spite of the agreement reached in Peza and his solemn pledge before the national flag that he would fight the Italians.[8]

The rhetoric of these articles did not affect Abaz Kupi in any way. A pragmatic fighter, in the summer of 1944 he realised that the communists, who dominated the National Liberation Movement, were in fact fighting for postwar power rather than for the liberation of the country. Kupi was concerned about the arrival of the First Division of the NLA in the north of the country and was shaken by the attacks the partisan division had carried out on his vanguard troops. Hoxha knew that Abaz Kupi was possibly the only obstacle to his rise to power and that he was a tough nut to crack. By destroying Kupi, Hoxha hoped to win the war and strengthen his authority in the north, where the communist movement was weak. In a letter he sent to Gogo Nushi in late 1943, he asked Nushi to speak to Ymer Dishnica and Sejfullah Malëshova and tell them not to have any illusions about Bazi i Canes, as he would never be on their side – he would always fight for their main enemy, Ahmet Zogu.

Dušan Mugoša had expressed the same opinion to Xhelal Staravecka, a former commander of the First Assault Brigade. In the last months of the war, Staravecka deserted the partisan forces, accusing them of terrorism, and joined the opposition camp. In a 1944 leaflet Staravecka denounced the terrorist tendencies of the CPA and cited the following conversation:

I asked Dušan: 'Dušan, what do you think of Baz?'

He looked at me and said: 'Which Baz? Baz, the motherfucker? You will hear about him soon enough. He has betrayed us, but he'll pay with his life!'

'That won't be easy,' I said, 'he's very careful.'

'Our partisans can greet you with a "*dobar dan*" [good day] in the middle of the night,' he added. 'I was aware of Baz's games and had decided to eliminate him, but a comrade said Baz was the chieftain of northern mountains tribes and he would work with us and for us. It serves me right for having heeded his words,' said Dušan.[9]

A bit further down in the text, Staravecka related what Dušan Mugoša thought of some Albanian military leaders:

'Dušan, do you think Haxhi Lleshi will go the way of Bazi i Canes?' I asked.

Dušan started whispering, although there was no one around us: 'Do you know anything about the Lleshis of Dibra?'

'Yes,' I said.

'They have long been our friends,' he said. 'That family does not need to give any guarantees to us. They will never betray us.'[10]

The last time Enver Hoxha met Major Abaz Kupi was on 7 December 1943 in the house of a friend of the latter in Shëngjergj. Accompanied by Ymer Dishnica and Fetah Ekmekçiu, the leader of the CPA sat across the table from the veteran fighter for two and a half hours. Only one record of that conversation exists, the one Hoxha provides in his memoirs. One thing is clear: there was no love lost between them and both had their own political agendas. Hoxha believed in his military power, while Bazi i Canes was hoping for an Allied landing. Between the two, there would ultimately be only one victor.

Kupi fought against Hoxha's partisans for several months. His troops shrank and were forced to retreat. They were no match for the well-organised and well-armed First Assault Brigade. In November 1944 Kupi lost two of his major strongholds, Preza and Kruja. But the most severe blow came from the British. To avoid exacerbating their relations with Hoxha, the Allied Command based in Naples ordered the British mission attached to Abaz Kupi to return to Italy and Kupi was not to be among the evacuees. This treatment at the hands of his old allies must have wounded him to the quick. He was running out of options. After managing to escape from a partisan ambush, he fled by boat to Brindisi. In the meantime, the members of the British mission had informed foreign secretary Eden and prime minister Churchill about Kupi's role and how he had been abandoned by the British. Henry Maitland Wilson, supreme Allied commander in the Mediterranean, then issued an order for Kupi's evacuation. Maitland Wilson was unequivocal: 'The fellow's been our friend and we must get him out. We'll do it quite openly; and we'll tell Hodja too; but not until your man's safe in Italy.'[11]

By then, though, Kupi had already made his way to Italy. The major was treated as a British ally and the United Kingdom refused Hoxha's requests – and threats – to surrender him to the communist authorities. Hoxha even sent a mission to the Allied Command in Naples for this purpose.

Abaz Kupi played an active role in the anti-communist movement abroad. Hoxha never forgave the fact that Kupi rose against him. He was among the top three names on the list of people wanted by the communist regime and the Sigurimi went to unimaginable lengths to track him down abroad. Abaz Kupi spent the last years of his life in Brooklyn, New York, where he died on 9 January 1976, at the age of 84. His funeral, attended by thousands of people, drew the attention of the American press. The ceremony was led by Julian Amery, now an important member of the British Conservative Party and holder of several ministerial posts in Her Majesty's Government, and a former member of the British mission to whom Kupi had kindly lent 40 gold coins at the moment of his evacuation from Albania.

According to documents from the former archives of the Central Committee of the PLA, Enver Hoxha was informed of Kupi's death on 10 January 1976, by an urgent telegram sent by the Albanian mission to the United Nations. The message was brief: 'Abaz Kupi died last night in New York. Death is confirmed. Arrangements are being made today for his funeral. Further details will follow.'[12]

It is not known what effect the news had on Hoxha, but the battle between the two was now definitely over. Enver Hoxha must have felt he was the winner.

10

The Plenary Meeting in Berat – An Interlude

I n autumn 1944, Enver Hoxha was in effect the most powerful man in the country. The old political class, most of whom were prominent figures from the time of the declaration of independence and other major historical events, were not able to stop the momentum of this new, highly disciplined political organisation, known for its strong ideals, strict ideological position and vigorous decision-making.

The new government formed within the framework of the National Liberation Movement had now moved to Berat and enjoyed wide support among the population. Anarchy, uncertainty, destruction and confusion reigned supreme in the country but, on the other hand, there were exciting moments, it was a time of high hopes and expectations – emotions which the old strife-ridden and corrupt political class had long ceased to inspire.

On 20 October, Enver Hoxha, all dressed up in his military uniform as colonel general, appeared at the Kolombo café in the centre of Berat. It was his first public appearance as the new leader of the country. By now his agenda was clear.

Two days later, the Anti-Fascist National Liberation Council changed its name to the Provisional Government of Albania. Enver Hoxha kept the posts of prime minister and minister of the interior, but added that of minister of foreign affairs for good measure. Myslim Peza was elected deputy prime minister. Initially the government set up office in the villas of the old landowning Vrioni family in Berat, but preparations were under way for the final transfer to the capital, Tirana.

By the end of October, Ibrahim Biçakçiu, the last prime minister of occupied Albania, tendered his resignation to the High Regency Council. The capital and all the major retreat routes were still under the control of German troops, while Enver Hoxha's Provisional Government controlled the rest of the country. On the same day, the outgoing prime minister sent Hoxha a personal message telling him that his administration would continue in office until the handover to the new government.

On 26 October, Mehmet Shehu, commander of the First Assault Brigade, received orders to attack Tirana. The previous day, a publicly distributed leaflet and a message on Radio Bari had called on all intellectuals who 'had not steeped their hands in blood', who had not collaborated with the occupiers and who considered themselves patriots, to leave town and go to the liberated areas. The liberated zone started only a few kilometres from the outskirts of the capital. The General Staff was by now stationed in the Priska area. The battle for the liberation of Tirana went on for some 20 days, until the morning of 17 November, when Commander Mehmet Shehu sent the following telegram to prime minister Hoxha: 'Tirana is now liberated! The enemy is retreating towards Lezha. Stop. The road is clear! Death to fascism – Freedom to the People!'[1]

On 17 November, Liri Belishova received orders to travel from Berat to Tirana to make preparations for the handover of power. Belishova clearly recalled the moment when she arrived in the liberated capital and met with Mehmet Shehu, commander of the forces that took the capital, at Hotel Dajti. He had taken care of everything. In fact, Belishova and Mehmet Shehu did not have much left to do. Enver Hoxha himself decided to enter Tirana on 28 November, the anniversary of Albanian independence and a date of great historical significance.

Enver Hoxha's triumphant entry into Tirana was, however, jeopardised by an unforeseen event, possibly the most difficult moment in his career as leader of the CPA. At the second plenary meeting of the party, which started on 23 November, the majority of the Politburo members, including the Yugoslav envoy Velimir Stojnić, rose against Hoxha. Of course, this revolt against the new leader did not just happen. The group seemed well organised and intent on removing him from the top position and divesting him of all the other functions he held. In her speech at the 1948 plenary meeting convened to condemn Nako Spiru, Naxhije Dume, who had been present at the meeting in Berat, reported the following exchange with Nako Spiro in the presence of Pandi Kristo: "'Hoxha will have to go!' 'And if he doesn't?' she asked. "Well, if he refuses [to go], a gun will persuade him to do so," he retorted.'[2]

This is Hoxha's version of events. But other people present at the meeting remembered differently. According to them, Naxhije Dume had simply reported that Spiru had paraphrased something said by Alqi Kondi, an activist of the Anti-Fascist Youth of Albania. Kondi himself died at a very young age, in a road accident.

Nako Spiru and Sejfullah Malëshova were undoubtedly two of Hoxha's harshest critics at the plenary meeting in Berat. Hoxha was accused of serious crimes committed within the party, of embarking upon a sectarian and criminal course against his political opponents, of constructing a cult of personality around himself, of keeping all the credit for the achievements of the party, and more. He was held responsible for the wanton crimes committed by partisan forces and their supporters in urban areas. Although he had little support, Hoxha managed to weather the storm. He wrote a lengthy self-critical speech, which he read out in two parts. On the evening of 26 November, things really looked grim for Hoxha. The next day he proposed that the meeting be adjourned in order to allow the government enough time to travel to Tirana, where its triumphant entry was set for the 28th. Hoxha argued that the roads were not safe and they might be late for the midday military parade on that day. It was decided that the meeting would resume later, once they had arrived in Tirana. It never did. Enver Hoxha went on to lead the CPA/PLA for another 41 years.

11

Tirana and the Wedding

Hoxha's entry into Tirana was captured on film by a crew of British reporters. This day, 28 November 1944, was arguably the most glorious in his entire career, the heights of which he never reached again, not even when he was at the zenith of his power and widely revered as a demigod. That November morning, Enver Hoxha was the embodiment of hope. People believed in him and began to nurture great expectations for the future. In the entire history of Albania no single individual ever failed people's expectations more spectacularly. Several decades later, when Hoxha's remains were unceremoniously transferred from the Cemetery of the Martyrs of the Nation to one of Tirana's municipal graveyards, his family chose precisely the picture taken in November 1944 to put on his gravestone. They, too, knew that this was his most triumphant day. For the Albanian people, it was the day that marked the rise of a tyrant and the death of all hope.

In the evening, once the music and excitement of the military parade had died down, the new government celebrated its first day in office with an event rather uncharacteristic for a communist regime – a grand ball in Hotel Dajti, where the members of the government had temporarily set up their offices and living quarters. Enver Hoxha was given suite no. 5 on the second floor, the largest in the hotel. It had a drawing room, a bedroom and a wide balcony overlooking the main boulevard. A sentry from the Special Battalion kept guard out on the balcony day and night.

At the ball the new head of government made his first public appearance with his fiancée. Nexhmije Xhuglini was a young woman whose family had

moved from Monastir in Macedonia to Tirana in 1920. She had attended the
Nëna Mbretëreshë (Queen Mother) school for girls, the most prestigious
female pedagogical institution in the country. Enver Hoxha and Nexhmije
Xhuglini first met on 23 November 1941, two weeks after the founding of the
CPA, at a meeting held for the founding of the organisation known as the
Communist Youth. In her memoirs Nexhmije Hoxha described how she had
in fact seen Hoxha prior to that meeting, at a major demonstration held in
the centre of Tirana on 28 October 1941, albeit from a distance:

> I remember seeing a stocky young man, much taller than the rest of the
> youths around him, who was trying to tear a young fellow away from
> the grip of a policeman. Who was he? I was with Meli Dishnica, Esat
> Dishnica's sister, who never missed a rally. I asked her who he was. She
> said he was a former teacher who had recently moved to Tirana from
> Korça and had a tobacco shop nearby. 'What is his name?' I asked. 'He's
> called Enver Hoxha,' she answered.[1]

It is said that Enver Hoxha fell for the young activist from the time he first
laid eyes on her. They had other opportunities to meet at various bases used
by the underground movement in Tirana, and it appears the young woman
had sensed the new leader's interest in her. In her memoirs written 57 years
later, Nexhmije Hoxha recalled the day in 1942 when Enver Hoxha proposed
to her at one of the communist bases near the Tirana Secondary School.
The house had been rented by Syrja Selfo, on Hoxha's behalf. At the time
Selfo was the greatest financial supporter of Hoxha and his family, as Hoxha
himself admitted in his memoirs:

> Syrja was a good friend of mine; we often discussed things together and
> he understood me. Although not a communist, he was an anti-Italian and
> an anti-fascist patriot. He liked me a lot, and I had great affection for
> him. Syrja helped the war effort as much as he could. He had rented two
> houses and put them both at the disposal of our movement. He supported
> the war effort and me personally with funds. And he was there for my
> family when I went underground.[2]

In 1946, the same Syrja Selfo, 'great supporter of the movement', would be arrested, charged with 'conspiring against the people's power', and sentenced to death. In his *Kur u hodhën themelet e Shqipërisë së re* (*Laying the Foundations of a New Albania*), Hoxha explained that Selfo had been a victim of Koçi Xoxe's vile intrigues and that he had signed the execution order only after Xoxe had produced an admission of guilt signed by Selfo himself. The unfortunate man had of course been completely innocent. Nearly forty years after his execution, Hoxha expressed his regret about his former benefactor's tragic death, probably the only time he expressed regret in his entire life.

This is, at any rate, how Nexhmije Hoxha described the moment Hoxha proposed to her:

> I was standing with my back to him, making some coffee, when Enver spoke from where he was sitting, 'Listen Nexhmije, I don't know whether you really haven't noticed anything, or you are just pretending not to notice anything, so I will cut to the chase: I want to marry you!' I froze. A marriage proposal, blurted out just like that, came as a bolt out of the blue.[3]

A few days later, having made up her mind to accept, she made her way to the base where Enver Hoxha was staying to let him know of her decision:

> I said to him: 'The resistance front has fallen, I surrender!' He was so surprised that for a moment he stood there speechless, and his eyes seemed to be asking, 'Did I hear it right?' 'Yes, yes,' I laughed, 'I surrender!'[4]

This conversation occurred in 1942. In the next couple of years Hoxha and Xhuglini continued their separate underground activities and they would often be unable to see one another for months on end. On the day Hoxha died in April 1985, they had been living together for 43 years. Mrs Hoxha's role in the life of the communist leader is shrouded behind a veil of mystery and has generated much discussion. In a 1995 interview given from her prison cell in Tirana, she claimed that a role had been attributed to her that she never played: 'I had no part in Enver's decisions, except for when he was unwell and I had to communicate his messages to the comrades.'[5]

But Liljana Hoxha, Mrs Hoxha's daughter-in-law, remembers differently:

> This is the saddest thing in Albanian history. For years, when I looked at them as a couple, I used to think that Enver Hoxha could not have wished for a better wife. Her commitment, her devotion, her attention to the smallest detail, everything led one to think that. I was convinced that no other woman could take care of her husband like she did. But later I realised that it was the opposite. This was her way of keeping things under control – a demonic duality presented in the guise of a woman devotedly serving her husband, but who was in fact capable of much more, perhaps even more than he was.[6]

And further:

> This duality manifested itself in many forms; it was terrible when things were said in Enver Hoxha's name. She would do that. For instance, when she said, 'Enver said this,' or, 'Enver said that,' she was imposing her own will on the Central Committee, the government and so on.[7]

The bonds between Enver and Nexhmije Hoxha seem to have become even stronger after a heart attack he suffered in 1973. A few years later, a short entry in Hoxha's diary read: 'Nexhmije is unwell and, when she is ill, I feel ill. When she is well, I feel well, too.'[8]

People who knew or had dealings with Nexhmije Hoxha all agree on one thing: Mrs Hoxha was a cold and stern woman who seemed capable of committing any crime. She reinforced Hoxha's paranoia, which got worse and worse as more and more power was amassed in his hands. Some say that she changed over the years – obviously she was no better than many others whose character was corrupted by power. A letter she wrote to Hoxha in 1944 clearly shows that she was as cold-hearted in her youth as she was later in life. As such, it could hardly be expected that she would change Hoxha for the better. In the letter, of 14 October, signed under her code-name 'Delikatja', she complained about the disobedience of the comrades Gogo Nushi, Ymer Dishnica and Nako Spiru from the Tirana chapter of the CPA, who had apparently refused to comply with her fiancé's orders to liquidate Anastas Plasari and others:

> In relation to the purging of certain individuals – I did communicate your instructions to the comrades. As Deti [Nako Spiru] wrote, they do not agree with what we decided there. They are not convinced that I reported the issue of Anastas Plasari and the others properly. They are dithering for fear of acting unjustly. I'm loath to respond to minor allegations, but you should know that it was not my decision to have Anastas Plasari sent there […] Delikatja[9]

During 1942 the couple lived with the Omaris, Hoxha's sister and brother-in-law. This is how Nexhmije Hoxha remembers the first time she met her sister-in-law, in a house on Bami Street, next to the residence of Qazim Mulleti, former prefect of Tirana:

> She said, 'This is the room where Enver works when he stays with us. Now you can use it, too. You can stay here, talk and work together. At night I'll bring a mattress in for you; Enver can sleep in my sons' room.'[10]

Further on, Nexhmije wrote:

> That night I went down to the ground floor and was introduced to Bahri Omari, the master of the house. He gave the impression of an intellectual in his appearance, his demeanour, and the way he spoke. It was clear that he loved his wife very much, so much that he consented to providing shelter to her communist brother and his fiancée.[11]

Enver Hoxha and Nexhmije Xhuglini stayed with the Omaris off and on for a period of eight months. Bahri Omari himself was involved with the nationalists and in 1944 accepted the post of minister of foreign affairs in Rexhep Mitrovica's government. It is not known what the state of relations between him and Hoxha were at the time, whether there were any heated discussions or arguments. Hana Klissura, Ali Këlcyra's daughter, was present at her father's last meeting with Bahri Omari. The conversation between the two men went something like this:

> 'Bahri, what are you going to do?' [Ali Këlcyra] asked.
>
> 'I certainly don't intend to leave the country,' he answered.
>
> 'But what are you going to do?'
>
> 'I'll stay here,' replied Omari.
>
> 'Bahri, you were implicated with the Italians, how can you stay?' [Ali Këlcyra] insisted.
>
> 'I gave refuge to Enver Hoxha,' he answered, 'and he promised me, saying, "I cannot guarantee you will get a post in the government, but you can certainly stay on as a private citizen."'[12]

It is not known whether Hoxha really made the promise reported in this conversation. It certainly does not seem that he did if you read a telegram he sent to General Dali Ndreu on 28 September 1944. There Hoxha had nothing but disdain for his brother-in-law, the man who had always been there for him in his time of need, as testified to by many people, including his own fiancée, Nexhmije Hoxha. Here is the text of the telegram, first made public in 2004:

> To General Daliu,
>
> Re: Bahri Omari and his associates. Do not give heed to any calls for special treatment. They are no better than the rest of those lowlifes.
>
> Enver[13]

Bahri Omari's end was tragic. In November 1944 he was among the 60 prominent Albanian political and public figures who were arrested and made to appear before the so-called 'Special Court'. The trial, one of the first held under the communist dictatorship, began on 15 December 1944. Among his co-accused were signatories of the declaration of independence in 1912, former prime ministers, speakers of parliament and government ministers. Most of them had been educated in Western Europe and had ended up as collaborationists for one reason or another.

The chief prosecutor in the case was Bedri Spahiu, a former lieutenant in King Zog's army who was dismissed in 1935 and had no legal background whatsoever. The presiding judge was deputy prime minister Lieutenant General Koçi Xoxe, a former tinsmith who had completed only elementary education. The trial was held in Kinema Kosova (today the National Theatre Building) and thousands of people followed the proceedings on the streets, from the blaring loudspeakers installed all around the capital. The sentence was pronounced on 13 April 1945, at 10.00 hours. Seventeen of the accused were sentenced to death; the rest were given long prison terms, between 20 and 30 years. Only five were acquitted. Bahri Omari was among those who were given capital punishment. Nevertheless, there are indications that he believed to the end that his life would be spared. On New Year's Eve in 1944 he received a small parcel from Nexhmije Hoxha, now the wife of his brother-in-law, with three pieces of baklava in it. The parcel was probably intended to wish him happy New Year and let him know of the marriage that had taken place. Four months later he received another present: his death sentence.

Bahri Omari was sentenced to death, although many others, who had held much more important government posts – like Ibrahim Biçakçiu, the last prime minister – were only given lengthy prison terms. One cannot help but think that this was meant to be a gesture to let the public know that the new regime was not going to tolerate any opponents, even if they happened to be related to the leadership. Bahri Omari, who had helped Hoxha so much over the years, was to serve as an example of this uncompromising stance.

Bedri Spahiu, the prosecutor in the case, had been Hoxha's classmate in primary school in Gjirokastra. At the time of the trial he was one of the strongmen of the regime, but later he would find himself sentenced to prison for 30 years. In 1991 he was one of just a handful of former communist officials who made a public apology for their past actions. In an open letter published in the daily *Republika* on 6 June 1991, entitled 'Bedri Spahiu revises Bedri Spahiu', he wrote:

I, Bedri Spahiu, a complete layman in matters of law, was twice appointed by Enver Hoxha to be chief prosecutor in the most important trials in the history of our country. The first was the Special Trial of the so-called 'enemies of the people', and the second was the trial of Koçi Xoxe. Today I feel ashamed to have served as prosecutor in those trials. Communists may well remember the rhyme that was popular at the time, '*Tradhtarët porsi miu / i dënoi Bedri Spahiu*' [The traitors were like mice when Spahiu cast the dice]. Today I would say, too much glory for the inglorious![14]

This is how Bedri Spahiu remembered the moment when Bahri Omari and the other 16 men were executed by firing squad:

At the order of the commander of the firing squad, the convicts turned their backs to the guns. Only one had the courage to disobey, 'No one should turn his back on the guns. Only traitors are shot in the back. History will redeem us!' This was Bahri Omari, a wise man and patriot.[15]

The 17 men were all buried in a common and nameless grave, which was discovered by chance 60 years later, in a neighbourhood on the outskirts of Tirana. A house has been built on top of the mass grave. The men's last plea was for their families to be spared any punishment. In fact all the members of their families, with the exception of Omari's, spent long years in prison or internal exile under the communist regime.

Hana Klissura had a vivid recollection of the moment when Ali Këlcyra, Mid'hat Frashëri and Faik Quku, then languishing in a refugee camp at Barletta, learned about the execution of their old friend:

On that day we were at the camp, listening to the radio – the set was on the table – when we heard that he had been executed. I can still picture my father, his eyes welling up with tears. He jumped to his feet and left the table. There was nowhere to go – we were enclosed in a camp – but for two hours he was nowhere to be found.[16]

The executions did not end with the Special Trial. For the best part of the next five years, the communist regime waged a fierce campaign against all individuals of influence, and against those who had expressed reservations about the way the new regime was wielding power.

Soon after the government moved to Tirana, 15 members of the social democratic group were arrested. This group consisted of a number of mainly left-wing intellectuals who had founded a social democratic party with the aim of running in the next general elections. The group was condemned as one 'incited by reactionaries'. Eight of them were sentenced to death; the rest received prison terms of up to 30 years.

Among them was a woman, Musine Kokalari, daughter of a rich lawyer and one of the most cultivated, attractive and emancipated women in Albania, author of three successful books published in the last years of the war. Two of her brothers, Muntaz and Vejsim, though politically inactive, were summarily executed in the basement of Hotel Bristol on 12 November 1944, before Hoxha's arrival in Tirana. Her remaining brother, Hamit, Hoxha's classmate for many years, survived due to a fortuitous circumstance: on the night his two brothers were taken away, he was in bed with high fever and the partisans decided he would be too heavy to carry.

Musine Kokalari's stand at the trial was impressive. She declared:

I do not need to be a communist to love my country. I love my country even though I'm not one. I long to see it make progress. It is true that you won the war, you won the elections, but that is no licence to persecute people whose political opinions are different from yours. I think differently from you, but I do love my country. You are punishing me for my ideas. I won't ask for pardon because I have not done anything wrong![17]

The young woman spent the next 18 years in prison. After serving her sentence, she was interned in Rrëshen, where she spent the rest of her life working as a street-sweeper. Hers was an extremely lonely existence – she was cruelly ostracised by the community, but held her head high until the day she died of cancer in 1983. Musine Kokalari was refused medical help even as she lay on her deathbed. A week before she died she wrote in her notebook:

I got to know democratic culture and witnessed the tragedy of great revolutionary upheavals. I went through a Special Trial. I spent 18 years in prison and 22 years in internal exile, thrown around from place to place. I

worked as a manual labourer on piece-rate pay; I worked on construction
sites and collective farms. I experienced self-induced loneliness, chance
friendships in prison and all the changes caused by the constant earthquake
that is the 'consolidation of the dictatorship of the proletariat'. Sometimes
I wonder whether I gained anything from remaining alive. For 38 years I
never knew what family life was. It would have been much better if I had
just closed my eyes forever. That would have put an end to my affliction
and tragic predicament.[18]

On the day Musine Kokalari died, her neighbour, an elderly man, also persecuted by the regime, was summoned by the Sigurimi operative for Rrëshen.
He was warned, in no uncertain terms, that anyone attempting to attend
her funeral would be immediately arrested. She went to her grave alone –
the only people trailing behind the funeral carriage were the two municipal
gravediggers.

After the 1990s, relations between Hoxha and Musine Kokalari, and the
latter's punishment, became the subject of much discussion and speculation.
It has even been suggested that she once turned down his marriage proposal,
or that she used to make fun of him, but there is little evidence to substantiate these stories. It was surprising, however, to discover in the Central State
Archives that Musine Kokalari and Enver Hoxha had once corresponded
intensively with each other. The letters were written in the 1930s, when she
was a student in Rome and he was a teacher in Korça. Hoxha's letters were
typical messages of a well-wisher, in which he congratulated her on her
articles published in the press of the time. The last letter in the collection,
from 1939, reveals that Hoxha and Kokalari were in fact distant relatives. It
is still a mystery how and why their relationship fell apart thereafter. In 1960,
PEN Club International officially demanded Kokalari's release as one of 30
writers imprisoned by dictatorial regimes around the world. When this was
reported to Hoxha by one of his aides, his reaction was: 'Why, you mean the
whore is still alive?'[19]

A Reign of Terror

Set up prisons and concentration camps and imprison all those charged
with serious offences, high treason and open collaboration. Do not show
mercy to anyone who collaborated with the occupiers; execute them on
the spot. Assemble all prisoners in concentration camps; try to avoid mass
arrests because such actions will frighten people. Be careful. Stop, arrest
and execute influential individuals, make them an example for others. This
is sure to have an impact on people.[1]

The above telegram, dated 17 November 1944, was sent by Colonel
General Enver Hoxha, prime minister of the Provisional Government, to
General Dali Ndreu, who was in charge of clean-up operations in the north
of the country. It is a clear reflection of the new regime's political ideology
and of its intentions – uncompromising, cold and calculated punishment for
all opponents and sceptics.

As early as the summer of 1944, Hoxha focused primarily on the liqui-
dation of influential individuals, as revealed in this letter he wrote to Gogo
Nushi: 'Irfan Ohri must be tracked down and killed. Start making enquiries.
I believe he is staying at a house near the Rex cinema.'[2]

On 10 November 1944, just a week prior to the telegram to Ndreu, Hoxha
sent an order to Mehmet Shehu, the commander in charge of the liberation
of Tirana. Written by Hoxha himself, it read:

Our stance towards traitors and criminals who are apprehended or who
surrender must be severe and unwavering. They must realise immediately

that they are in the hands of the court. They are strictly prohibited from moving freely in town and talking to anyone. They must be detained and kept under guard.[3]

Whether as a direct result of this telegram or not, two days later, on 12 November 1944, as the battle for the liberation of Tirana raged, partisan forces knocked on the doors of 52 people for 'verification' purposes. Thirty-seven were taken away, 14 were not at home, and one, Hamit Kokalari, could not be moved because of a high fever. The 37 who were detained – a mixture of fascist collaborators, politically inactive intellectuals, anti-Yugoslavs and former army officers who had refused to take sides during the war – were all taken to the basement of Hotel Bristol. There they were executed on the spot, without any explanation, trial or court decision. Among them were two Kokalari brothers, founders of the Mesagjerië Shqiptare publishing house, who were staunch opponents of the occupation but otherwise politically uninvolved, and Hoxha's distant relatives. The reason for their summary execution at a time when many collaborationists were spared remained a mystery for decades. In 1995, a letter was found in the Central State Archives that might provide an explanation. The letter, written on 8 November 1944 by Muntaz Kokalari to Makbule Vrioni, a friend of the Kokalaris, said:

My own life and my friends' lives are now in peril because of the bastard of Gjirokastra. He has unleashed his red devils on us. It is perfectly clear – it is nothing but personal revenge, pure and simple. He cannot deny that we were opponents of fascism and that we did our bit for the country. We discussed this before; he is the bane of our poor Albania. It is such a misfortune that our long-suffering nation is in the hands of a monstrous, sneaky, vengeful, bitter, sly, selfish and autocratic megalomaniac, a gambler and liar, who did not pass a single exam abroad as he was too busy wasting his time in clubs and casinos. Not to speak of all the debts he amassed. We, the intellectuals of Gjirokastra, know exactly what he is worth and this is why he wants to get rid of us. I can only hope that this scoundrel and his red devils will be exposed sooner than later.[4]

The letter does not seem to have reached its destination. It fell somehow into the hands of Mehmet Shehu, the partisan commander in the city. Four days later Muntaz Kokalari and 36 other men were dead, shot in the basement of Hotel Bristol.

The summary executions that took place on the night of 12 November – and many others that followed, at least until the start of regular judicial proceedings in December 1944 – were by no means spontaneous or accidental. In some cases, it was merely a settling of scores, inspired by old grudges and resentment harboured by some partisan leaders against certain individuals. Yet, there can be no doubt that lists of victims had also been prepared. After the fall of the dictatorship in 1991, Kristo Themelko, once one of the most feared senior officials on the Sigurimi, who subsequently fell from grace, published a book called *Tirana e përgjakur* (Bloodbath in Tirana), in which he wrote about the early executions and Hoxha's awareness of them: 'I spoke to Enver, whose advice was that, once we were in the capital, all dangerous elements had to be cleansed. So, as soon as I got there, I asked our people to compile a list of them.'[5]

The summary executions in Tirana even caused alarm among some senior leaders of the CPA. According to Hoxha's memoirs, Sejfullah Malëshova was the first to express his deep concern about the execution of officers who had recently switched sides to the communists, or those who had not collaborated with the enemy at all. Malëshova was aggrieved that 'there was a lot of terror in Tirana, many "repented officers" were being killed.'[6] Hoxha's answer, according to his book *Titistët* (published in English as *The Titoites*), was: 'The great battle for the liberation of the capital is still raging. What is it that you are calling terror and who are these officers you are complaining about?'[7]

A few days later, at the plenary meeting in Berat, Gogo Nushi, one of the communist leaders for Tirana, expressed his 'repentance':

All our political opponents, even if they were not criminals or quislings, were regarded as enemies and we tried to erase them from the face of the earth [...] In the wake of our forces entering Tirana, 60 people were liquidated; there is a list of them. I knew those names and none of those people deserved to die. We are sure that there were others. The number must be over 100. We believed that by eliminating these enemies we were helping safeguard our victory.[8]

Such executions were not confined to Tirana. According to a letter addressed to Colonel General Enver Hoxha, sent from Shkodra by a certain Vaskë Koleci on 30 January 1945, similar lists were drawn up for all major towns. According to Koleci, on 28 January Shkodra was surrounded by two brigades and a curfew had been imposed. Further down he wrote: 'On the first day we prepared the lists with the help of comrades from the local chapter. The lists contained the names of 210 people to be arrested on various charges.' Here the wording becomes eerie: '[T]he charges are not that well founded. This is because the lists were not prepared beforehand. So far, about 120 people have been detained.'[9]

The officer then proposed a radical but effective solution, which is the only passage thickly underlined in the seven-page letter:

[K]eeping in mind our position in these parts, we need to take measures and strike both in town and in the surrounding areas. Some blood needs to be spilled and some houses burned down, both in town and in the villages, so that they can feel our power and submit to it. Today only a show of force can help turn the situation around for us.[10]

Then the officer suggests to the prime minister a list of 12 persons to be executed immediately and another 31 to be sentenced to prison terms of various duration.

Over the years, there has been open or hushed speculation that the executions that took place during the first months of the regime, and over the next four to five years after the war, were carried out without Hoxha's knowledge. The blame is invariably laid at the door of Mehmet Shehu, Shefqet Peçi or Koçi Xoxe. However, documents that became available after the opening of the archives in 1991 show that every execution, down to seemingly insignificant ones, was carried out with Enver Hoxha's full knowledge and endorsement, as shown by this message of 1 February 1945 sent to Mehmet Shehu:

Extremely urgent.

    To Mehmet Shehu, Shkodra.

    No one shall be executed without prior communication of their names to us and without our approval. Stop. Please advise who has been sentenced to death and await approval.

Colonel General Enver Hoxha[11]

It seems Hoxha's orders were complied with, as on many occasions he was indeed notified of the convictions for which he gave his approval, as shown by this telegram of 10 February 1945:

Extremely urgent.

    To the legal department; Second Corps.

    In response to the second telegram of 9 February 1945, approval has been given for the execution of 12 persons and various sentences for the others as per above. Stop. Please inform on date of execution.

Colonel General Enver Hoxha[12]

In at least five cases, approval for an execution was granted just 12 to 15 minutes after notification was received, which could only mean that the decisions were made directly by Hoxha or his close associates; in any case it does not seem that they were the result of a group deliberation. This was what happened with the order for the execution of Dom Lazër Shantoja and Sulçe Beg Bushati. According to the times registered on the telegrams, their execution was ordered only nine minutes after the reply of approval was received. The telegram of 10 February 1945 read as follows:

To the Third Corps

    Military Tribunal, Shkodra

    In response to your request of 10 February 1945, death sentence for Dom Lazër Shantoja and Sulçe Beg Bushati approved. Stop. Please inform on date of execution.

Enver Hoxha[13]

The issue of these executions seems to have been swept under the carpet and left untouched for years, but a careful look at the war records, especially the minutes of the plenary meeting held in Berat from 23 to 27 November 1944, shows that there was some unease within the CPA about so much blood spilled in vain. It seems Hoxha was obliged to accept the violence that occurred within and outside the ranks of the party, but he laid the blame on the Yugoslavs:

> The terrorist line was emphasised more by Dušan, Ali and Liri. I merely followed Ali on this. When someone came from the front and informed us that so-and-so was not acting properly, we decided that that person should be executed. We had no clear line on this issue.[14]

After the plenary meeting, the punishments continued; if anything, they became even more severe. Punishments reserved for the so-called 'overthrown classes' were particularly extreme. The first executions in Tirana, immediately after the capture of the capital, were just the beginning. They were followed by similar reprisals in other areas of Albania. Dozens of people were convicted without due process and nearly 2,000 were executed. Within a very short period of time, mind-boggling taxes were levied on merchants and other rich people, under what came to be known as the 'Extraordinary War Tax'. Those who did not, or could not, pay were arrested. Many of them perished in prison. Cars, houses and other property and assets were widely nationalised. Landowners were expropriated under the much-trumpeted Agrarian Reform and the land was distributed among the peasants. Within less than a year, however, the collectivisation of farmland started, and led to the creation of agricultural cooperatives in the style of Soviet kolkhozes. Initially a voluntary process, the collectivisation soon became mandatory and was often carried out under the threat of force.

The first wave of liquidations targeting mainly anti-communists and renegades, which continued into the early 1950s, achieved its undeclared mission. Many members of the Albanian elite, people educated in the West or prominent businessmen and merchants, either lost their lives as a result of this incomprehensible massacre, or languished behind bars, something that deprived them of any opportunity to contribute to society. The communists then tried to create their own elite, mainly educated in the East. These people achieved power in full force about ten years after the war, in the mid-1950s.

Soon after the war, the Sigurimi was set up within the Ministry of the Interior, patterned on the Yugoslav model. Its main task was to keep the regime safe. A few years after its creation, its founder, Koçi Xoxe, would explain how it came about, doing so at his own trial:

> The Sigurimi's organisational structure and methodology were taken from the Yugoslav model. I sent Nesti Kerenxhi to Belgrade in 1946 expressly for this purpose. In 1947 Safet Filipović came to see us, at my request, and worked with us at the Ministry of the Interior. He remained in the country as an employee of the Yugoslav legation. In December 1944, Lieutenant Colonel Mijat [Vuletić] of OZNA [the Yugoslav Department of National Security] came to Tirana to help us with the organisation of the work.[15]

The Sigurimi was without a doubt the most terrifying organisation Albania had ever experienced. It kept the country firmly within its grip, by means both fair and foul. At times it acted within the law, and at others it ignored the law completely. Shrouded in mystery, the organisation remains to this day the most obscure and least-known aspect of the communist regime. The Sigurimi created a sophisticated system of surveillance and denunciation. According to figures recently made public by the Ministry of the Interior, during the 46 years of its existence, the Sigurimi had an army of 200,000 'operatives'. Some of the 'eyes and ears of the regime' were coerced into collaborating; others were loyal volunteers acting on their convictions, and others still were enlisted in return for certain privileges. This so-called 'army of snitches' kept track of all people considered 'problematic' by the regime. By 1990 the Sigurimi reportedly had no less than a million files, which means a file for every adult citizen of the People's Socialist Republic of Albania. The files contained all sorts of information – from people's political beliefs to details about their personal lives such as adultery, betrayal or sexual preferences. Most of the files were destroyed in the spring of 1991.

Thirty-nine prisons were built in the country. Prisoners carried out hard labour in them with no compensation, mainly in the mining industry. The prisons were generally located in remote areas and the conditions in them were dire and undignified to say the least. In the prisons of Spaç and Burrel it was not unusual for over 20 inmates to be stuffed in cells with an area of less than ten square metres. According to the records of the Ministry of the Interior, prison food was very low in protein and fat. A daily ration consisted of 650 grams of bread, 7 grams of oil, 10 grams of sugar, 70 grams of rice, pasta or beans, and 150 grams of vegetables a day. Until 1982 the inmates were allowed to cook their own meals at specific one-hour periods of time, one in the morning and the other in the evening, when they would cook food purchased in the prison shop or brought in by their families. In 1982, this 'privilege' was revoked.

Pjetër Arbnori, son of a police officer who was killed in an ambush by partisan forces, was imprisoned at a young age, charged with 'attempting to form a social democratic group'. He was initially sentenced to death, but this was later commuted to 20 years' imprisonment, to which an additional consecutive sentence was added while he was in prison. By the time of his release, he had served a total of 28 years, starting from 1961. This is how Arbnori remembered his time in prison, in a 2004 interview:

> The conditions there were very harsh. Often, at the slightest pretext, they would reduce our food rations further, or submit us to beatings, torture and out-of-hours forced labour. Anyone who did not meet the target set for the day was put into a cell with walls made of barbed wire, out in the cold, and no movement was allowed. Every day we would walk several kilometres to the place of work, lugging heavy picks and wheelbarrows, and those of us who were stronger would even carry the sentry posts on their backs. Food was scarce: it consisted of just 300 grams of bread, and potatoes. Later they increased the quantity of hot food, but it was often full of maggots and flies. The days when they served beans were the happiest moments of our lives.[16]

Over the years Arbnori was transferred to various prisons, but he served most of his sentence in the notorious Burrel prison. He recounted how they once won a small victory over the prison authorities:

There was a period when family members were allowed to bring us food –
they could bring 2 kilos of biscuits, pasta, margarine and a bit of sugar –
those were the good times! But then this was discontinued on the pretext
that it was a burden to the families! [...] We went on strike for 19 days and
this was our grandest achievement: we were eventually allowed 15 grams of
cheese a day. They also allowed us 3 kilos of fruit a month. If a watermelon
weighed over 3 kilos, the extra portion would be cut off and sent back.[17]

Arbnori was released from prison one and a half years before the fall of the
communist regime, around the time when Solidarność won the elections and
came to power in Poland. After 28 long years in prison, the first thing he
noticed in the 'outside' world was that people in his native Shkodra were no
longer growing flowers in their gardens. In those tough economic times, the
flowers had been replaced by staple-food plants. Upon his release, he reported
to the offices of the PLA in town, asking them for help in finding a job as
a carpenter. The answer was unequivocal: 'You are an enemy; you can find a
job when the British and Americans come back.'

Within two years Arbnori became an MP for the Democratic Party, the
newly founded opposition force, and a year later he was elected speaker of
the first pluralist parliament in Albania. He was the one who received James
Baker, the US Secretary of State, who paid a visit to Albania on the occasion
of the re-establishment of diplomatic relations between the two countries,
which had been severed in 1946.

The postwar years were extremely bleak. The Ministry of the Interior, led
by Koçi Xoxe, held the country in a tight grip of fear and repression. In addition to imprisonment, a system of internment was put in place, very similar
to the models applied in some of the worst dictatorial regimes on earth, not
unlike the Siberian gulags. Dozens of families were uprooted from their
native towns and banished to isolated camps built on marshland, mainly in
the Myzeqe region, where they had to report to the police three times a day.
They were not allowed to leave the camps and most of them remained there
for the entire 46 years of the communist regime.

The regime also applied the principle of collective punishment for families. Anyone who had a family member or a close relative who had been a

member of Balli Kombëtar, or who had been convicted or declared 'hostile to the party line', would be interned. Their children, nieces and nephews, even their grandchildren, were barred from attending university or getting normal jobs and were forever marked by this indelible 'stain'. They did their military service in separate units and were even housed in separate barracks, called '(forced) labour barracks'.

The initial purging of the opponents of the regime, who were dealt with relatively swiftly, was followed by further persecution campaigns. Gjergj Kokoshi, member of the National Liberation Council and a delegate at the Congress of Përmet, was among the first former partisan fighters to be taken to task. Minister of education in Hoxha's Provisional Government, he protested against the initial purges, the lack of democracy and the role played by the Yugoslavs in the country. A few months after the government's grand entry into Tirana, Kokoshi was dismissed from his ministerial post, arrested and thrown in jail, where he died a few years later. Todi Lubonja, Kokoshi's one-time student, was a political commissar in Burrel when he met his former teacher in one of the cells of the notorious prison:

Here in the infamous Burrel prison, in 1946 (it must have been towards the beginning of that year) I ran across a man of some intellect and knowledge, sitting alone in a cell. He was suffering from tuberculosis. I recognised him; he had been my teacher for a while. In 1943 he left the capital to join partisan forces in Peza and the National Liberation Movement. He came from a poor Orthodox family from Shkodra. I was not on duty in the prison; I was just curious to see the prisoners. Some of them had been important officials of the regime, such as Koço Kota, for instance. At the time I was serving as a commissar at the command headquarters and they would let me in. I must admit, it was shocking to see him in that condition. In Peza his presence had filled me with enthusiasm and I had embraced him with great affection. But now I just stood there, frozen. He did not move either. He simply raised his head to see who I was. I don't know whether he even recognised me. 'Hello, professor,' I said in a trembling voice. 'How are you?' I can't remember whether he answered or not. 'How did it all come to this?' I blurted out, not really knowing what to say. I wanted him to speak, to say something. 'Time will tell, my son!' That is all he said. This man was Gjergj Kokoshi, former minister of education of our first Provisional Democratic Government after the victory over fascism. He had dared to speak his mind in parliament, as a free and democratic man. Enver Hoxha threw him in prison. He died there.[18]

Todi Lubonja himself ended up in Burrel prison, too, together with his son.

In May 1947 another wave of arrests followed. This time the target was a group of members of the People's Assembly (the parliament) and their family and friends, about 40 people in all, both former communists and non-political individuals. The group had attempted to form a parliamentary grouping in opposition to the government, or at least this was the charge brought against them. In his memoirs, Enver Hoxha explained what Riza Dani was seeking to achieve:

Riza Dani, a henchman of the old regime and, of course, of the former bourgeois parliament, sought to turn our parliament into a place for prattling away, where everyone could ramble on for as long as they liked, say whatever they liked with no restrictions. Riza Dani and his associates even expected that everything they were going to say would be published in the papers.[19]

And here is how Enver Hoxha reported Riza Dani's opinion on the new constitution of the People's Republic of Albania:

[H]e attacked the constitution because, according to him, it was an ideological, rather than a national constitution. As he stated, his credo was, 'I am for a free democracy and I had hoped the constitution would be inspired by the same principle!'[20]

Riza Dani was not allowed to speak his mind in parliament much longer. He was arrested with ten other MPs in May 1947, about one and a half years after being elected to parliament. The total number of those detained reached 40. On 30 August 1947 the sentences were pronounced: 17 of them were sentenced to death, including prominent individuals like Shefqet Beja, Riza Dani and Selahudin Toto, the brother of Et'hem and Ismet Toto, who had lost their lives after a failed uprising against King Zog. Another name on the death list was Enver Zazani, Hoxha's one-time schoolmate and best friend. After the sentencing, Zazani's French wife, her young baby in her arms, waited outside Hoxha's door for 12 long hours to ask for mercy. But she was unable to stop the execution. She was eventually sent back to France together with her daughter. The latter returned to Albania a mature woman, to find the remains of a father she never knew and give them a proper burial.

These liquidations were just one aspect of the terror campaign. Close surveillance of people, including some of the most senior communist leaders, was another method used by the regime to maintain its grip on power. In his trial in 1949, responding to charges that he had wiretapped the president of the republic, members of the Politburo and almost all government ministers, Koçi Xoxe said: 'As for the surveillance of the leadership, I did discuss it with the general secretary of the party and had his approval.'[21]

Punishments within the ranks caused unprecedented trauma. There were some voices who would meekly question the meaning of all this, but the majority continued to behave in the same way, accepting the punishment of the next 'culprit' in line, not daring to ask or think whose turn it would be next. In 2008, Bedri Koka, a former officer at the Ministry of the Interior, who had often driven convicts to their place of execution, appeared at the door of the Ndreu family home. He was there to help the son and daughter of former general Dali Ndreu and his wife Liri Gega, two former senior communist officials and one-time protagonists of the reign of communist terror in Albania, find the place where their parents and another communist, Petro Bullati, had been executed on a rainy day in 1956. Despite his good intentions, they were not able to locate the remains. It is possible that the bodies were subsequently moved elsewhere, a frequent practice at the time. In a 2008 interview in the newspaper *Panorama*, the same man related how Petro Bullati's family was interned after his execution:

A few days after the execution, I was told to go to Petro Bullati's home. An order had been issued for the family to be interned. I was part of the group that would help move them from Tirana. We went into the house and communicated to them the order issued by the internment committee. We took their belongings and bundled them into the car. As we were leaving the house, I noticed our chief reach up to take a large photograph off the wall. I went to help him by holding the chair he was standing on. After managing to get the string off the nail on the wall, he turned and swore at Petro Bullati's wife, 'You witch, what are you doing with a photo of the heroic Vasil Shanto here?' 'Please don't,' the woman pleaded. 'Go and wash your mouth when you use his name!' snarled the major, holding the frame in both hands. The woman explained tearfully, 'He was my brother; he was friends with Enver and Vojo Kushi. He gave his life for the country.' We froze. We both knew that something was not right, but it was not our duty to think about such things. We drove Vasil Shanto's sister and her children off to the camp. The chief of the operation held on to the photo all the time we were in the car and kept muttering to himself. On the way back he told us that Vasil Shanto had once saved his life during a battle on the outskirts of Tirana.[22]

Vasil Shanto was a founding member of the CPA, one of those who supported Enver Hoxha unconditionally in his bid for the post of the first secretary of the Central Committee of the CPA. He was killed in a battle on the shores of Lake Shkodra, in 1943, leaving behind a sister, herself a communist – the same sister who was now being punished so mercilessly.

13

Departure of the British and the Americans

The grand ball on 28 November 1944 and the prime minister's future wife dancing with an officer of the British mission in Tirana were the first and last grand gestures of the new government and prime minister. Enver Hoxha entered his new office overlooking the main boulevard in Tirana with a clear goal in his mind: to consolidate his power and to eliminate all political figures and organisations that stood in the way of a Soviet-style communist dictatorship. In the 41 years he ruled over Albania he had many love-and-hate relations with foreign countries and their leaders; he built and destroyed alliances that marked the way the Albanians lived, and often changed his political style on a whim. Only one thing remained unchanged over the years: his hatred for the United States and the United Kingdom. From 1946, when diplomatic relations with the two Western powers were severed and the US and British missions were expelled from Albania, Hoxha never wanted anything to do with them again. The next time the Americans and the British came to Albania was in 1991, when his regime collapsed six years after his death.

The British had an important role to play during the war years, while Hoxha was consolidating his position as leader. From the arrival of the first British mission in Albania in 1943, until November 1944, they were practically the only Allied presence in the country, if one does not count Tito's envoys, with whom Hoxha had a totally different kind of rapport. The Americans arrived later, while the Russians only sent an army major to Helmës in August 1944, when the war was practically over: a token gesture simply to register their presence with Hoxha's forces in Albania. Documents uncovered later have shown that the Russians regarded Hoxha as Tito's subordinate and as a figure under his responsibility.

The first British officer to arrive in Albania was Billy (Neal) McLean. The young major transferred to the country from Palestine and was not very familiar with Albania. Educated at Eton and the son of a wealthy business-man who had made his fortune trading with India, Billy McLean decided to enlist with the Special Operations Executive, one of the most dangerous jobs in the war. Forty years later, this is how Hoxha remembered McLean's arrival in Albania:

By the end of April 1943, the party chapter for Gjirokastra informed me that a group of British officers, led by a certain Major Billy McLean, had entered our area from Greece. The group, who were in possession of weapons and radio equipment, claimed they were an official military mission sent by Allied headquarters for the Mediterranean based in Cairo.

I instructed our comrades from the Gjirokastra chapter to cut the British men off at Zagori and interrogate them in detail to establish their identity (corroborated by official proof of ID), where they came from, who their leader was, what their real mission was, and so on.

The members of the McLean mission remained there until they received their ID papers from their headquarters. In June the comrades in Gjirokastra sent them to us, in Labinot, with a security escort for their safe passage. They were completely exhausted when they arrived. I met them the next day. McLean introduced himself as head of the mission. He looked young, not more than 30 years of age, lean, of average height, with fine features and a cleanly shaven face. He was blonde and had sharp blue eyes, a bit like those of a wild cat. Later we learned that McLean was from the Scots Greys and had had experience in the colonial wars in Palestine and elsewhere.

I asked him, 'What is your mission?' In essence, Major McLean [who later became a colonel and a Conservative MP after the war] said the following, 'We are the first British mission to be seconded to the Albanian partisans. The British government has sent us here on a reconnaissance mission to gather information about your country and the resistance against the Italians. We shall inform our headquarters of your opinion on the war and of any needs or requests you might have.[1]

In the space of one and a half years, several other British groups were dropped into Albania, considerably increasing the size and level of the mission. In October 1943, His Majesty's Government sent to Albania Brigadier Edmund Frank Davies, nicknamed 'Trotsky', together with a staff team. Davies's Albanian mission did not last long as he was captured by the Germans in January 1944. After his capture, the British sent about seven other missions to Albania, which were attached to various anti-fascist resistance groups across the territory of Albania and Kosovo.

The purpose of the British missions was clear: to maximise combat forces and capacities in the fight against the Italian and German occupiers in Albania. According to Julian Amery, who was attached to Abaz Kupi's forces, the more German forces were kept tied up in the Balkans, the more successful the British mission would be. To achieve this, by the end of 1943 through to the end of the war, the British stimulated large operations by supplying weapons, uniforms and other war materiel to the Balkan countries. The existence of these supply operations, amply documented in most World War II history books, was denied by Hoxha in his memoirs. For many years after the break-up with the British, Hoxha maintained that British aid consisted of just odd boots and weapons without munitions. This was not true. The First Assault Brigade, which was formed in the summer of 1943, was entirely armed by the British. Not only did the British supply weapons, but they also provided large quantities of gold in support of the resistance effort.

While the British focused on uniting the entire spectrum of Albanian forces in the fight against the common enemy, irrespective of their ideological affiliation and internal disagreements, Hoxha's objective was totally different. He demanded of the British that they sever all contacts with the other forces active in Albania. Initially the demand included only Balli Kombëtar, but later it extended to Gani Kryeziu, Muharrem Bajraktari and especially Abaz Kupi. Securing political power after the war was much more important to Hoxha than a few more months of a united front against the German occupiers, who were clearly on their way out. This was his first major disagreement with the British. Enver Hoxha spoke to Brigadier Davies after the latter had met representatives of Balli Kombëtar in an attempt to engage them in the fight against the occupier. The conversation, according to Hoxha's memoirs, went something like this:

> 'Mr Hoxha,' the brigadier said, 'I had a conversation with Mr Lumo Skëndo and others and I spoke to them openly. I told them that, to my knowledge, only the National Liberation Movement were fighting the Germans, while they were not doing anything. They rejected the suggestion and pretty well accused me of being a communist. I stuck to my arguments and, in the end, I think I persuaded them. They promised they would fight.'
>
> 'No, they will fight against us,' I countered.
>
> 'Oh no, Mr Hoxha,' the brigadier answered, 'they will fight against the Germans.'
>
> 'Then allow me to assure you that you've been lied to. They never fought in the past and they will not fight the Germans in the future. Mark my words. They will continue to betray their own people and will side, arms and all, with the Germans.'[2]

We are unable to ascertain whether or not this is a true account of that conversation. In their memoirs, the British officers rejected almost all of the claims made by Hoxha in the early 1980s, just a few years before his death. However, it seems that the essence of what was discussed is more or less accurate, which can provide an explanation of how Hoxha's aversion to the British started. It is equally likely that his feud with the British was made worse by ideological differences. In his memoirs Hoxha describes a conversation he had with Mustafa Gjinishi, after the latter's return from Brigadier Davies's headquarters. Davies had apparently proposed that Gjinishi send a National Liberation delegation to London to meet with British authorities. There they could speak to the British about the partisan resistance and the relations between the communists and nationalists, and ask for more military aid in support of their resistance. Gjinishi's proposal, totally sensible in the circumstances, was regarded by Hoxha as nothing short of open treason. Here is the end of the conversation with Gjinishi:

'No, Mustafa, we must not do such a thing. I am totally opposed to the idea,' I said, trying not to give him any cause for alarm.

'All right,' Mustafa said. 'Still, why don't you discuss it with the rest of the comrades first?'

When I met the other comrades, I told them that Mustafa seemed to have fallen into a trap and described the conversation to them.

'The scoundrel, he's surely an Intelligence Service agent!' one of the comrades cried out, and he was right.

'Patience,' I said, 'let us not rush to conclusions. We'll keep him under observation. Let's see what he does next.'[3]

Hoxha's relations with the British became even tenser when the British decided to attach permanent missions to the headquarters of Abaz Kupi and Gani Kryeziu. The rift between him and the British command in Bari grew even wider. He sent Allied headquarters a telegram saying that Gani Kryeziu and Abaz Kupi were collaborators and foes; that they would be arrested and executed, and that the British officers attached to them would be treated as collaborators, too. He called for their immediate withdrawal to Italy. Some of these telegrams were published in his book *Rreziku anglo-amerikan për Shqipërinë* (*The Anglo-American Threat to Albania*).

It seems Hoxha's show of force achieved the desired objective, probably because Britain did not want any additional problems in the Balkans, but also because, realistically, the partisans were the only numerically significant force consistently engaged in the fight against the Germans.

Hoxha won the battle of wills: headquarters at Bari ordered all the British missions that were not attached to the NLA to abandon the local commanders and to withdraw immediately. Hoxha prevailed, but in doing so he made sworn enemies of two young English officers who would become very influential in postwar Britain: Julian Amery, formerly attached to Kupi, and David Smiley, also attached to nationalist forces. Between 1952 and 1992 Amery was a Conservative MP and held a number of governmental posts, including minister of aviation, undersecretary of state for war, minister for public works and minister of state for foreign and Commonwealth affairs. As the son-in-law of Harold Macmillan, he was a very influential politician for many years. Amery never forgave Hoxha for what he did and was openly opposed to the postwar communist regime in Albania. He was willing to cross swords with anyone who sought to soften the British stance towards the Stalinist regime in Albania.

In the autumn of 1944, as Hoxha was steadily consolidating his position of power, a provisional landing of British commandos in Spile near Himara and in Saranda turned into another source of conflict. According to Hoxha, the British forces aimed at reinstating King Zog and were forced to retreat under the threat of a partisan attack. According to British documents, the landings were part of local operations to strike at supply routes between the German garrisons at Corfu and Durrës.

At the military parade of 28 November 1944 Colonel Palmer, head of the British mission to Albania and a supporter of Hoxha, and Thomas Stefan, an American of Albanian origin, were both standing on the podium with Hoxha. The members of the British mission were also invited to the grand ball that evening, where they showed up looking very smart in their ceremonial uniforms. It looked like Albania would maintain normal relations with the two Western powers, but the problems between Hoxha and the British started almost immediately. Hoxha's intention was to establish a regime identical to Stalin's, while the British were still hoping for a Western-style regime, free elections and a multi-party system. They had reason to hope – Enver Hoxha was the only communist leader among their Eastern allies who had not been to Moscow; he did not seem to have any contacts with the Comintern; and, more importantly, he had spent the most important years of his youth in France.

One day in early autumn 1945, a few months prior to the elections of 2 December, General Hodgson, head of the British mission, invited Hoxha to dinner. The British mission was based in the villa of King Zog's brother, near the Tirana football stadium, which had just been named after Qemal Stafa, the fallen communist hero. Enver Hoxha, his wife and Nako Spiru arrived at the mission escorted by a squad of partisan guards. Hoxha must have known that the conversation of that evening would have a bearing on his political future. He was determined not to budge from his course. The contents of the conversation, related in Hoxha's book *Rreziku anglo-amerikan për Shqipërinë*, seem accurate and are corroborated by the memoirs of British officers:

'However, Mr Hoxha,' the general retorted, 'you do not allow the existence of other political parties. People can only express their free will if there are other political parties.'

'Mr Hodgson,' I laughed, 'it seems you have been losing some sleep over the fact that the "poor" Albanian people do not have other parties through which to have their say.'

The questions that General Hodgson was asking were not by chance.

'So, will there be any other groupings running in the election, in opposition to the front?' he asked after hearing my answer on the political parties.

'From the indications we have so far, General,' I replied, 'there are no other groups and there is no reason why there should be. You know why? The war that the Albanian people waged solved the issue. The opposition was eliminated by the revolution and the war; they sided with the occupiers and compromised themselves.'

'But, Mr Hoxha, aren't there at least some independent candidates who could stand in the elections?' the general insisted.[4]

Enver Hoxha stood his ground to the end of that conversation. He had already made his choice. From that moment Albania could be counted as part of the Soviet-led Eastern bloc, a menacing political power extending from the heart of Berlin to the Far East.

That dinner in September 1945 was Hoxha's last-known visit to the seat of the British mission in Tirana, or, for that matter, to any Western embassy or mission in the country. Three months later he held the general elections. In each polling station there were two ballot boxes – a red one for the National Liberation Movement and a black one for the 'reactionaries'. The former, that is, the CPA, won 93.6 per cent of the votes. The opposition was not even allowed to constitute itself as a political force. The unfortunate individuals who had naively believed they could express their discontent freely by casting a ballot in the black box were promptly identified and arrested. Many of them were executed.

The first constituent meeting of the People's Assembly that emerged from the December elections was held in Tirana on 10 January 1946, in a building which was formerly known as the Dopolavoro, built by the Italians. The next day the assembly unanimously voted for the new form of government and declared Albania a 'People's Republic'. King Zog and his family and heirs were banned from ever returning. In order to create a semblance of normal procedure, Enver Hoxha's government offered to tender its resignation, but this was flatly rejected by the MPs. A Presidium of the People's Assembly was constituted and a Statute of the People's Republic of Albania adopted. The assembly charged Enver Hoxha with forming the new cabinet, which was sworn in on 22 March 1946, amid tumultuous applause and cheering. In addition to the post of prime minister, Hoxha also held the posts of minister of foreign affairs and minister for national defence. His grip on power was now secure.

One of Hoxha's first actions as the new prime minister was to order the arrest of anyone known to have close ties with the British and American missions. On the list were friends of Harry T. Fultz, a prominent American who had opened two vocational schools in Albania during King Zog's reign, and who now worked at the US legation. Many of those accused of being 'American agents' had attended the Fultz Vocational Schools. Others, like Kol Kuqali, had worked at the US legation before the war. An MP and father of two sons who had perished in the war – one was killed in combat and the other died in a German concentration camp – Kuqali died under torture while in detention, before even appearing in court.

Britain and the United States delayed recognising Hoxha's government and then placed conditions on it such as its recognition of the concessions signed between King Zog and British and US companies before the war. Hoxha refused emphatically. The British annoyed the head of the Albanian government even more by supporting the Greek delegation headed by prime minister Konstantinos Tsaldaris in the Paris Peace Conference in August–September 1946. By attempting to portray Albania as a country that sided with Fascist Italy during its aggression against Greece, Athens was once again seeking to reconfigure the borders between the two countries. The accusations of the Greek delegation were so serious, and the situation at the conference became so tense, that Hoxha hastened to Paris, where he spent the end of August and beginning of September. In his speech Tsaldaris called Albania a fascist country and an aggressor. A copy of the fascist Albanian-language newspaper

Tomori (named after an Albanian mountain) from 1940, with a public appeal by Omer Nishani stating: 'I call on the Albanian people to join the Fascist Party,' was distributed to the participants. 'This man, a former fascist, is today the president of Albania,' Tsaldaris said to the delegates. Then he waved a daily order issued by the commander of the Tomorri Battalion, Spiro Moisiu, during the Greek–Italian war. 'This is an order for an attack. It says: Attack on Greek territory at 12.30 hours. This man, now leader of the Albanian army, committed atrocities as deep within Greek territory as Kastoria.'[5]

There was little Hoxha could do to change the atmosphere at the conference. He knew that behind the scenes the Greeks had the full support of the British. The situation improved somewhat when Moša Pijade, a member of the Yugoslav delegation, announced that just a week earlier Tsaldaris had made a proposal to Tito for the division of Albania between Yugoslavia and Greece. The proposal had been rejected and Pijade denounced it publicly. Soviet influence was also a factor that played in Albania's favour.

In September 1946 Hoxha held a press conference in Paris. This was to be his last ever visit to France or any other Western country, and his last meeting with foreign journalists. In the next 39 years, until the day he died in 1985, he would never set foot in a democratic country again.

British–Albanian relations were also tense for another reason. At the 1945 Yalta conference, Albania's fate was not discussed and it was left to the Albanians to decide for themselves on the form of the future regime they wanted. Enver Hoxha had made his choice, and the British and Americans were aware of it.

One can only speculate as to what course relations between the two countries might have taken, had it not been for the Corfu Channel incident in October 1946. This incident held British–Albanian relations hostage from 1946 until 1991. This is how Hoxha described it in his memoirs:

On 22 October 1946, four British warships were seen sailing on a northbound course through the Corfu Channel. They left international waters on their left and, without notifying us, entered our territorial waters. It was clear – they were seeking an excuse to cause an international conflict. I instructed [the forces] to keep calm and attack only in case of a landing.

Then more news came from Saranda: as the warships approached the coast, there were explosions and two of the ships burst into flames. An Albanian vedette sailed out to offer assistance and enquire as to why they had trespassed into our territorial waters. The English did not even deign to provide an explanation for this flagrant violation of our sovereignty and sent our men back.

At The Hague we publicly reiterated once again that Albania had no knowledge of the placement of the mines, that we did not possess any mines, and that we had neither the equipment nor the experts to lay them. Our delegation supported our claims with evidence. Mr Pierre Cot, a French lawyer and politician, spoke in support of our position, and said that the incident had its roots in the attitude of British reactionary circles who wanted 'to teach others a lesson as to how they should behave'. He told the court that not only the small and the weak, but the great and mighty, too, needed to learn how to behave.

In April 1949, based on the evidence submitted by the Albanian representatives and the defence mounted by our friends and well-wishers, it [the International Court of Justice in The Hague] dismissed the possibility that the mines had been laid by us. It did, however, bow to UK pressure and machinations, and found Albania guilty 'of being aware of [the mines] and not providing notification of their existence.'

It was obvious that Albania had to be declared guilty because those were the orders and wishes of the 'mighty'. Thus, in December 1949, the court ordered Albania 'in the name of justice' to pay £843,947 to the United Kingdom. We refused to accept the judgement, not only because we were not guilty, but also because the court had no jurisdiction to assess the amount of compensation. We did not pay it in the past and we do not intend to pay it in the future. We are not the ones who should pay.[6]

For nearly 40 years Hoxha refused to pay the reparations on the grounds that Albania was not responsible for laying the mines and was not aware of their existence. In retaliation, Great Britain kept Albania's gold reserves, which had been looted by the Germans when they retreated, in the Bank of England. Later research has thrown light on the Corfu Channel incident. The

British ships had entered Albanian territorial waters without prior warning. In July 2009 sections from the bow of one of the damaged British ships, HMS *Volage*, were found in Albanian waters. But the Albanian delegation at The Hague was not telling the truth when it claimed that Albania had no knowledge of the mines. After his release from prison in June 1991, Bedri Spahiu, former senior government official and general prosecutor, declared that the mines had been laid by the Yugoslavs at the request of the Albanian government in order to prevent a British landing. Spahiu stated he was ready to appear before the International Court of Justice in The Hague to confirm the correctness of the judgement. But it was too late and, by then, the incident belonged in the past. Communism collapsed and the new democratic government recognised the international legal obligations that stemmed from Albania's previous conflicts.

In 1946 the British were the first to leave Albania. A few weeks later, on 14 November, Henderson, head of the US mission to Albania, formally asked the French ambassador to represent and protect the rights and interests of American citizens in Albania. On the afternoon of 14 November, an American destroyer lay in wait ten miles off the Albanian coast. Tirana was buzzing with the trial against the so-called 'Maliqi saboteurs'. Some engineers working on a major land-reclamation project in Maliq, former students of the Fultz schools, had been arrested and charged with being 'agents of Washington'. Statements of the payments they had received from the Americans had been published for several days on the front page of the daily *Bashkimi* (Unity).

At 16.00 hours, Manol Konomi, general secretary at the Ministry of Foreign Affairs, rang Enver Hoxha's office to inform him that Henderson had lowered the American flag in the legation courtyard and had handed the building over to the French. At 17.30 hours, four cars carrying the members of the US mission, escorted by two Albanian security vehicles, left for Durrës. At 20.30 hours, after submitting to a thorough check, the members of the US mission got on the speedboat sent from the US destroyer that was waiting in international waters to take them to Naples. At 20.35 hours, an officer who introduced himself as Captain Zoto sent an urgent telegram to prime minister Hoxha's office, with this simple message: 'The Americans have left.'[7] The Americans next set foot in Albania 45 years later.

14

The Yugoslavs: A Matter of Love and Hate

Koçi Xoxe, number two of the regime, was deputy prime minister and minister of the interior in the new government of 22 March 1946. Originally from Negovan, a nondescript little town between Greece and Macedonia, Xoxe, a one-time tinsmith with a good knowledge of Slavic and Greek but with no formal education, had risen swiftly in the ranks to become one of the most powerful men in Albania. Supported by the Yugoslavs and clearly their favourite, he was sometimes seen to have more power than Hoxha himself. Nearly all the Yugoslav envoys after the departure of Miladin Popović – who had supported Hoxha – favoured Xoxe rather than the leader of the party. As Milovan Djilas said, describing an occasion when Stalin asked him about Hoxha:

> I avoided a direct and clear answer, but Stalin expressed precisely the same opinion of Hoxha as the Yugoslav leaders had acquired. 'He is a petty bourgeois, inclined towards nationalism? Yes, we think so too. Does it seem that the strongest man there is Xoxe?'[1]

The Yugoslavs preferred Xoxe for a number of reasons. In addition to being a working-class man, he was also an Orthodox Christian and had proven himself to be very useful. In mid-1944, at Xoxe's proposal and with Nako Spiru's support, Velimir Stojnić, head of the Yugoslav mission attached to the General Staff, was invited to attend the meetings of the Politburo of the CPA. Later he was also a constant presence at military meetings and at those of the Provisional Government. The Yugoslavs expressed their preference openly.

At the plenary meeting in Berat, in November 1944, they almost succeeded in having Hoxha isolated and removed as leader of the party. He was saved by a fortuitous circumstance. Hoxha pretended to accept their criticism, promised the Yugoslavs more access to the country, and managed to postpone the decision-making till later. But documentary evidence reveals two other factors that worked in Hoxha's favour. Firstly, although he was the Yugoslavs' favourite, Xoxe always admired Hoxha and was loyal to him. Secondly, Hoxha was just as obedient and willing to do the Yugoslavs' bidding, in spite of their giving him the cold shoulder. Clearly, between 1944 and 1948, the Yugoslavs felt themselves masters of Albania. Not only did Hoxha not try to prevent that impression, he put himself to the service of reinforcing it.

Tito's Yugoslavia was the most important foreign partner of the new government. Tito became Hoxha's mentor and great patron. The Albanian prime minister met Tito in Belgrade on a visit which did not attract much publicity and about which very little is known. During the war Hoxha sent an entire division in support of Tito's partisans, which, after passing through Kosovo, marched up as far north as Bosnia. Its mission was not so much to assist the Yugoslav partisan army to liberate the country as to help consolidate Tito's power, especially in Kosovo, where his leadership was expected to be fiercely contested. It was during that time that what came to be known as the Bar massacre occurred – thousands of young Kosovar men were forcibly mobilised and marched from Kosovo, through the territory of Albania, to Bar in Montenegro, where they were killed. It was a massacre that the communist regime never spoke about, not even when relations with the Yugoslavs became tense and hostile.

Hoxha's relations with the Yugoslavs were extremely complex. Towards the end of his life, he published a bulky volume of memoirs on them entitled *Titistët* (*The Titoites*). Hoxha's stance towards Yugoslavia and its CPY was ambivalent. Although he was identified quite early as one of the strongmen of the CPA, Hoxha only became leader with the help of Miladin Popović and Dušan Mugoša. He was certainly grateful to Popović and the Yugoslavs. But after the break with Yugoslavia in 1948, his aversion to Tito and Yugoslavia inspired many of his political decisions in future years. His subsequent breaks with the Soviet Union and with China were precipitated by news of a rapprochement with Tito by Khrushchev and later by Mao Zedong. Hoxha seems to have hated Tito to his death and he never tried to hide this feeling, right to the end of his life. There was only one man from Yugoslavia for whom Hoxha had something good to say – Miladin Popović. Because of the latter's early death, Hoxha never came into conflict with him, as he did with other Yugoslav communists. In his memoirs, Hoxha had some very harsh words to say about Dušan Mugoša, whom he professed to have called an agent and chauvinist from the time of the war. A letter found in the CPY archives, written by Hoxha to Mugoša soon after the latter was ordered by Tito to leave Albania, seems to contradict that claim:

Dear Comrade Dušan Mugoša,

I now feel stronger than on the day we parted, but I still miss you. It seems Ali was the strongest of us all, although I know how emotional he was on the day of departure. I am not alone. The rest of the comrades were also extremely touched. Dr Nishani started crying and commiserated, 'All those vile things the enemy said about Dušan and Ali, these worthy, determined comrades, who left their families and their country behind to come and help us and fight with us' [...] But let us talk about work now. Almost all of us are gathered here: Tuk, Besnik, Hulo, Dali, Beqir Balluku, Nexhip, Pëllumb, and so on. Nako and Shule have not arrived yet. We have already held some briefing sessions. Tuk and Besnik started first; they briefed us on the operations carried out by their brigade, the morale of the partisans and so on. We intend to start a short course, in the form of a series of sessions, on the following topics:

– Imperialist wars, the first and the second, just and unjust wars;
– Role of the party in the army;
– Organisation of power;
– The National Liberation War.

A number of military courses will also be organised.

Tuk is not very happy with Mehmet – please do not read more into this than is meant – however, Tuk is saying that since Salo left, Mehmet has taken heed of no one. At the brigade meeting he played down the operation against Haki Blloshmi and the one in Pogradec. He gave some very strange orders to Tuk and did a number of other things. Do not worry, we will look into these things very carefully, in an unprejudiced way, and we will act in the way we decided.

The election of delegates to the congress is going according to plan in the free zones, but I fear very few will be able to attend from the occupied areas. I will let you know how things progress. Please write more often.

A warm embrace from

Taras[2]

Hoxha's grudge against Mugoša was clearly linked to the fact that, at the height of the Albanian–Yugoslav dispute, Mugoša appeared on TV, where he publicly reminded Hoxha of the fact that it was Yugoslav support that propelled him to his position as leader of the CPA.

Relations became equally tense with Vukmanović Tempo, who in 1972 published his multi-volume war memoirs, where relations with Hoxha occupy a considerable place.

But back in the spring of 1946, Hoxha seemed completely under the sway of the Yugoslavs and willing to make any concessions to them. This stance caused reaction among many leading nationalists, who were less than impressed with the way Albanian–Yugoslav relations were going. Serbia and Yugoslavia were traditionally seen as Albania's enemies. The Kosovo question remained unsolved and was a source of considerable tension between the two countries. Alfred Moisiu, son of Spiro Moisiu, former chief of staff of the partisan army, and a senior officer in the Albanian army, recalled how his father came home one evening very upset. He had had an altercation with Hoxha, and was being ostracised as a result. The subject of the argument had been the Yugoslavs. This is how Alfred Moisiu, president of Albania from 2002 to 2007, remembered the conversation that cost his father his career and led to his forced early retirement, in a 2002 interview:

In 1946 the Albanian state was still finding its feet. Enver said, 'Let's ask Marshal Tito to send us some military experts.' My father did not agree. 'Enver, we are officers, they are officers, we were guerrilla fighters, they were guerrilla fighters. What more could they possibly teach us? Why don't we ask Stalin – he conducted a frontal war. His army could help us.' 'No,' countered Enver, 'they are very busy.' 'But they have thousands of officers; can't they spare 500 or a thousand men to help us with our army?'[3]

The strength of Hoxha's relations with the Yugoslavs was also proven by an incident that occurred towards the end of 1945, which involved another political leader with the same surname as his – Fadil Hoxha, the leader of the Kosovar communists. Educated in Albania, and a member of the Shkodra Communist Group, Fadil Hoxha had transferred to Kosovo during the war to help organise the anti-fascist movement there. He was one of the organisers of the Bujan conference of 1943, at which Kosovo expressed a wish to be united with Albania, and, after the victory of Tito's partisans in Kosovo, he became a leading figure there. In 1945, Fadil Hoxha and Zekeria Rexha, another communist militant, travelled to Albania with a simple request for the communist leader. They asked for 100 language teachers to be sent to Kosovo, and a Latin-script printing press, to be used for printing textbooks for Kosovar children. Until then, the printing machines used in Kosovo could only print in Cyrillic script.

Fadil Hoxha was received warmly by his numerous friends in Tirana. He also met Enver Hoxha for about three hours. This was the first and last *tête-à-tête* between the two Hoxhas, during which they discussed a number of issues, including the many problems ethnic Albanians were facing in Kosovo. A recording of the conversation between them had somehow fallen into the hands of the Yugoslavs. Upon arriving in Prishtina, Fadil Hoxha was interrogated by the UDBA, the Yugoslav secret police, who wanted to know about the talks. In 2000, Fadil Hoxha explained: 'There were no exaggerations in the transcript; they were all the things I had actually told Enver Hoxha. We discussed the political situation in Kosovo and Albania.'[4] Fadil Hoxha thought that it was the work of Koçi Xoxe, the interior minister, who had also signed the cover telegram. It remained something of a mystery, however, how the Yugoslavs were able to obtain the transcript of a meeting at which only Enver Hoxha and he were present.

Fadil Hoxha passed away in 2001, after serving for many years in top
political positions in Kosovo. He was in secret contact with Enver Hoxha
later, too, especially in the early 1970s. He never blamed Hoxha for the latter's
policy in relation to Yugoslavia. But he never forgave Enver Hoxha for one
thing. On his visit to Yugoslavia in June 1946, Enver Hoxha did not set foot
in Kosovo and did not meet any Kosovar leaders. Here is what Fadil Hoxha
said in an interview:

> Enver Hoxha did not meet anyone from Kosovo when he visited Yugoslavia.
> The Kosovar people were very saddened that he came to Yugoslavia and
> did not come to see his own people, or at least visit one of the towns. Also,
> he never invited any delegation over. He never said, 'Let a delegation from
> Kosovo come.' At the time when Enver Hoxha visited Yugoslavia, the
> relations were not yet exacerbated. He did not even send a telegram to
> the Provincial Committee or to the Kosovo Assembly. All they did was
> to fly over Kosovo from Albania.[5]

To add insult to injury, Enver Hoxha had insisted on meeting the mother of
his friend Miladin Popović, who had been killed a few months earlier by a
Kosovar Albanian in Prishtina. Popović's mother lived in Peja, but as Hoxha
did not intend to visit Kosovo, the Yugoslavs sent a governmental Mercedes
and a police escort to drive the woman all the way to Ljubljana in Slovenia,
where Enver Hoxha received her. On her way there she was accompanied by
the number two of the Albanian embassy in Belgrade.

Hoxha's visit to Yugoslavia marked the zenith of Albanian–Yugoslav relations. He arrived in Belgrade in June 1946 on a Yugoslav charter plane. Tito
and Hoxha had never met before and the Albanian prime minister seems to
have taken the visit very seriously. This was the most important official visit
made by an Albanian prime minister since the declaration of independence
in 1912. Until June 1946 no other prime minister or president, not even the
king of Albania, had ever gone abroad on an official visit, with the exception,
perhaps, of the difficult visit Ismail Qemali paid to London in 1913, during
the Conference of Ambassadors. In Belgrade Hoxha was seen for the first
time in civilian attire. He wore a double-breasted striped blue suit, *d'étoffe*

anglaise, made to measure by Albanian tailors. In addition, he had brought with him two full ceremonial military uniforms.

Hoxha was surprised by Tito's lifestyle, which was much talked about in the West. Although heavily bombed during the war, Belgrade had by then recovered and had the charm of a European city, with the boulevards and tall buildings that Tirana lacked.

Hoxha had a number of issues to discuss with Tito: the Greek threat in the south, the recognition of the Albanian government by the great Western powers, and, above all, the economic aid that Albania wanted to receive from Yugoslavia. In his memoirs Hoxha mocked Tito's luxurious lifestyle and described relations between Albania and Yugoslavia with what sounds like surprising naivety. To him, Albania was sincere, willing and open to collaboration, while Tito and the Yugoslavs had a hidden political agenda. Enver Hoxha's visit to Belgrade is one of the least documented and most obscure of all official visits he ever made. Nevertheless, he did not deny the fact that one major problem, that of Kosovo, stood between the two leaders. In his memoirs Hoxha claimed that he was emphatic on the question of Kosovo:

> You are aware of the historical injustice committed by various imperialists and Greater Serbian reactionaries against Albania. You also are aware of the principled stand of our party during the National Liberation War, and our feelings of goodwill and friendship towards the Yugoslav peoples.[6]

And further:

> Then I informed Tito of the opinion of the Albanian party that Kosovo and other Albanian-inhabited regions in Yugoslavia belong with Albania and must be returned to Albania.
>
> The Albanians fought, I said, for a free and sovereign Albanian state, which must now be joined by the Albanian-inhabited regions in Yugoslavia. The time has come for the national issue to be solved justly by our parties. President Tito replied, 'I agree, but for the time being this cannot be done; the Serbs won't understand.'[7]

Yugoslav historians and other participants in the meeting reject the suggestion that the topic was ever raised in the talks. There are no other documentary sources to corroborate what Hoxha said in his memoirs. Quite apart from his obvious jealousy towards Tito and the hatred he whipped up against Yugoslavia over the years, Enver Hoxha never raised any claims for Kosovo. Under pressure from nationalist elements in the CPA and accusations that the regime was practically 'giving Kosovo away' and 'betraying Kosovo', Enver Hoxha was forced to provide explanations to the extraordinary plenary meeting of the Central Committee of the CPA, held from 18 to 20 December 1946:

> Some members of the party wonder whether the people will raise questions about what is happening with Kosovo. The party members that are clear about the party line are also clear about the Kosovo issue. Democratic Yugoslavia is more advanced than we are. It is in our interest that it be strong, because a strong Yugoslavia means peace in the Balkans. Is it in our best interest to claim Kosovo back? That would not be progressive. In this situation we must do our utmost to promote fraternal relations between the Kosovars and the Yugoslavs.[8]

Hoxha did not raise a finger to help the Kosovo Albanians. He did nothing to stop the Bar massacre, which was carried out before the very eyes of the high communist officials of the time. Thousands of Kosovar young men were marched from Kosovo to Bar in Montenegro, via Albanian territory, as Zoi Themeli, the second most important official of the Sigurimi, testified in his trial in 1949:

> Around mid-1945 the Yugoslavs who were escorting the Kosovars to Montenegro were killing many of them en route, for no apparent reason. Some of the Kosovars managed to escape and surrendered to our authorities, begging for mercy and protection. In our dispatches we suggested that the men should not be handed back to the Yugoslavs, because they risked being killed. But Koçi Xoxe ordered us to turn them over. From the information I have, the repatriated men met their deaths in Yugoslavia.[9]

In his diary Hoxha explained that, when the 1981 mass protests and rallies started in Prishtina, he was still against a 'republic' of Kosovo. The argument was that, although there were two German states, two Koreas and two Vietnams, it was not possible to have two Albanian republics. He had conveyed this message to Fadil Hoxha and Tito through Rexhep Duraku, father of war hero Emin Duraku, who lived in Kosovo but visited Albania frequently. Rexhep Duraku and Bije Vokshi (the aunt of Asim Vokshi, another war hero), who had provided shelter to Enver Hoxha and Qemal Stafa during the war years, frequently carried messages between Hoxha and the Kosovar Albanian leaders, and, through them, to Tito.[10]

After Hoxha's visit to Belgrade, relations intensified and concrete steps were taken towards the unification of the two countries. It is not known whether Hoxha was powerless, or whether he really thought concessions to the Yugoslavs were the best way forward, but in 1947 he took two extremely important decisions: a customs union and a currency union with Yugoslavia. These were the decisions that led to the suicide of Nako Spiru, one of the main leaders of the CPA.

Enver Hoxha was in his office at home when the door was pushed open and Koçi Xoxe, deputy prime minister and interior minister, appeared in the door frame:

'What did I tell you!' he shouted. 'He was an enemy; a lowlife. The dog has killed himself. He has now proven that he was worse than an enemy.'
    'Who did?'
    'Nako Spiru killed himself, a well-deserved end.'[11]

The above conversation was reported by Hoxha in his book *Titistët* (*The Titoites*). Relations between Xoxe and Spiru had been extremely tense and the rivalry between them was practically holding the Politburo hostage. Xoxe had the powerful backing of the Yugoslavs, while Nako Spiru, minister of economics – a very intelligent figure and son of a wealthy family from Durrës who had interrupted his studies in Italy to return to fight in Albania – had positioned himself against them. A Politburo meeting had been called in which Yugoslav envoy Savo Zlatić and Koçi Xoxe attacked Nako Spiru for being an anti-Yugoslav and even threatened him. With tensions running high, the meeting was adjourned to the next day, 20 November 1947.

On the morning of 20 November, Nako Spiru knocked on Hoxha's door. According to Hoxha, his old friend asked for five days to prepare his defence. Hoxha did not give the time to him.

Nako Spiru was anxious that day – he knew that the Yugoslavs had decided to eliminate him and they had all the power to do so. In 1946, after the tragic execution of his first wife, Ramize Gjebrea, by partisans in 1944, Spiru had married a very intelligent young woman, Liri Belishova. They lived in a villa on the edge of the Bllok. On the morning of 20 November 1947 he was extremely depressed, as Liri Belishova recalled:

> The last day was the hardest. He went to the Soviet embassy. He had asked for a few days' time till the next meeting, in order to prepare his defence. He was also hoping that by informing the Soviet embassy, they would intervene and save him from the trap. The chargé d'affaires at the Soviet embassy, a certain Gagarov, refused to see him. He had received [Nako] on several other occasions, but not this time.[12]

Half a century after her husband's suicide, Liri Belishova conducted a search in the Soviet archives, to find out why Nako Spiru was not received that day:

> Today I understand why he was not received. According to documents published by the Soviet archives recently, Enver Hoxha had called Gagarov and told him that grave errors had been committed concerning the policy of friendship with Yugoslavia, for which Nako Spiru was responsible. 'We are analysing the issue at the Politburo but he is being stubborn, he does not accept responsibility and is asking for time. We intend to take serious measures to put things right and strengthen friendship with Yugoslavia.' This makes everything clear – this was Enver Hoxha's position, one that sided with the accusations mounted by Tito and the Yugoslav chauvinists and was supported by Koçi Xoxe. Had Enver Hoxha been on the side of justice, he would have asked the Soviet chargé d'affaires to help. He could have told him that the Yugoslavs were making unjust

allegations. Enver Hoxha had done so once in early July 1947, when the Yugoslavs made their first claims. At that time, he had asked Nako Spiru to gather evidence and responded to the Yugoslavs by telling them, 'You are wrong.'[13]

Liri Belishova was at Mehmet Shehu's house when she learned that her husband had shot himself in his office. She had been extremely worried about him. That morning, when Spiru left the house to go to his office, his last words were: 'I do not see a way out. The Soviet embassy slammed the door to my face; Enver Hoxha did the same. Nothing else is left, except to get rid of myself.'[14] When Belishova started crying, he turned round to comfort her: 'Did you really believe that? It's just an expression. You know how Albanians always say "Things couldn't get any worse if I killed myself."'[15]

Nako Spiru shot himself, but he did not die immediately. He was taken to hospital where the battle for his life continued for several hours. His wife went to see him, but was not allowed to stay by his side in those last moments. In her 2004 interview she vividly recalled the day:

He was still alive, but I was not allowed to see him. I remained there until 22.05, when he expired. It is still a great mystery to me why I was not allowed to see him while he was alive. Mehmet Shehu was allowed to go in, I wasn't. Before they told me he was dead, I heard a loud gasp: 'Oooh!' I ran to the door, but it was locked. Then, seconds later Mehmet came out and said, 'It's no use, Liri, he died, just wait till they get him ready.' A few moments later I was taken in. He was already dead.[16]

Both in Albania and abroad Nako Spiru's suicide was widely regarded as a liquidation. There are many who still believe that Spiru was murdered by Xoxe, and that the death was made to look like a suicide. According to Liri Belishova, who was only 20 at the time, and who went on to enjoy an important career in the party and suffer an equally painful end, the arguments for and against a suicide are not important. Fifty-seven years later, Liri Belishova expressed her anguish that she was not able to see him one last time while he was still alive:

I think he did kill himself. But I believe [Russian poet] Yevtushenko was right when he wrote: 'In this world there are no suicides, only murders.' Regardless of who pulled the trigger, nearly 60 years on, it is now practically impossible to establish whether Nako Spiru was a victim of the Yugoslavs, of Enver Hoxha or of Koçi Xoxe. They forced him to do what he did by accusing him of being an agent of imperialism and an enemy of the friendship with Yugoslavia. He was right when he told me: 'They are not looking for a self-critical statement, they want my head. They are not talking about mistakes; they are talking about an enemy.'[17]

Nako Spiru was buried, exhumed and reburied several times, sometimes as a 'hero', other times as a 'traitor'. The reason for his last posthumous fall from grace seems to have been a letter he had sent to Dušan Mugoša, which was found in the archives of the CPY. The letter, which contained a kind of outline of Enver Hoxha's career, was published in 1949 in a book on Yugoslav–Albanian relations by Tito's biographer, Vladimir Dedijer. It is possible that the letter was used to blackmail the politician, who was standing in the way of Yugoslav policies and who had stood up to Koçi Xoxe in the Politburo. According to testimony by people who were close to him, Hoxha recognised Nako Spiru's handwriting and went berserk when he read its contents. Written in Italian and published in the Albanian press in 1993, the letter stated:

Enver Hoxha: mediocre intelligence as a student abroad; equally mediocre as a teacher. During all this time (before the founding of the party), he led an erratic lifestyle. Sectarian in the party. Now he wants to be worshipped. He wants to be the centre of everything, the first in everything, and is ready to trample on anyone. He wants to see everyone belittled and berated. His inferiority complex is obvious. He has no leadership qualities and hinders every initiative. He originates from a family of small traders; recently a bit worse off. He is not widely known among people – where he is known, he is not popular. The party is trying hard to popularise him and he is becoming known as a result, but people are not very convinced of his abilities.[18]

Nako Spiru's suicide opened the way to Xoxe's revenge. The majority of the Politburo members were pro-Yugoslav anyway; most of them were even ethnic Macedonians by origin. On 14 March 1948 the Politburo of the CPA approved the union of Albania and Yugoslavia and, according to Edvard Kardelj, the Federation Palace on the banks of the Sava River was already making offices ready for the seventh republic.[19]

Albania would surely have become the seventh Yugoslav Republic with Stalin's blessing, had it not been for the rift between Stalin and Tito and the subsequent public denunciation of Tito by the Soviet Politburo on 27 March 1948.

Stalin's first letter arrived in Albania on 15 April 1948. By then Hoxha was trying to break loose from the Yugoslavs, who were now seeking to replace him with Koçi Xoxe. It is surprising that Hoxha did not travel to Moscow to meet Stalin in those days when he needed the most support. Many years later he revealed in his memoirs that before undertaking the campaign for purging the party of pro-Yugoslav elements, he took part in a secret meeting held in Romania. In Bucharest he met Vyshinsky, former state prosecutor in Stalin's tragic trials of the mid-1930s.

The contents of their conversation are still largely unknown, with the exception of a couple of passages cited by Hoxha himself. They are no doubt preserved in the Soviet archives. The general thrust of the conversation must have been Hoxha's demands for guarantees that Stalin would not allow a Yugoslav attack on Albania and that Hoxha would have a free hand to purge the party of pro-Yugoslav elements. His demands were evidently accepted.

Upon his return to Tirana, Hoxha acted swiftly. He called a meeting with Mehmet Shehu, a well-known wartime commander, whose relations with Xoxe were tense to say the least, and they drew up an action plan. The Politburo of the CPA officially endorsed Stalin's position on 28 June 1948. Yugoslavia was lambasted as a hostile country, and Yugoslav experts were expelled from the country. The second step was the purging of pro-Yugoslav elements and of any other people Hoxha no longer trusted, as well as an 'amnesty' for some prisoners who were serving time for 'anti-Yugoslav agitation'.

Koçi Xoxe was in for an unwelcome surprise in mid-November 1948 when, at a party meeting in Korça, his birthplace and the cradle of the communist

movement in Albania, members of the audience started asking him provoca-
tive questions. Some even dared to use sarcasm. The man who had terrorised
Albania was baffled by the courage shown by the audience. The gathering
seemed more like a trial than a party meeting. When he returned to Tirana
that afternoon, Xoxe discovered that he was no longer interior minister of
the country. His fall from grace proved to be dramatic over the next few days.
He was dismissed from all posts he held: deputy prime minister, minister of
industry, secretary of the Central Committee of the CPA and, lastly, vice
president of Albania. Divested of all his functions, Koçi Xoxe, the former
number two of the regime, was arrested on 28 November 1948 in his house
in the Bllok, next door to Enver Hoxha's. He was dragged out to a car, to
the terrified screams of his neighbours in the exclusive neighbourhood. A
number of other senior government and Sigurimi officials were also arrested
at the time.

Koçi Xoxe was sentenced to death and executed in the spring of 1949. In
his last letter from prison, signed on 11 June 1949, one day before his execution, he addressed Hoxha with the following words:

> Comrade Enver,
> My plea for a pardon was rejected by the Presidium. So be it. Long live
> the party, and you, Comrade Enver Hoxha. I wish you success in achieving
> Albania's prosperity and the furtherance of the cause.[20]

Among other things, Koçi Xoxe, who for four years had lived under the same
roof or next door to Hoxha, expressed one last wish: 'I'm writing to let you
know of my last wish, which I will pronounce before they execute me: that no
harm be done to my family and my beloved son.' Xoxe's request was that his
family be spared from persecution, that they be allowed to live in Tirana or
Korça, and that his son be allowed to pursue his education. The letter ended
in three words: 'Farewell! Koçi Xoxe.'

No part of Xoxe's last wish was respected. The family was persecuted for
41 years and his son was not able to pursue his education. This poignant message, published only after the 1990s, raises many questions about the history
of Albanian communism. All the more so if we consider that it was neither

the first nor the last liquidation that was carried out on Hoxha's orders. In the mid-1970s, a group of army officers who were sentenced to death expressed their last wish to have Hoxha's last published work and a photo of him sent to their cells on the night before the execution. A letter written by one of them said:

> Comrade Enver. Today we asked for your latest book to be brought to us. I will take careful note of everything you have written in it, in the knowledge that I have gravely erred, that my punishment is well deserved, and everything is done for the good of the party.[21]

Thirty-two years later, the man who was directly responsible for Xoxe's death, prime minister Mehmet Shehu, would himself leave a suicide note. This one said:

> Yes, Comrade Enver, I was always ready to give my life for the party. And this is exactly what I am doing now. I'm giving my life for the party, so that I, your closest friend in times of trouble and success, as you yourself rightly called me, can use this as a last resort to give you yourself, my friend, my teacher and my dear brother, an opportunity to learn the truth.[22]

Kadri Hazbiu, another government minister, who was condemned to death in 1983, wrote the following note in the spring of that year: 'I shouldn't have been arrested now, when the party needed me more than ever.'[23]

On the night before their execution, what was it that inspired these people to ask to read Hoxha's works, instead of worrying about the children and relatives they were leaving behind without any support? Were they really happy that their executioner was still at the head of the party? Was it a last-ditch attempt to obtain a pardon? Were they putting on a show in an attempt to save their families from persecution? Or was it extreme, inexplicable indoctrination – of the same kind seen in many of Stalin's disciples, who, even as they were being executed, did not want to believe that they were the victims of their idol?

The Yugoslavs stood by their man in Albania to the end. After the execution, a street in Peja and one in Belgrade were given Koçi Xoxe's name. While Xoxe's was the most sensational execution in the ranks of senior communist leaders, it was by no means the last. The story of liquidations would continue at an unrelenting pace for the next 32 years, ending on the night of 17 December 1981, when prime minister Mehmet Shehu was eliminated.

15

Stalin and the Soviets

'So comrade Enver, do you eat pork?' Stalin asked suddenly, as he was prodding the cold food in his metal bowl with a fork.

'Yes, I do,' Enver Hoxha answered.

'Islam forbids its followers from eating pork,' he noted, and then added, 'An outdated custom, I'm sure. Nevertheless, the question of religious faiths must be followed closely and tackled with care, without hurting people's feelings. These feelings have been cultivated for centuries, so we must be very prudent in dealing with them. These things have a bearing on the unity of the people.'[1]

This dialogue, recorded in April 1949, was probably the most interesting excerpt from Hoxha's meetings with Stalin. Seated opposite each other, a former seminary student who never became a priest and an imam's son whose first school was a *mektep*, the two seemed at a loss as to what else to discuss with each other.

This was Hoxha's second and most important meeting with Stalin. This time round Hoxha was calm and relaxed – by now he was in full control of the CPA and government of Albania. His first meeting with the Soviet leader, on 16 July 1947, had been rather formal and held in the presence of Koçi Xoxe, who would surely have reported everything to the Yugoslavs. In 1949 Hoxha returned to meet Stalin as the leader of a party which had overcome Yugoslav hegemony, convinced that this 'victory' over the Yugoslavs would have Stalin's seal of approval.

Enver Hoxha met Stalin five times in all. The last encounter was in April 1951, two years prior to the Soviet leader's death. In 1979, on the occasion of the centenary of Stalin's birth, Hoxha wrote another book of memoirs, *Me Stalinin* (published in English as *With Stalin*), based mostly on Albanian documents and records, uncorroborated by any Soviet archival sources. Reading Hoxha's memoirs, one cannot help but notice Stalin's marked lack of interest in Albania. In a meeting with Yugoslav special envoy Milovan Djilas in 1945, Stalin had slighted the tiny country completely. In his *Conversations with Stalin* Djilas recalled how, when he raised the subject of Albania and asked for an opinion on what to do with that country, Stalin had implied that Albania could be made part of the Yugoslav federation. According to Djilas, Stalin said: '"We have no special interest in Albania. We agree to Yugoslavia swallowing Albania!" At this he gathered together the fingers of his right hand and, bringing them to his mouth, he made a motion as if to swallow them.'[2]

Of course, in 1979 Hoxha knew all this. By then, Djilas's book had been published in the West and the Yugoslav dissident had done several years in prison and confinement. But Stalin was always kind and warm to Hoxha when they met in person, although he seldom showed any interest in anything related to Albania. The only exception was the advice he gave Hoxha not to get involved in the Greek civil war. Also, it was Stalin's suggestion that the CPA change its name to the Party of Labour of Albania (PLA), like the party had done in North Korea, to reflect the larger number of peasants than workers in its membership. The rest of their conversations were just the usual mix of small talk and curiosities that two strangers would exchange in a coffee shop anywhere on the globe. Stalin would invariably ask Hoxha about the origins of Albanians, relations between the religious faiths in the country, its landscape, geography, problems with neighbours, and the like. Had he had any real interest in the country, any one of his aides could have put together a fact sheet in less than an hour.

Stalin advised Hoxha not to rush with the collectivisation of farmland, not to overdo the fight against religion and the clerics, to refrain from showing his hostility to the United Kingdom and the United States too openly, and to avoid meting out harsh punishments to his opponents within the party. When Stalin asked him about Albania's relations with Britain, Hoxha replied that the British were conditioning their recognition of Albania on the establishment of military bases on the Adriatic coast. According to Hoxha, Stalin reacted as follows:

'Do not give them access to any of your bases! Defend your ports well!' Stalin insisted.

'We'll never give anything up to anyone,'I assured him. 'If worse comes to worst, we'd rather die than surrender them.'

'Keep them and don't die,' Stalin laughed. 'These things must be done with diplomacy.'[3]

Even Stalin, one of the most despotic leaders of modern times, appears more moderate and less intransigent than Hoxha in this exchange. But his attitude could also be an indication of how low on Stalin's agenda Albania was. Hoxha, on the other hand, like all other Eastern European leaders, was in awe of Stalin. Stalin was his idol. On the centenary of Stalin's birth in 1979, Hoxha was the only self-proclaimed Stalinist leader in the world and the only one who refused to acknowledge the heinous crimes committed by the Soviet leader. As late as December 1990, foreign visitors to Tirana were greeted by a monumental statue of the Soviet leader looming over the town's main boulevard. In addition, a number of factories around the country and one of the main squares in Tirana were named '21 December', after Stalin's date of birth. In 1953 the southern oil town of Kuçova was renamed 'Qyteti Stalin' (Stalin town).

It is hard to say whether Hoxha was really a fanatical disciple of Stalin or whether Stalinist philosophy was the one that best suited his political goals. The second hypothesis seems more plausible. In 1979, in the introduction to his book *Me Stalinin*, Hoxha wrote:

No, Stalin was not a tyrant; he was not a despot. He was a principled, fair, unassuming and kind man, who paid attention to people, cadres and his associates [...] No single error of principle can be found in the works of this renowned Marxist–Leninist.[4]

But in the spring of 1956, just a few weeks after Stalin was publicly denounced by Khrushchev at the Twentieth Congress of the CPSU, Hoxha was singing from a different hymn sheet. In an editorial published in the daily newspaper *Zëri i popullit* (The people's voice) on 14 April 1956, entitled 'Marxism–Leninism teaches us that the masses are the makers of history', signed by him personally, Enver Hoxha wrote the following:

> Stalin made some mistakes which cost the Soviet peoples and the cause of socialism dearly [...]
>
> The CP of the Soviet Union rightly denounced the cult of personality created by J. V. Stalin during the last years of his life, which caused so much harm to the Soviet Union [...] It has to be said that, after the CP, the Soviet Union and the Soviet peoples achieved so many victories that led to the triumph of socialism, J. V. Stalin began to place himself above the people and the party. He distanced himself from the masses, which led to very costly mistakes that greatly harmed the Soviet peoples and the cause of socialism.[5]

These lines show that Hoxha's ideology was not simply blind adoration for Stalin. He was more interested in Stalinism, which he upheld and applied to the end of his days.

By the time Hoxha and Stalin met for the second time, in 1949, the situation had changed dramatically. The break with the Yugoslavs had opened the way to a honeymoon in Albanian–Soviet relations. Albania became part of the Eastern bloc, a member of the Warsaw Pact and of the Council for Mutual Economic Assistance (COMECON). The subservience and dependence of Albanian politicians on the Soviet Union was evident: all important decisions were now taken in Moscow. The Soviet ambassador to Tirana was the most important man in the country and he had a decisive say in Albanian politics at the time.

Stalin died in March 1953. On the day his death was announced, Enver Hoxha had all the Albanians – himself included – kneel before the bronze statue of the Soviet dictator, which was temporarily transferred to Skanderbeg Square for the occasion. Albania held 14 days of mourning, more than the Soviet Union itself.

But his love of Stalin did not prevent Hoxha from building an equally

obsequious relationship with Khrushchev and supporting the Twentieth
Congress of the CPSU, at which Stalin's cult of personality was attacked.
Concurring with Khrushchev's policy, in the above-mentioned article pub-
lished in April 1956, Hoxha wrote:

> After the denunciation of the cult of personality at the Twentieth Congress
> and open recognition of the damage caused by it, the Communist Party
> of the Soviet Union and all communist and workers' parties around the
> world have been drawing conclusions of practical importance.[6]

Hoxha applied the same critical approach to developments within the PLA:

> In many cases punishments were a result of exaggerated accusations,
> especially in the period leading up to the First Congress of the party
> [...] The party condemned the attempts to give the Sigurimi precedence
> over the party itself, the application of policing methods within the ranks
> of the party, and the infringement of civil rights through arbitrary acts,
> persecution and unjust punishments.[7]

Hoxha's relations with Khrushchev remained normal until 1955, the year
when the latter moved towards a rapprochement with Yugoslavia. As a
foreign-policy strategist, Nikita Khrushchev decided to lure Yugoslavia –
the black sheep – back into the Eastern bloc and trumpeted it as a personal victory. He condemned the attack that Stalin and the Communist
Information Bureau (Cominform) had mounted on Yugoslavia in 1948 and
sent messages of open reconciliation to Tito. Khrushchev's visit to Belgrade
in 1955 set alarm bells ringing and put Hoxha on a different course from the
Soviet Union.

   In the summer of 1955 Hoxha was holidaying in a villa outside Moscow. It
was probably around midnight when an officer of the national guard knocked
on his bedroom door. Nexhmije woke up in panic, but the late-night call had
nothing to do with their family back in Tirana. The officer explained politely
that Anastas Mikoyan, Khrushchev's closest associate, was on the phone and
had asked to speak to Enver Hoxha. Mikoyan told Hoxha that he was having

dinner with Vukmanović Tempo, one of Tito's most trusted men and Hoxha's old acquaintance, and suggested that the two meet up.

Hoxha and Tempo met the next day, in what seemed to be an informal meeting. No official records exist of what was discussed there. According to Hoxha, the conversation was a rather uncomfortable one and all the two men discussed were things like agriculture and the general situation in the two countries. However, it seems very unlikely that a two-hour conversation between two senior state leaders could focus only on the lack of rain and the low yield in agricultural produce that year. Mikoyan's insistence that Hoxha meet Tempo and the pressure that the Soviet ideologist Mikhail Suslov had brought to bear on the Albanian leader to revise his policy towards Yugoslavia failed to achieve the intended result. All that was achieved was that Hoxha became more distrustful of the Soviets.

Hoxha refused to reconcile with the Yugoslavs. His loathing of Tito had been the driving force of many of his decisions in the past, but it became even more pronounced in April 1956, after the Twentieth Congress of the CPSU. At a conference of the Tirana chapter of the PLA, Enver Hoxha, Mehmet Shehu and a number of other leading members of the party found themselves in the eye of a political storm. Hoxha was convinced that the attacks against him were inspired by the new political course announced by the Twentieth Congress and incited by the Yugoslav embassy in Tirana. He was right. Annoyed by his unwillingness to change course, the Yugoslavs, perhaps in collusion with the Soviets, were plotting to oust Hoxha from the political scene (as Mahmut Bakalli confirmed in his yet-to-be-published memoirs).[8]

Under pressure brought to bear by Khrushchev himself, the Stalinist leaders of Eastern Europe were being replaced. In some cases, such as in Poland, former disgraced communists like Gomulka – who had even been to prison – were restored to power. Hoxha interpreted all this and Khrushchev's rapprochement with Tito as a personal threat. On 15 April 1956, he cut his holiday in Vlora short and appeared in person to face rebellious conference delegates in Tirana. He managed to turn the situation around by applying very effective tactics. While he launched a vicious attack on some of the rebels, he treated others as 'misguided and misinformed' and sought to appease them. As soon as the storm abated, both groups were arrested and handcuffed in front of their fellow conference participants – 44 of them ended up serving lengthy prison sentences.

Khrushchev was furious. He sent word to Hoxha to release the imprisoned communists, especially Liri Gega and Dali Ndreu. According to Agim Popa, who acted as interpreter in the talks between the Albanian and Soviet leaders, Khrushchev was stunned to learn that not only had they not been released, they had been executed by a firing squad:

> Then Khrushchev suddenly said something that left Hoxha speechless.
>
> 'You did not execute two people, but three,' he said to the visitor from Albania, alluding to the fact that Liri Gega had been pregnant at the time of her execution.
>
> This caught Enver by surprise; he was unable to come up with anything to say.[9]

In spite of everything, Hoxha did not give in to Khrushchev's pressure, nor did he lose his composure. He managed to get himself out of this difficult situation, and it would not be the last time he did so. In order to nip any such future rebellions in the bud, he swiftly proceeded to punish two leading communist figures: Bedri Spahiu and Tuk Jakova.

Bedri Spahiu, a well-known partisan commander during the war and member of the Politburo, was dismissed from his post and arrested. He was the same age as Enver Hoxha and was born in the same neighbourhood, and the two of them had been classmates in the first year of primary school. Their names were next to each other on the same page of their school register, now preserved in the Central State Archives. After finishing fourth grade, Spahiu moved to Turkey for four years, first to Izmir and then to Istanbul, where he graduated with distinction from an Italian school, after which he returned to Albania and pursued a military career. He served as an artillery officer in King Zog's army, but was arrested and convicted for violating his oath of allegiance to the king during the 1936 Fier uprising. Spahiu was spared execution and joined a cell of communist army officers until the foundation of the CPA. Brave, charismatic and a skilled orator, he was a key communist figure during and after the war. He served as minister for reconstruction, general prosecutor of the Republic of Albania and minister of education, at the same time being a member of the Politburo. Bedri Spahiu's brave speech at the meeting that had been called to expel him from the party was described as nothing short of remarkable. Kiço Ngjela, then minister of economics, who was present at the meeting, recalled Spahiu's outburst at Hoxha's accusations:

> Bedri kept silent during the entire meeting and requested the floor only at the end. He pointed his finger accusingly at Enver Hoxha and bellowed, 'Who do you think you are, acting so high and mighty? How do you dare tell lies and hurl accusations left and right? You called Sejfullah an opportunist, Tuk an opportunist, Bedri a so-and-so? [...] What about you, who are you? I'll tell you: you are a shadowy figure from the cul-de-sacs of Paris [...] an unprincipled philanderer.' No one had ever dared to speak to Enver like that.[10]

Spahiu's arrest was dramatic. He denied all charges and did not bow under pressure in the interrogation room. He declared that he had spent half of his career under the threat of death from various regimes and dying did not scare him at all.

After a short stint of solitary internment in Kanina, Bedri Spahiu was sent to prison. Every year, without fail, he sent prime minister Mehmet Shehu a letter from his cell, which started with the words 'Your Excellency'. Later on, he published all these letters in his *Testamenti politik* (Political testament). The letters denounced the Sigurimi's use of torture on prisoners and other violations of the constitution and Albanian law. He kept detailed notes of the barbaric acts committed on inmates and of the atmosphere in the prison. His letters were never answered. General Bedri Spahiu spent most of the rest of his life in prison, until his release in March 1991. He died in Tirana in 1998 and was among the very few former communist leaders who publicly apologised and admitted responsibility for the crimes committed under communism.

Tuk Jakova, one of the founding members of the CPA, former member of the Politburo and former speaker of the parliament that emerged from the first postwar elections of 2 December 1945, was convicted at the same time as Spahiu. Jakova died in prison in 1959, never learning what crime he had committed. He left behind a number of love letters he sent to his wife from prison.

In 1954, Omer Nishani, one-time chairman of the Anti-Fascist National Liberation Council, Albania's first communist president, and foreign minister, died under mysterious circumstances a year after leaving his post as head of state. On 27 May 1954, the daily newspapers *Zëri i popullit* (The people's voice) and *Bashkimi* (Unity) announced that Dr Omer Nishani had passed away 'after a long illness' at the age of 67. His funeral was attended by the dignitaries of the time and the investigation into his death was shelved. Nishani's case was reopened in 2010, after researcher Kastriot Dervishi published some documents of the initial investigation, which were found in the safe of the interior minister. Nishani's file contained a death certificate drawn up by the investigative department of the Sigurimi, headed by Lieutenant Colonel Nevzat Haznedari, dated 27 May 1954. It started with the words: 'Dr Omer Nishani committed suicide by shooting himself twice on 25 May 1954 at 23.00 hours.'[11]

By 1959, relations between Hoxha and Khrushchev had become extremely tense. Khrushchev paid an official visit to Albania that year. It was the first visit of a Soviet leader to Albania. Khrushchev, who was the highest-level foreign politician ever to have visited the country, was accompanied by his minister of defence, Marshal Malinovsky, and a 250-strong delegation. It so happened that Peng Dehuai, the Chinese minister of defence, was visiting Albania at the same time, which briefly placed the small country at the centre of attention of international news. Khrushchev spent 12 days in Albania. The visit was deemed so important that Hoxha agreed to Khrushchev's condition that there should be no speeches against Tito and the Yugoslavs.

Hoxha did his best to please Khrushchev and to find a possible compromise with him. Old footage from the time shows Khrushchev laying the cornerstone of the new Palace of Culture to be built in the centre of Tirana. Hoxha is heard saying: 'May you live a long life!' However, the visit did not solve the differences between the two political leaders. In November 1960, at the meeting of the 81 communist parties in Moscow, Hoxha openly sided with the Chinese against the Soviets.

The Albanian delegation consisted of Enver Hoxha, Mehmet Shehu, Hysni Kapo and the young Ramiz Alia, who also acted as interpreter for the delegation. The debates with Khrushchev and the other Soviet leaders were fierce. Here is how Alia, who interpreted the heated discussions between Hoxha and Khrushchev, remembered that time in an interview given 45 years later:

> The truth is that we did not agree with the Russian stance towards Yugoslavia; they were saying that the Yugoslavs had not been in the wrong. According to them, Stalin had erred when he denounced the Yugoslavs in 1948 and, consequently, everything that followed was also a mistake. They went so far as to demand the rehabilitation of Koçi Xoxe.[12]

Ramiz Alia denied that the Soviets had asked Hoxha to leave the country, but this was certainly implied. Suddenly Albania found itself at the centre of world attention, as seen in the international press of the time. In April 1961, *Time* magazine dedicated a two-page article to Hoxha, calling him the Red Boss. It was the first time the Albanian communist leader had enjoyed so much press attention in the West.[13]

An eerie atmosphere reigned during Hoxha's visit to Moscow on the occasion of the meeting of the 81 communist and workers' parties held from 10 November to 1 December 1960. By that time, he had become paranoid with the thought that they were out to liquidate him and refused to stay in the accommodation provided by his hosts. He only ate food prepared at the Albanian embassy and the groceries were bought daily from different shops in the neighbourhood, rather than from the diplomatic store. In fear of his life, Hoxha decided not to stay until the end of the meeting and even refused to fly over Soviet skies. Instead, he took the train from Moscow to Vienna, and from there to Bari, where he caught a government charter back to Tirana. He did not stop anywhere on his return journey and did not contact any of the political leaders of the countries he passed through.

While Hoxha was still in Moscow, his differences with the Soviet leaders having become public, the Soviet ambassador to Tirana approached Beqir Balluku, the highest-ranking official remaining in Albania, with a proposal for a coup d'état with Soviet assistance. The other four leaders would be arrested in Moscow and extradited upon a request by Albania. Balluku loyally rejected the proposal. His answer, as reported later by Balluku's son, Çlirim, was something like: 'If anything happens to the Albanian leaders, the Soviet ambassador and all the other Soviets working in Albania will be held hostage and treated as such.' His loyalty did not gain the interior minister any kudos: 12 years later he was executed and his family were interned.[14]

The break with the Soviet Union became official a few months later, at the Fourth Congress of the PLA. The chasm had grown so deep that prime minister Shehu even heckled Yuri Andropov, head of the Soviet delegation, as the latter was speaking to the delegates. Andropov was no small fry. In 1982, after serving as head of the KGB, he became Brezhnev's successor as first secretary of the CPSU and one of Gorbachev's key supporters. Albania and the Soviet Union broke off diplomatic relations in 1961, and the leadership in Tirana began a new love story, this time with China.

While the break had already taken place in effect, it was only sanctioned *de jure* eight years later. On the night of 21–2 August 1968, Soviet-led troops of the Warsaw Pact invaded Czechoslovakia. Alexander Dubček, first secretary of the Czechoslovak Communist Party at the time, had embarked upon a new, more liberal political course, which came to be known as 'socialism with a human face'. Within the space of a few months Dubček's movement – the Prague Spring – caused quite a stir in the entire Eastern European bloc. In order to prevent any further insurgence, Leonid Brezhnev, first secretary of the CPSU, ordered the invasion of Czechoslovakia.

Enver Hoxha was holidaying in Durrës, when Mehmet Shehu asked to see him urgently. Albania was officially a member of the Warsaw Pact, and, although it had not attended any meetings since 1961, the empty seat with the Albanian flag in front of it was a reminder of its membership. Tirana did not know anything about the invasion yet, but prime minister Shehu sensed something and expressed his concern for the staff of the Czech embassy, which was situated right across from the building of the Albanian Ministry of the Interior.

The days of the invasion of Czechoslovakia must have been among the most difficult for Hoxha and Shehu. Brezhnev came up with the doctrine of the 'limited sovereignty' of Warsaw Pact member states, and Albania was under serious threat. Hoxha, Shehu and Kapo met for about 16 hours at Hoxha's house. A logbook of the leaders' security unit shows that the service was on red alert, as was the entire Albanian army. In late August 1968 Hoxha sent a message to Josip Broz Tito via Fadil Hoxha, as the latter testified without disclosing the communication channel. He asked for guarantees that Yugoslavia would not allow Soviet forces to pass through Yugoslavia in case of an attack on Albania. The answer came at the beginning of September – Yugoslav territory would not be open to any occupying force, and if such a step were to be taken, both countries would fight together. On 13 September 1968 Albania announced its formal and unilateral withdrawal from the Warsaw Pact and denounced the attack on Czechoslovakia.[15]

Robert Frowick was then a young diplomat working for the Albanian and Romanian Desk of the US State Department. He followed the Albanian press closely and received daily translations from Vienna of statements broadcast on Radio Tirana. In the second week of September, Frowick wrote a memo warning his superiors that it looked likely that Albania would withdraw from the Warsaw Pact. On 11 September he was called to attend a meeting of the National Security Council and the US president. In a 2000 interview he described how he briefed the president, informing him that the Albanian press and PLA statements pointed towards Albania's imminent withdrawal from the pact. The withdrawal was announced two days later. Albania became Frowick's key to success; it marked the start of his long career as a diplomat, which culminated in his involvement in the peace process in Kosovo and Macedonia at the turn of the millennium.[16]

The break with the Soviet Union had its political casualties in Albania.

Koço Tashko, a founding member of the CPA, former head of the Korça Group and the man who invited Hoxha to the founding meeting, expressed his concern about the break-up with the Soviet Union. He continued to have contacts with the Soviet ambassador in Tirana even after relations went sour, and was the first to be struck. Although no longer a prominent figure, his punishment was exemplary. Tashko was divested of all his functions, banished from Tirana and then arrested. After serving a long prison term, he died in internment, haunted by the thought that he had inadvertently been the cause of Albania's greatest misfortune. He remained a staunch champion of communism and the Soviet Union to the end.

In his book *Nën peshën e dhunës* (Under the weight of violence), published in 1994, Todi Lubonja remembered the 70-year-old Koço Tashko when he was still serving his sentence. His love of the Soviet Union and communism remained unabated:

> In prison, Gjin Marku [a war general and member of the first Politburo of the CPA, later purged and thrown in jail] used to lead the commemoration of all sorts of national and international holidays, but there were two days when he let Koço do the honours: the anniversary of the founding of the Third Communist International and 7 November, the anniversary of the great October Revolution. On 7 November, Koço would put on his best clothes and a new Soviet-style beret. He took a serving tray, heaped it with biscuits, pieces of Turkish delight and so on, and went from one prisoner to another, treating them with sweets.
>
> There would invariably be someone who would tease him: 'You know you should be held to account for the bad choice you made.' He would laugh (he had a pleasant, frank laugh) and answer: 'Even Lenin made Malinovsky a member of the Central Committee, and it later transpired that he had been a secret agent of the tsarist police.'[17]

Koço Tashko was often treated brutally in prison, as Lubonja testifies:

> I will never forget the morning when I saw Koço in solitary confinement. That day I was scheduled to help in the kitchen. It was 7 November 1977. Koço had turned 70 by then. I was horrified when they gave him 31 days in the isolation cell. The winter was extremely cold that year – thick icicles hung from the eaves of the terraced roof, reaching about three-quarters of a metre down. The isolation cells did not have wooden floorboards; the cement floor was frozen and the cell was frightfully damp. He was given just one blanket for the night. Koço got up slowly and looked at me with almost opaque eyes: 'Is it you, Todi?' I felt like screaming: 'Damn you heartless criminals!'[18]

Around the same time, Liri Belishova, who had held some of the highest
positions in the Albanian communist leadership, including member of the
Politburo and secretary of the Central Committee, was also relieved of all
her duties and posts:

> I was expelled from the Politburo, then from the Central Committee,
> and then the grass-roots organisation decided to expel me from the
> party altogether. Initially I was sent to work as a teacher at the Hasan
> Vogli Primary School. Then my husband was expelled from the Central
> Committee and dismissed from his ministerial post, but not on political
> grounds. Our family was banished from Tirana on 9 November 1960 and
> we were sent to a farm near Gjirokastra. I was appointed head teacher and
> he became director of the farm. It was there that we were expelled from
> the party altogether, and two months later we were banished to Kuç near
> Vlora. From Kuç we were then transferred to Progonat and, after that, to
> Zvërnec, where we lived for ten years. Then on to Cërrik, where I lived for
> 20 years. Initially I worked on the farm, doing very hard physical labour.[19]

Liri Belishova's internment lasted for nearly 30 years, and during that time
she suffered the greatest tragedy of her life: the death of her 22-year-old
daughter. Belishova vividly recalls that as her daughter was slipping away in
a Tirana hospital, she was ordered to return to Cërrik because her pass had
expired. Her daughter had just a few hours left. Belishova pleaded with the
officers to be allowed to stay at her daughter's bedside a bit longer. The secret
police were unmoved. As a last resort, she asked for permission to contact her
former best friend from school and the war years, and appeal to her humanity:

> I begged the officer there with me, who was ordering me to go back,
> 'Please, let me stay.' I had just been to see my daughter and the doctors
> said it was a matter of hours. My daughter was fully conscious but it was
> clear she was going to die. She was extremely weak; only oxygen was
> keeping her alive – when they removed the mask she went completely
> numb. While I was with her she would constantly ask for water as her
> mouth was parched and dry. I begged the officer, 'Please let me stay with

The communist leaders arrive in Tirana on 28 November 1944. Front row, left to right: the short Koçi Xoxe, the bearded Baba Faja Martaneshi, Enver Hoxha holding a bouquet, Omer Nishani and Myslim Peza (Archives of the Centre for Albanian Studies, London).

Congress of the Democratic Front on 5 August 1945, with Enver Hoxha watching the camera (Archives of the Centre for Albanian Studies, London).

Portrait of Enver Hoxha, ca. 1945
(Archives of the Centre for Albanian Studies, London).

Enver Hoxha and jubilating party members, 1972
(Archives of the Centre for Albanian Studies, London).

Stalin and Enver Hoxha in Moscow
(Archives of the Centre for Albanian Studies, London).

Enver Hoxha and the mostly aged members of the Politburo, on the occasion of the
7th Party Congress in November 1976. The purged members have their faces scratched
out in the publication (Archives of the Centre for Albanian Studies, London).

my daughter, you can see for yourself what condition she is in.' He refused. For a brief moment, Nexhmije Hoxha's name came to mind and I said to myself, 'We fought together during the war, she is a mother, too, she will surely understand.' So I plucked up my courage and asked the officer to make the call for me and enquire if they would let me stay with my dying daughter. 'You must be kidding!' he replied. 'Do you still think you are a member of the Politburo?'[20]

The young woman passed away three hours after her mother departed for Cërrik, where she was serving her internment. Liri Belishova, who had joined the communist resistance movement at the age of 14 and contributed to the consolidation of the regime that was now crushing her with its weight, was refused permission to be with her daughter in the girl's last moments. Belishova remained interned in Cërrik until 1991. After nearly 30 years of combined imprisonment and internment, she returned to Tirana. In spite of her advanced age, she joined a veteran association and became actively involved in other public activities. She was also among the few former communists who admitted their responsibility for the harm that communism did to Albanians. Sixty-two years after she first joined the communist movement, she apologised publicly for what had happened:

> Not only did we not fulfil the promises we made to the people, but we also failed to realise our own dreams, for which we sacrificed our youth, and the dreams of our comrades who laid down their lives. The most iniquitous and painful aspect of the regime we helped set up was the repression. And yet no one has ever made a public apology for that [...] I take this opportunity to say sorry not only to the victims that suffered directly, but also to the entire Albanian people. The road to hell is paved with good intentions.[21]

Another high official who was targeted at the time was Admiral Teme Sejko, commander of the Albanian navy. His treatment was probably intended to send a message to the Western countries on the eve of Albania's break with the Soviet Union. In May 1961, Sejko was charged with being an American,

Yugoslav, Greek and Italian agent. A former partisan fighter originally from Chameria, he was tortured so savagely that he admitted to all the charges, namely that he was an agent of all the imperialist states and had attempted to overthrow the 'people's power'. Sejko was sentenced to death, but did not make it to his execution day. The truth about his death was revealed in 1983, in the trial against former interior minister and minister of defence Kadri Hazbiu. When it was put to him that he had failed to carry out the order for Teme Sejko's execution, Kadri Hazbiu responded:

> Before the execution, Rexhep Kolli and Nevzat Haznedari took Teme Sejko from prison for interrogation, in the hope that he would confess under duress to anything he had kept from them. I remember that in the evening I went to the place where Teme Sejko was being interrogated. Rexhep and Nevzat reported to me that Teme had died under torture. They told me that he died when they had tightened a rope round his neck during interrogation. I'm not sure whether I saw Teme's body in the room; also I don't know where he was buried.[22]

In 1983, Qemal Birçe, a Sigurimi officer, described Teme Sejko's last moments:

> We went to Maminas and stopped in the middle of a vineyard, where there is an isolated house, known as the Bey's Manor. We got Teme out there [...] We took Teme to a room. Mihallaq [Ziçishti] then sent Qemal Xhaferri out to cut off about 20 hornbeam branches. When the rods arrived, Mihallaq himself, in the presence of Rexhep [Kolli] and Nevzat [Haznedari], began beating Teme. He beat Teme with the rods, which were over an inch thick, hitting him everywhere on the body, including his head. He struck him so savagely that the rods would break. When Mihallaq got tired, Rexhep took over, and then Nevzat. This continued the whole day, till the evening. Teme was half dead from all the beating, he could barely breathe. His body was all bruised and split open, and bleeding everywhere, his face, his head, his ribs, his thighs and his feet. He was in such a state that he could not have survived. By the time Kadri Hazbiu arrived, he was not responding. I saw the whole thing with my own eyes – I was in

the corridor and the door to the room where they were beating Teme was open. I just watched. There were two other comrades who were on guard further away, to keep anyone from getting close to the place. When Kadri arrived, we shook hands and he asked me, 'So, what is going on?' I told him that Teme was dying from the beating. Kadri went into the room and met Mihallaq Ziçishti, Rexhep Kolli and Nevzat Haznedari. He went into the house alone; his driver and bodyguard stayed in the car about 15–20 metres from the house. I must add that the house was not inhabited at the time. Kadri stayed for about five minutes and then left. When he departed, we wrapped Teme in a blanket – his hands were still handcuffed behind his back, just as when he was being beaten – and we threw him into the seven-seater jeep. Nevzat, Islam, Qemal and I got in, too, and we set off for Tirana. I did not know where exactly we were going; it was Nevzat who received the orders. Before reaching Vora, Islam Gjondede and I put a rope round Teme Sejko's neck – he was lying on the floor between us – and we started pulling at it from both ends until he died. Teme was not showing any sign of life. Nevzat Haznedari gave us the order to kill him. We drove up to the hills opposite Linza. It was dark. Mihallaq, who was in the car in front of us, stopped, and we stopped, too. Rexhep Kolli was not with him; I don't know where he had gone. He ordered us to get the body out, wrapped in the blanket. Qemal Xhaferri, Islam Gjondede and the driver, who was Mihallaq's cousin, carried the body. I just stood there, with Mihallaq Ziçishti, while the others lugged the body about 20 metres downhill from the road, where a hole had been dug. It was dug by the driver who had driven us to Maminas earlier. After leaving us there, he drove off and came back later in the evening to pick us up. He took his orders from Mihallaq Ziçishti. I joined them as they were preparing to lower the body into the grave. To make sure that he was dead, I took a pick that was lying close to the grave and hit Teme several times on the head, until the skull was shattered. Other comrades also hit him with picks. Then we threw him into the hole, covered him with earth, and left.[23]

Teme Sejko was not the only member of his family to suffer a tragic fate under Hoxha's regime. Sejko's youngest son, Sokol, was tried in court for attempting to blow up the textile plant in Berat and was executed. Another son was sentenced to eight years in prison for 'agitation and propaganda against the people's power'. Shpresa Sejko, Teme's wife, committed suicide a few hours after her husband was arrested. Only their eldest son, Raimond, survived. He emigrated to the United States in the 1990s.

The ups and downs of Hoxha's relationships with foreign countries were prominently reflected in the dictator's attire. In the late 1940s he would appear wearing a Yugoslav-style military cap, very similar to the one worn by Marshal Tito. Later he donned kolkhoz shirts like those of Khrushchev, and wore a Soviet-style semi-brimmed fedora; while after 1969 he would often be seen wearing a Chinese beret, like the ones worn by Mao Zedong.

Every time Enver Hoxha broke up with his one-time allies, his wrath was as exemplary as his expressions of affection had been for them. Far from reflecting a well-balanced strategy that had the best interests of his country and his people in mind, his language and accusations were more like the rantings of a scorned lover.

In 1961 Hoxha dumped the Soviets for the Chinese. His relationship with China lasted for 17 years, though he never seems to have taken it very seriously. During the entire period of his last love affair, he never once visited China, nor did Mao Zedong visit Tirana. The main purpose of the relationship was to provide a deterrent against a potential Soviet attack and to secure economic aid for the country. In his speeches, Hoxha frequently stressed: 'We are not 2 million strong. We are 1 billion and 2 million strong!'

This was a clear allusion to the country's alliance with China, which provided Albania with much-needed economic support. But China also introduced Albania to the practices of the infamous Cultural Revolution, which wiped out the Albanian middle class, deepened the country's isolation and reinforced Hoxha's xenophobic paranoia. It was at this time that the Albanians constructed about 750,000 bunkers, air-raid shelters, trenches and other military fortifications throughout the country, from the beaches to the mountains, to defend the country against an imaginary foreign invasion, evocative of Dino Buzzati's novel *The Tartar Steppe*.

In 1978, after the normalisation of Sino-American relations, Hoxha broke up with his Asian friends and Albania was more isolated than ever, a period that lasted for 12 years. The once popular couplet, '*Dy luanë ka sot bota / një Azia dhe një Evropa*' ('Two lions on this planet, one in Asia and one in Europe'), which referred to Hoxha and Mao Zedong, was reformulated and replaced by another:

> *Pula vezë e veza pulë,*
> *Ç'na ngatërroi një formulë,*
> *Një formulë me tetë pika*
> *Në kuzhinë tek Amerika.*

> [Was it the chicken or the egg?
> What confusion, what a mess,
> Eight-point project in a keg,
> Steamed and boiled by the US.]

16

The Bllok

On that cold December day in 1960, while the government charter – a four-engine Antonov – was landing at Rinas airport, Enver Hoxha would never have imagined that this would be his last trip abroad. For the next 24 years he practically quarantined himself, not only in Albania, but also within the boundaries of the so-called Bllok. The Bllok, short for 'Blloku i Udhëheqësve' (the Leaders' Block) was a centrally located neighbourhood in the capital, barely a quarter of a mile across, guarded by soldiers and plainclothes servicemen of the Second Directorate of the Sigurimi. Hoxha moved into the Bllok in 1944 and had lived there ever since.

The history of the Bllok is intriguing in itself. It began in November 1944. Conceived as a sort of Kremlin, it became a way of life, a marker of hierarchical standing and a catalyser of the cult of personality.

When she arrived in Tirana in November 1944 to make preparations for the transfer of government from Berat to Tirana, Liri Belishova was pleasantly surprised to find that Mehmet Shehu, the partisan commander in town, had already taken care of everything. After an initial short stay at Hotel Dajti, the members of the new government were to be accommodated in a neighbourhood to the west of the main boulevard, right opposite the government offices and the British legation. Enver Hoxha was to move into the house of an Italian engineer by the name of Belloni, who had fled Albania, while Koçi Xoxe was to get the house next door. The Bllok was almost square in shape, with a wide street running through the middle of it that stretched from the main boulevard to one of the newly laid streets of Tirana e Re (New Tirana).

It was clear who would be allowed to live in the Bllok: only full members and candidate members of the Politburo and the chairman of the Presidium of the People's Assembly, as well as their immediate families. Members of the government who were not members of the Politburo were to reside elsewhere.

Up until 1947, there was free public access to the entire area of the Bllok, including the street where the Hoxhas lived. This street was then the first to be closed off, and eventually the ban extended to several parallel streets. In 1985 the Bllok was a neighbourhood of approximately 151,400 square metres (0.058 square miles) and, by this time, not even members of the Politburo who lived there were allowed free access to Hoxha's street.

Life in the Bllok was shrouded in secrecy and fanatically guarded from the outside world. From the beginning, the inhabitants began to intermarry and establish alliances through other kinds of kinship relations, as a way of strengthening their positions. These marriage alliances continued well into the second and third generations, as Bashkim Shehu, son of Mehmet Shehu, Albania's prime minister for 27 years, explained later. In his book *Vjeshta e ankthit* (Autumn of angst) published in Paris and Tirana after his release from prison in 1991, Shehu provided an interesting snapshot of the intricate tangle that was the Bllok's nepotistic web:

> The trend of intermarriages appeared very early on. It started with Enver Hoxha's niece marrying Gogo Nushi's brother; then Hysni Kapo married the sister of Alqi and Pirro Kondi. The latter is the brother-in-law of Manush Myftiu, whose sister is Pilo Peristeri's wife. Ramiz Alia's sister married Reis Malile; the latter's sister married Xhaferr Spahiu, and Bilbil Klosi's wife is Ramiz Alia's wife's sister. All these people were members of the Politburo, of the Central Committee, ministers or deputy prime ministers [...] The intermarriages between the good and the great of Albanian politics produced children who came of age and intermarried, too [...] For example, Adil Çarçani's daughter married Manush Myftiu's son [...] Around the same time, one of Enver Hoxha's sons got engaged to Ramiz Alia's brother's daughter [...] Even Kadri Hazbiu became related to Enver Hoxha when Hoxha's daughter married the brother of the husband of Kadri Hazbiu's wife's niece.[1]

Liljana Hoxha, Hoxha's daughter-in-law, echoed the same view in a 2010
interview:

> Intermarriages in the Bllok were all about forging political alliances,
> although care was taken to avoid very close blood affinity. For instance,
> the children of some Politburo members would marry nieces or nephews
> of other Politburo members. All marriages were within the confines of
> the Bllok.[2]

These alliances and ties did not pass unnoticed and people would discuss
them, albeit not openly. After the fall of communism in 1991, Frrok Çupi
wrote an editorial for *Rilindja* (Revival), the daily newspaper of the then
recently founded opposition party, entitled 'Pse nuk çahet Blloku?' (Why
can't the Bllok be broken up?). The author posited that the Bllok was not
a mere geographical notion or just another neighbourhood, but a way of
life. Its inhabitants were all part of a tightly knit political clique, with
thousands of visible and invisible kinship and affinity threads holding
them together.

The Bllok inhabitants received special treatment: they all had waiting
and housekeeping staff, special shops where they bought their groceries and
Western clothes, government villas and holiday homes across the country,
and a host of other privileges. But these privileges did come at a cost – life
there was fraught with complications and uncertainties. This is how Bashkim
Shehu described the atmosphere:

> Once you were at that level of the system, friendships went out the door.
> What glued these people together was their joint enterprise and complicity
> in keeping the majority under their sway. The man at the very top, Enver
> Hoxha, had no illusions: there was no friendship or camaraderie to talk
> of. He held everybody on a tight leash and they, in turn, would strive to
> give proof of their loyalty, friendship and so on, hoping to secure a place in
> his good books. I saw this in the way my father behaved towards Hoxha:
> I would describe it as total adulation for a man he felt it was his duty to
> be loyal to and work closely with.[3]

The lack of sincerity in personal relations in the Bllok had of course a great deal to do with Hoxha himself. In a propaganda documentary shot in 1981, he is seen walking side by side with Myslim Peza and Haxhi Lleshi, two of his comrades-in-arms from the time of the war. The script, written by Nexhmije Hoxha in the form of a narrative addressed to Hoxha's first-born granddaughter Valbona, began with the words:

> Here is grandfather with his friends. They are slowly climbing the stairs together, one step at a time. Years have passed and life's challenges have weighed on their shoulders, but they have not aged. They are all just 41 years old, because that is how old the party is.[4]

On several occasions, Hoxha appeared quite emotional and misty-eyed about old times and about the strong comradely bond between him and the other leaders. Not long before this documentary was shot, he awarded Myslim Peza the highest decoration in the country and gave a magnanimous speech at the ceremony:

> This title is bestowed on you not because of your age. The medal has a significant political meaning for the reasons I just mentioned. It is an acknowledgement of your contribution to the cause, starting from King Zog's time, when you were the first to give the signal for revolt by killing Osman Bali, the man who had tortured and executed Haxhi Qamili, and who was a henchman of both [Shefqet bey] Vërlaci and Ahmet Zogu. Your brave and manly gesture was not just an act of revenge, nor was it a terrorist act; it was a political gesture which symbolised the rise of our patriotic peasantry against the tyrants. Because of the relentless persecution you suffered under King Zog's regime, you had to flee the country and live abroad as an Albanian patriot and honest man, in the bosom of the Albanian community living in poverty under the Serbian krals [the Kingdom of Serbs, Croats and Slovenes, i.e. Yugoslavia]. While you were living there, you never stopped thinking about your village of Peza, about your beloved Albania, suffering under a king who was Albanian only by name – because in truth he was an alien, a traitor, an evil man who caused

so much pain to our noble and suffering people. I got to know you through a mutual friend and patriot, Esat Dishnica. We've been together through thick and thin, and had many happy moments as well, as the country progressed on the road of Marxism–Leninism.[5]

Documents from the Central State Archives made available to the public in 1992 present the other side of the medal. Precisely at the time when the documentary was being shown in movie theatres up and down the country, Hoxha wrote the following about Myslim Peza, Haxhi Lleshi and their friendship, in his diary:

Monday, 21 June 1982

I discussed with comrades Ramiz [Alia], Simon [Stefani] and Kadri [Hazbiu] the behaviour of Haxhi Lleshi, who has been far from morally correct recently. The path he has chosen has caused much dismay among the other comrades who work at the Presidium of the People's Assembly. The latter have warned him about the [anti-communist] stance of a certain D. S., who works at the Presidium. They are also worried that by having this improper relationship with her, Haxhi is giving this scheming troublemaker of a woman free rein to do as she pleases.

Tuesday, 22 June 1982

Another problem – a dangerous problem – is brewing. Who is caus-ing it? What is its source? At the time when we uncovered the coup that Beqir Balluku and co. were plotting, a conflict broke out between Haxhi Lleshi and his wife and children. Haxhi's wife, who originates from a leading family (several members of the Jegeni family defected to Titoite Yugoslavia), began to speak openly to everyone against Haxhi. Hers is a scandalous act against the president of the Presidium of the People's Assembly. Hysni [Kapo] and I talked to Haxhi a couple of times and told him what was going on. We told him to take steps – she would have to stop blabbering or she would be banished to a remote village. Haxhi's response was, 'Whatever the party says!' Around the same time, the children rose against their father [Haxhi]. His son, R. (who used to work at the Central Committee), called his father an adulterer. He was summoned to explain himself; but he wouldn't budge from his opinion. Hysni summoned Haxhi again. Haxhi said that there was nothing he could do about his son. Hysni then suggested, 'Why don't we send him to the same farm as his mother [Haxhi's wife], and they can till the soil together there?' Haxhi, of course, agreed as always, 'Whatever the party says!' This is how the issue was resolved, but we still have some lingering doubts. What caused all that?

Over the years, relations between Myslim Peza and Haxhi Lleshi were always excellent. But recently, out of the blue, dark clouds have been gathering in the sky of their friendship.

Myslim Peza, who received due recognition from the party and from me for the role he played during the National Liberation War, suddenly decided, at 80 years of age and almost totally blind, that he wanted to write his memoirs 'in three volumes'. He discussed this with Haxhi Lleshi, who suggested that his secretary go to Myslim's house to record and then transcribe the memoirs. And that is what they did. The recording began, but Myslim was impatient, he wanted the tapes transcribed right away. Why? No one knows.

Myslim was angry, 'This woman is not doing a good job; she is keeping my tapes in her filing cabinet so that Haxhi Lleshi can use them for his own memoirs.' In fact, Haxhi Lleshi, too, had started recording his memoirs. Both of them were doing this in parallel and the same woman, D. S., was doing the recording and transcribing. In his frustration, Myslim demanded that his tapes be returned, convinced that Haxhi 'was eating his cake'. So the tapes were retrieved – initially the woman refused to hand them over, but following some loud protests and an order by the Central Committee, she gave in.

Then a different person was assigned to work with Myslim. He recorded the memoirs, transcribed them and gave one copy to the Central Committee of the party and the other to Myslim himself. Myslim was expecting the Central Committee to send them to the publishing house straight away. As this was taking too long, he decided to send his own copy to the publishing house. The editor who read the manuscript was so shocked by their contents that he notified the Central Committee immediately. Officials at the Central Committee had also read their copy and had decided that it was not fit for publication. The memoirs consisted mainly of Myslim's personal adventures before he got in touch with us and the National Liberation Movement, which he presented as 'acts of heroism, patriotism, etc.'

There was nothing in his memoirs about the momentous historical events that occurred in Peza – which were the major achievements of our party – or about the Peza fighters and their resistance. He had even downplayed his own role in the war. Not only were his memoirs a stream of erratic, opinionated and repetitive statements about miscellaneous insignificant events in the villages, but he had gone so far as to provide smug descriptions of his many adventures abroad, in the Yugoslavia of the Serbian krals. He told of how he received money from the Yugoslavs, how they had wanted to recruit him as their agent but he 'had declined'. Nevertheless, the Yugoslavs still kept him on their payroll. Even before that, when he was living in Albania under King Zog, the Yugoslav lega-tion had given him 500 gold pieces, but Myslim 'did not touch them, all the money went to the poor.'

And so he rambled on, with his stories about proposals to collaborate with Gani Kryeziu, Lleshi's family and Irfan Ohri, against King Zog. At the suggestion of the Yugoslavs, Myslim had chosen the Lleshis, 'a clan that commanded significant authority in Yugoslavia and Belgrade'. It was in Belgrade that Myslim Peza met Haxhi Lleshi and the pair embarked upon adventures that he recorded in his own voice.

In the entire time that Myslim and I worked together, he never men-tioned anything about these aspects of his life. Why did he keep them from me and the party? Why is he revealing all these things now, after the uncovering of Mehmet Shehu's plot? Is this a pre-emptive strike? Is he afraid that others might come forward with these stories? With these memoirs, which he insists so much on publishing, he casts a dark shadow on himself and what he became thanks to the party and the liberation war. If Myslim's adventures are published, they will become a weapon in our enemies' hands and people will think, 'Are these the kind of people the party has promoted?' No, we are not going to give Myslim or the Yugoslavs that satisfaction. Not if we can help it!

Tuesday, 22 June 1982

The Myslim Peza question is entangled with the Haxhi Lleshi question. Haxhi seems to have woken up from his slumber after the suicide of the traitor Mehmet Shehu. D. S., a woman from a good family and employee at the Presidium of the People's Assembly, is his secretary. It seems Haxhi has crossed the line with her. Other employees at the Presidium are talking about it and some have been writing to the Central Committee 'to stop the scandal'. But the worst part is that this woman has become so very conceited that she is causing trouble in the administration, laying down the law in the name of the president. What law? What does she think she is doing? She is a troublemaker. She speaks ill of the highest leaders of the party, and has even gone so far as to tell a communist comrade, one that works at the Presidium of the People's Assembly (who immediately reported this to the Central Committee): 'when Enver Hoxha dies, Haxhi Lleshi will take power.' It is clear that these are things she must have heard from Haxhi Lleshi. The only explanation for it is that Haxhi has taken leave of his senses. *In vino veritas.* This is the first thing.

Second: it seems Haxhi Lleshi recommended this woman to Myslim to record and transcribe the latter's memoirs of the time he was interned in Yugoslavia. Was this offer made because Haxhi wanted to know what Myslim would say about him, his father, his uncles and Aqif Lleshi? Haxhi feared that Myslim's memoirs would compromise his family's good name by linking it to the Yugoslavs. Haxhi refused to return the transcripts to Myslim, until the latter went off the handle and D. S. was eventually forced to hand them over.

It is abundantly clear to us that Haxhi felt he was put in a tight spot by his old friend, so he came up with a new intrigue, which could very well have an element of truth to it. Myslim Peza's niece also works for the administration of the Presidium of the People's Assembly. She must have told Myslim about Haxhi's affair with D. S. The jealousy and unbridled ambitions of these two women have been causing problems in the

administration for some time now. After the altercation with Myslim over
the latter's memoirs, Haxhi Lleshi called a meeting with other members
of the Central Committee who work at the Presidium of the People's
Assembly – comrades Spiro Koleka, Shefqet Peçi and Xhafer Spahiu – and
proposed that a male employee of the Presidium and Myslim Peza's niece
be dismissed from their positions on the grounds that they were involved
in a sexual relationship with each other. The other comrades asked Haxhi
if he had any proof to substantiate his claim. He refused to provide any,
and stubbornly insisted: 'You must do what I say.' The other comrades
declined to go along with this and Haxhi, our 'comrade president' said:
'Then let's take it to the grass-roots organisation.'

Myslim Peza learned about the scandal and reportedly told Xhafer
Spahiu, 'If Haxhi goes ahead with this, I will consider it a personal insult
and won't have anything to do with him.' Haxhi declared: 'I'm ready to
take up the fight,' and the scandal ensued. He blackmailed Myslim Peza,
who in turn threatened him back.

By this time it was clear to us that this was a provocation by Haxhi
Lleshi, and the members of the Central Committee who worked at the
Presidium of the assembly were advised to keep a cool head. Contrary
to what Haxhi had requested, neither of the two people in question was
to be dismissed or transferred to another job and there was nothing to
discuss at the grass-roots organisation.

All the while, the Central Committee and myself were receiving
anonymous letters about Haxhi's affair with D. S. Ramiz had also received
letters signed by a communist comrade who works at the Presidium and
who described the hostile (i.e. anti-communist) opinions of this woman
who is Haxhi Lleshi's secretary. Simon Stefani, secretary of the Central
Committee, forwarded the anonymous letter to Haxhi, who responded in
writing to Simon (all these letters are kept in the archives of the Central
Committee). Haxhi Lleshi withdrew his request for the dismissal of
Myslim Peza's niece, but insisted on the dismissal of the male employee,
providing some very lame reasons. The comrades told Haxhi that his
reasons were not well founded and that, if there were to be any dismiss-
als, then D. S. had to be one of the first to be dismissed, given that she

was the root of the scandal. They had told him about all her arrogant and anti-communist behaviour and actions (without mentioning that they knew about the affair). Haxhi Lleshi said he did not agree. 'I will not have D. S. dismissed from the Presidium; let's take this to the grass-roots organisation.' The members of the Central Committee working at the Presidium told Haxhi that it would be better if this were not discussed with the grass-roots membership, as many other things could come to light that could undermine his prestige as president of the Presidium. Haxhi went so far as to say: 'If the party wants me to retire by dismissing me from the Presidium, then so be it!'

This was just a personal matter between two men whose fight has now come out into the open, causing so many problems for the party. Both made their contribution to the Anti-Fascist National Liberation Movement. The party and I personally have recognised their contributions and have publicly pointed out their merits to the people, who look up to them as leaders. Why are Myslim and Haxhi opening their old unsettled accounts at this time, when the party is successfully recovering from the very hostile activities of Mehmet Shehu, the Yugoslav agent? They are causing us new trouble. Could it be that the Yugoslavs are behind all this? Our experience in the fight against external and internal enemies has taught us many lessons. We always were, and always will be, alert in the defence of our homeland, the party and socialism.

I really hope that the enemy is not behind this quarrel, but I will be vigilant and I will act in such a way as not to give our Yugoslav foes that satisfaction, and I will not fall prey to these comrades' provocations, if indeed they are provocations. I will keep a cool head so that the country is protected, the scandal that the enemy is trying to cause is avoided and the actions of these two 'old' comrades are rendered harmless. It is in the interest of our party, which is constantly under attack by the enemies, that we take measures to defeat the enemy and ensure the triumph of the party and the people.

A handwritten note on the margins of this diary entry, probably by Nexhmije Hoxha, said, 'For Comrade Ramiz's eyes only.' Until about 1976 or 1978 every entry in Hoxha's diary was in his handwriting. In later years he began recording his thoughts, which were transcribed and typed for him. He would then select parts he thought were fit for publication – the rest, like the two entries above, never made it into print. Hoxha's diaries are now preserved in the Central State Archives, bound in numerous folders.

Liljana Hoxha, Hoxha's daughter-in-law, moved into the Bllok in 1973. She was a university student when Hoxha's second son, Sokol, proposed to her. This was one of the few marriages from outside the Bllok and Liljana is convinced her mother-in-law never forgave her for the fact that she came from 'the outside world'. For a long time she felt ostracised. This is how she described her experience in a 2010 interview:

> I got married in 1972 and I vividly remember that the atmosphere in the Bllok was always very tense. Everybody was under strict surveillance. It can safely be said that it was a place with an extreme lack of freedom. Everyone and everything was under surveillance: they knew who came in, who went out, who befriended whom and everything they got up to.[6]

Asked who the most important families in the Bllok were, she answered:

> The families of Enver Hoxha, Mehmet Shehu and Hysni Kapo. But it was clear that relations between these three families were nothing short of pure hypocrisy. There was hypocrisy and there were disparities, which of course led to jealousy. Fiqirete Shehu and Vito Kapo were both more intelligent than Nexhmije Hoxha. They were assertive and would take part as equals in all sorts of discussions. Nexhmije was the quiet type; she would generally sit and listen and observe, playing the part of an unassertive wife whose role was to support her husband.[7]

The Hoxhas, the Kapos and the Alias were the only families who never left the Bllok; the other leaders and their families were constantly moving in and out. Purges were the most frequent reason. What is surprising is that even after the political changes of the 1990s, most of them continued to keep their silence about their experience in the Bllok. In many ways, they resemble a sect whose members are bound together by a pledge or a threat, and refuse to disclose anything about that part of their lives. One exception was Spartak Ngjela, son of Kiço Ngjela, who was minister for trade for 28 years. In 2011 Ngjela published his memoirs, which shed some light on life in the Bllok.

A central feature in Ngjela's memoirs was the so-called 'Party House'. This was a sort of exclusive club inside the Bllok, adjacent to the Central Committee building. It was an imposing edifice, built in the late 1930s as the residence of former prime minister Koço Kota, who never got to move in. Just as the house was finished, Kota had to flee the country with King Zog. He went to Thessaloníki, where he settled and lived from 1939 to 1945. Early in 1945, three Sigurimi officers, aided by some Greek communists, kidnapped Kota from a club in Thessaloníki and brought him secretly back to Albania. He appeared before the so-called Special Court and was sentenced to 30 years in prison. He died in 1949 in the Burrel prison which he himself had ordered built when prime minister. From the early 1940s, his intended residence became a club venue and was christened the Party House. It had several lounges, a billiards hall and a cinema room where the leaders would watch movies banned for the general public. Dropping by at the Party House was a daily ritual for the party leaders; every evening they would spend a couple of hours there. The most senior leaders would be on the first floor, often lost in long discussions, which Hoxha was wont to dominate. The topics ranged from mundane matters to foreign policy and other issues of vital importance for communism in Albania. According to Spartak Ngjela, Hoxha was very particular about attendance at the club and demanded that all the other leaders be there every day without fail. It was probably a way to keep them on a tight leash, much like Stalin had done before him. He wanted to be able to look his associates in the eye and gauge their loyalty. He felt so strongly about this that one of the charges he raised against Bedri Spahiu in 1955 was that 'he had not shown up at the Party House for two entire months'.

Whenever he was not engaged in conversations with his associates, or delivering one of his long political speeches, Hoxha's favourite pastime was to play billiards. He was good at it. Those who played with him then remember that he was unbeatable. It was one of the few sports-related talents he had cultivated in his youth. Hoxha was not particularly fond of drinking; he would take a shot of ouzo on the rocks on the odd occasion. He also liked spicy food and his waiter would invariably add some strong wine vinegar to his plate. The serving staff at the Party House and at home called him Commander, a trend set by the partisans who had served him back in 1944.

After the break with the Soviet Union, Hoxha's cult of personality grew out of all proportion. Hoxha was increasingly becoming a carbon copy of his mentor, Stalin, and was consumed by the same overwhelming paranoia that the Soviet leader had displayed 40 years earlier. An entire media and film industry was put at the service of creating and maintaining his cult of personality and building the image of an infallible and good-natured leader. All photos and footage of him would be scrutinised to the minutest detail to create the perfect image. Hoxha was always immaculately combed and dressed and always smiling, and no picture ever showed him in a moment of weakness. His printed images always exuded euphoria and enthusiasm.

But footage that has been released recently portrays a very different man. At a 1982 Politburo meeting called to discuss Kadri Hazbiu's case, he was caught on camera swearing: 'Fuck his sister!'[8] At another meeting, he addressed Kadri Hazbiu sarcastically: 'Is it Beqir Balluku you are talking about? Do you want to know what we think about him? He is nothing but a piece of shit!'[9] Incidents of the use of such unsavoury language at Politburo and Central Committee meetings were surprisingly numerous. According to people who knew him, such behaviour was the norm rather than an exception.

Starting in the 1960s, security at the Bllok was tightened even further and Hoxha's growing paranoia meant that thousands of people needed to be employed to provide personal security for him on a daily basis.

17

Enver Hoxha and Mother Teresa

O ne day in 1968 Enver Hoxha asked to see the confidential report of a meeting that had been held earlier that year between Maurice Couve de Murville, French minister of foreign affairs, and Javer Malo, Albanian ambassador to France. The Albanian diplomat had added an accompanying note, explaining that the issue discussed with France's chief diplomat had been brought to the attention of various Albanian embassies in the West many times over the past couple of years.

The story had started a few years earlier, when the Albanian embassy to Rome received a letter from a certain Mother Teresa, a Catholic nun based in Calcutta, India. Founder of the order bearing her name, Mother Teresa had asked that her frail and infirm 80-year-old mother be permitted to travel from Albania to Rome for medical treatment. In her letter, Mother Teresa explained that she herself had left Albania in 1928 but her mother Drane and sister Age remained in the country. She had not been able to see her mother since the day she left the country, over 30 years earlier. This would probably be the last chance for her to kiss her mother's hands and take care of her in the remaining years of her life. The letter was also signed by Mother Teresa's brother, Lazër Bojaxhiu, a former artillery captain in King Zog's army who had left Albania during World War II and had settled in Palermo, Italy.

Born into an ethnic Albanian family from Skopje, Mother Teresa, or Gonxhe Bojaxhiu as she was known before becoming a nun, had moved with her family to Albania after Skopje became part of the new Kingdom of Serbs, Croats and Slovenes. She knew from an early age that her calling in life was to serve God. She took her religious vows as a nun under the name of Sister Teresa and, after a short spell in Ireland, she moved to Calcutta, India.

Sister Teresa's father died when she was still very young. Her mother Drane and sister Age remained in Albania, living in relatively difficult circumstances. The more famous Mother Teresa became, the more they would try to keep their relation to her a secret. The two women did not even dare to mention her name, fearing punishment by a communist regime that had declared open war on all religious faiths. In 1959 Mother Teresa and her brother Lazër met in Rome. It was their first meeting in 31 years, and one that was marked by sorrow because neither of them had been able to see the other half of the family that was still in Albania. For over ten years, Mother Teresa had not received a single letter from them. Eventually she learned that they were still living in Tirana and were only allowed to send one letter per month. But even then, all personal letters were subject to strict state censorship. Biographers of Mother Teresa all note that she had an ardent wish to visit Albania and she would often talk with her friends about it. But Albania would remain a forbidden land for her for a long time.

By the mid-1960s, Drane's health took a turn for the worse, so mother and daughter plucked up the courage to write to Lazër, asking for some medicines that were not available in Albania. Lazër thought the best solution would be if his mother went and stayed in Italy for a month or so. There she could be seen by doctors at an Italian hospital and he and his sister would finally be able to see their mother, who had sacrificed so much for them. They sent a letter to the Albanian embassy in Rome, but no response was forthcoming. A second letter and a request made on their behalf by the political director at the Italian Ministry of Foreign Affairs, urged by the Vatican, produced no results either. Immediately after this intervention, the Albanian ambassador contacted Lazër and informed him that the elderly woman could not travel out of Albania, that the hospitals in Albania were very good, and that the son and daughter who had chosen to leave the country should have thought about missing their mother before they left and abandoned her.

Mother Teresa's plight, which received considerable coverage in the Western media, touched many people's hearts. In the span of two years, nearly all the countries that had good relations with Albania were asking the Albanian Ministry of Foreign Affairs to do something about it; after all, the elderly lady would only leave the country for 30 days and this surely would not pose any difficulties. The Albanian regime remained unmoved. Mother Teresa made a last-ditch attempt: she asked permission to enter Albania for just a week. One of her biographers explains:

> By the early 1970s, when she learned about her mother's ill health, Mother Teresa intensified her efforts to visit her country. She went to meet the attaché at the Albanian embassy in Rome, in the hope that she would at least be allowed to visit Albania. 'As she was leaving the embassy building,' wrote Dom Lush Gjergji in his book *Our Mother Teresa*, 'I saw tears running down her cheeks for the first time. She stopped, turned her eyes to the sky and said: "Dear God, I can understand and accept that I should suffer, but it is so hard to understand and accept why my mother has to suffer. In her old age she has no other wish than to see us one last time."'[1]

This was the topic of the confidential meeting between the French foreign minister and the Albanian ambassador to Paris. The French minister had asked the ambassador to convey the request to Enver Hoxha personally and inform him that both President de Gaulle and the US First Lady Jacqueline Kennedy had taken a personal interest in the matter. They appealed to Hoxha to intervene so that a special permit could be issued on compassionate grounds.

Hoxha must have felt pressured. After going through the report, he summoned interior minister Hazbiu demanding more information about a nun called Mother Teresa, with the warning that it was very likely she was a dangerous agent. He also requested more information about the nun's elderly mother and sister living in Albania, as well as any people seen entering their home.

Although she was refused a visa to enter Albania, Mother Teresa continued with her efforts to get her mother and sister out of the country. She enlisted the support of some of the greatest personalities on the globe, but to no avail. Eventually she resigned herself to the thought that her dream of meeting them was not going to come true and wrote to her mother and sister: 'Nothing else is left for me to do but pray for you.'[2]

On 14 July 1972, Mother Teresa received a telegram from Lazër Bojaxhiu. It said simply: 'Pray for Mother. She passed away on 12 July.' Drane Bojaxhiu died with the pang of not being able to see her son in Italy and her missionary daughter in India one last time. After the 1990s, studies were published that revealed a poignant fact: Drane had sent a photograph to the daughter that she had not seen in 45 years, with this note: 'Gonxhe, I send you this with my kisses.'[3]

Aga, the sister, died in 1973. In a 1979 interview, after Mother Teresa received the Nobel Prize, Lazër Bojaxhiu stated:

> My little, humble sister, she who came to the aid of millions of abandoned people, she who gave her love and support to so many desperate people, was not allowed to sit by her own mother's deathbed. The poor woman died in desperation, clutching a tear-drenched photo to her chest.[4]

Lazër Bojaxhiu died in 1981, while Mother Teresa finally managed to visit Albania in 1990, five years after Hoxha's death and a few months before the communist regime collapsed. Under the watchful eye of the secret police, she went to the house where her mother and sister had lived and was able to touch some of their meagre possessions: an old Siemens radio set dating from World War II and a hand-held Turkish coffee grinder. At long last, the world-famous nun was able to put flowers on the graves of her mother and sister – her triumph over the regime which forbade her from seeing them while they were still alive.

Enver Hoxha's fight against religion was a campaign of unprecedented cruelty and one of the saddest chapters of his regime. Most historians, rather misleadingly, date the start of the campaign to his 'Open Letter' of 1967, which did in fact lead to the banning of religion, but the campaign had in fact begun much earlier. The persecution of clerics started as early as 1944, when Hoxha's position of power was not yet fully established. A letter sent from Shkodra on 30 January 1945, by Vaskë Koleci, a senior Sigurimi officer, provides the following information about Hoxha's request: 'Our plan is to arrest three priests against whom numerous charges have been raised. Our men will eventually carry out a thorough search of the Jesuit convent premises. For the moment, it has only been locked up.'[5]

The punishments exacted on the clergy, especially the Catholic clergy, went beyond anyone's imagination. All men of the cloth were swept with the same broom and declared collaborators with the occupiers and opponents of the new regime. Many were detained and executed. One of the first to experience the wrath was Dom Lazër Shantoja, who was executed even before the communists came to power. His execution was ordered personally by Hoxha, as shown by the following telegram:

> To the Shkodra Military Tribunal.
> Third Corps.
> In response to your dispatch no. 5 of 10 February 1945: Death penalty for Dom Lazër Shantoja and Sulçe Beg Bushati approved. Stop. Please inform of execution date.
> Enver Hoxha.[6]

Dom Lazër Shantoja was executed by firing squad the next day. Both his legs had been broken under torture and even crawling caused him excruciating pain. His body had been tortured so savagely, and reduced to such a state, that his mother, who went to meet him before the execution, pleaded with chief investigator Mehmet Shehu: 'Do him a last favour. Kill him! Don't let him suffer like this!'[7]

Although Dom Lazër Shantoja had indeed collaborated with the Italians, what was done to him was nothing short of barbaric. But the persecution did not end with him. Many other men of the cloth suffered a similar fate. One of them was Father Bernardin Palaj, who died in prison after contracting tetanus from the barbed wire in which his hands were kept tied day and night.

Contemporaneous documents speak of the unbelievable courage shown by these servants of God. A document reporting the execution of three Catholic priests, Monsignor Frano Gjini, Father Mati Prendushi and Dom Nikoll Deda, was placed on Hoxha's desk on 12 March 1948. It reported their last words:

This is to inform you about the execution of Monsignor Frano Gjini, Father Mati Prendushi, and Dom Nikoll Deda on 11 March 1948 at 5 p.m. Their last words were:

Frano Pjetër Gjini: 'Long live Christ the King! Long live the Catholic faith and Catholics all over the world! Long live the Pope! My body and my blood will remain here, but my soul and heart will go to the Pope. Long live Albania!'

Pater Mati Prendushi: 'I am innocent. I am dying in the line of duty. Long live Christ the King! Long live the Pope! Long live the Catholics! Long live Albania! I forgive the court and those who will shoot at our innocent bodies.'

Dom Nikoll Deda: 'Long live Albania! I am dying in the line of duty. Long live Christ the King! Long live the Albanian people!'[8]

In 1944, Father Zef Pllumi was a young seminarian. This is how he recalls the moment when his superior, Father Mati Prendushi, received his death sentence and spoke to him for the last time:

With tears in our eyes, we all embraced those who were sentenced to death. While I was embracing him for the last time, Father Mati said:

'Friar Zef, I commend you. Thank you for bringing honour to the name of the Franciscan Province. Always love it and protect it as you are doing now. May God protect you and bless you!'

Then he added: 'Hey, my Scythian, I hope one day we shall see one another in the other life.' His last message to me was: Live, live to tell the story of how the Catholic clergy and faith once suffered in Albania.[9]

Father Zef Pllumi was himself arrested twice and brutally tortured. He spent a total of 28 years in prison, but managed to survive the ordeal. Not only did he live to see the reopening of some churches in Tirana and Shkodra, but he also published his memoirs in three volumes entitled *Rrno vetëm për me tregue* (published in English as *Live to Tell*). Only after he fulfilled his mentor's last wish, by telling the story of the persecution of the clergy and the entire Albanian people, did he die in peace, surrounded by people who loved and respected him greatly. His funeral was attended by the president of the Republic, the prime minister and other senior officials, whose presence constituted a public apology for the persecution that he and other representatives of Catholicism had suffered in Albania.

While Father Zef Pllumi managed to come out of the whole ordeal alive, many others were not that lucky. Many were arrested on charges of hiding weapons in churches. In a 1948 trial in Shkodra, Pierin Kçira, a former Sigurimi officer, gave the following testimony:

> At Zoi Themeli's order, we used a master key to enter the Franciscan church in the Gjuhadol neighbourhood and planted some documents and other incriminating objects behind the altar. The next morning we surrounded the place, 'discovered' the guns and arrested many Franciscan priests, most of whom were later executed.[10]

Thousands of Catholics and non-Catholics who were following the proceedings live on Radio Shkodra were profoundly shocked by this testimony. The hearing was immediately adjourned, the trial was suspended, and Kçira was executed for disclosing a state secret.

The persecution campaign saw no sign of abatement in later years. Over 40 clergymen were killed or imprisoned. One of the most poignant stories is that of Dom Shtjefën Kurti. In 1971 Dom Kurti was arrested after performing a baptismal ceremony for the baby of a young couple at their own home. A disgruntled relative of the baby's father reported the priest and the young father to the Sigurimi. The father ended up in prison and the next time he saw his son again was in 1989 – by which time he was a young man of 19. Dom Shtjefën Kurti was sentenced to death in November 1971 and subsequently executed. In February 1972, a friend who went to visit him in prison with some food was simply told to take the food away: Dom Shtjefën had no more need for the food of this world. He had been executed. The date of his execution and place of burial remain unknown to this day. He was 74 when he died.

In January 1973, a Catholic woman who fled from Shkodra to Yugoslavia and subsequently settled in Austria spoke to the press about the priest's ordeal. She revealed details of Dom Kurti's trial and how painful it had been for him that the trial was actually held in a former church building. The Vatican's reaction was forceful and immediate. The world press reported it as one of the most poignant events of the year. Executing a man for performing his duties as a priest was one of the worst acts of the communist regime. A memo of the Albanian Ministry of Foreign Affairs reported that after Dom Kurti's execution, most Western democracies stopped inviting Albanian diplomats to official receptions. On 28 April 1973, Radio Tirana was forced to make a public announcement of the execution. In an article entitled 'Një shenjtor i ri për Vatikanin' (A new saint for the Vatican), the newspaper *Zëri i popullit* viciously attacked the Vatican and claimed that Dom Kurti had been an agent in the service of the Italians, the British and the Americans. According to Radio Tirana, Dom Kurti had not been executed for being a man of the faith, but for sabotaging the agricultural cooperative where he worked!

In a speech given in Brindisi shortly after his election as Pope, John Paul II launched fierce accusations against the Albanian regime, which banned people from believing in God. Dom Kurti's tragic story deeply touched Ronald Reagan. After his election as US president, he is said to have mentioned the story of the ill-fated priest at least twice, as one of the saddest stories he had ever heard in his life.

Twenty years after the fall of the communist regime in Albania, the Vatican sent its first envoy there. Vincenzo Foca's mission was to investigate the crimes committed against the clergy and fully document the fate of the 40 Catholic priests who were executed or died in prison during the years of Hoxha's regime. The Vatican also initiated procedures for declaring 40 men and one woman, Sister Maria Tuci, 'Martyrs of Christianity'.

Hoxha's vicious attack on religion was one of the darkest pages in the history of Albanian communism. Initially he restricted access to places of worship and religious venues, revoked the independence of the Church, reduced the number of clergymen to a minimum, and nationalised all assets of churches, mosques and *tekkes* (dervish lodges), and ultimately declared a complete ban on the exercise of all religious faiths. Hoxha knew that religion had deep roots among the people, as shown in a letter written by him in 1967, in which he directed all first secretaries of the PLA branches in the districts 'to be cautious, but ruthless, as religion is still very influential among the people'.

In addition to the brutal persecution of the clergy, numerous places of worship were closed down or demolished, while dozens of other churches, mosques and *tekkes* were turned into bars, restaurants, arts centres or youth clubs. The Great Cathedral in Shkodra, built at the end of the nineteenth century, became an indoor sports arena. The Heart of Christ Church in Tirana was turned into a movie theatre; and the ancient convent of Ardenica, where the Albanian national hero Skanderbeg, whose real name was Gjergj Kastrioti, is believed to have married, became a hotel and restaurant. The church of Vau i Dejës, the oldest one in the country, was blown up with dynamite, in spite of the fact that it was among the top ten on the list of historical buildings protected by the state. Countless religious artefacts of special interest, including icons and holy books, were hurled onto bonfires and consumed by the flames. The list of crimes committed against religious heritage sites is a long one.

Thousands of priests and imams were arrested and ended up serving lengthy prison terms. Many imams and dervishes of the Bektashi sect had their beards shaved off in public by the 'red guards' of the Communist Youth, in a bid to emulate the Chinese Cultural Revolution. People today still remember watching macabre scenes on TV of people vandalising the graves of Bektashi holy men and flinging their bones into the river.

According to the September 1967 issue of literary journal *Nëntori*, cited by Gjon Sinishta in his collection of articles on the persecution of the Catholic clergy in Albania, within the space of a few months, young people in Albania had totally or partially destroyed 2,169 religious sites – Catholic and Orthodox churches, Muslim mosques and Bektashi *tekkes*. Of these, 327 were Catholic churches.[11]

On 22 November 1967, the official gazette published decree no. 4,337, which banned the practising of all religious faiths in Albania. All remaining places of worship were closed down.

The exact number of clergymen who were executed or tortured to death, or who perished in prison, is unknown. Given that Muslims and Bektashis did not keep accurate lists of their members who were convicted under communism, the total number must be much higher than what is currently reported.

The 1976 constitution of the People's Socialist Republic of Albania pro-claimed the country an atheist state. Albania thus became the first and only atheist country in the world.

Enver Hoxha lost his battle with religion even before communism received the blow which led to its final collapse. In her first visit to Tirana in 1990, after putting flowers on the graves of her beloved mother and sister, Mother Teresa made a symbolic gesture that surprised everyone. She asked to be taken to the grave of the man who had tormented her and her family by forbidding them to see one another; and she placed a bunch of flowers on his grave. Her message of pity and forgiveness was the ultimate triumph of faith over the faithless regime that Enver Hoxha had set up in Albania.

18

Split Personality

I smail Kadare picked up the phone and a woman at the other end of the line introduced herself politely as Nexhmije Hoxha, the dictator's wife. She had been informed of Kadare's intention of writing a book on the breakdown of Albanian–Soviet relations and would be happy to meet him the next day to talk about it. How about coffee at her house around 5 p.m.? He could also bring his wife along.

It was March 1971. By this time, 35 years old and author of several successful novels, one of which was published in France, Kadare was undoubtedly the greatest literary talent in Albania. By the 1960s his fame was firmly established and he was widely admired by the younger generation. Towards the end of 1970 the idea occurred to him of writing a novel on Albanian–Soviet relations, with Enver Hoxha as one of the characters. Born in the same town as Hoxha and 28 years his junior, Kadare had lived as a child only a few metres across the street from Hoxha's house, but the two had never met. The two houses were separated by the rather curiously named street Mad Men's Alley.

Hoxha was not unaware of Kadare's work. According to Ramiz Alia, then political secretary for cultural affairs, Hoxha had identified him as a future talent in the early 1960s. In addition, the Kadares and the Hoxhas were said to be distant relatives, albeit so far removed that the initial link had been forgotten by both sides.

Ismail Kadare and his wife arrived at the house at exactly five minutes to five. The dictator's wife, director of the Institute of Marxist–Leninist Studies – which in fact was mainly concerned with the publication of the dictator's works – received them with a warm smile. The conversation was sluggish and awkward, in spite of the best efforts of all three to keep it alive. Nexhmije Hoxha said that Kadare would be given access to all the relevant classified documents, including the complete minutes of the Moscow meeting and the face-to-face talks between Hoxha and Khrushchev. As the polite conversation trudged along, heading nowhere, there was a light knock at the door. The person behind it did not wait to be invited in. The door opened slowly and Enver Hoxha appeared in the doorway. He greeted the guests warmly and almost shyly, as if seeking their approval to join in the conversation. Of course, he did not need anyone's permission to do so.

Here is how Kadare recalled the conversation in an interview he gave in 1998:

> There was a knock at the door. The door opened. Enver Hoxha entered and enquired: 'May I sit down and join in your conversation?' He addressed us as if we were old friends although this was the first time I had ever met or spoken to him in person, and, as things turned out, it was also to be the last. He stayed with us for the best part of two and a half or three hours. He did most of the talking. It seemed to be one of those days when he was in the mood for talking. He spoke about his memories of Gjirokastra. He gave such a vivid description that I felt the entire neighbourhood was parading before my eyes. He then turned to the long-established families of Gjirokastra – he had such an interesting way of describing things and had wide knowledge on many subjects. Then the conversation shifted to the topic of Moscow. Contrary to what one would expect, he did not embark upon a long ideological monologue; it was more like a factual, semi-literary narration of his stay in Moscow while the great communist gathering was taking place. He told us about his anxiety, uncertainties, and the meetings he had had with all of them. He described how the famous dinner in the Kremlin went. A large part of what you find in my novel is based on what he told me that day. The atmosphere I described in one of the chapters, 'Dinner in the Kremlin', is in essence what he described.[1]

It goes without saying that Kadare was summoned at the dictator's request. His wife was simply the messenger – a phone call from Hoxha would have had a whole different meaning. Aware of Kadare's plan to write a novel and convinced of his talent, Hoxha must have been intrigued and allured by the thought of becoming a character in the writer's forthcoming novel. Kadare was truly surprised by the meeting. Contrary to what he had expected, there was no mention of the party, there were no political slogans or clichés, and Hoxha appeared totally different from the man Kadare had thought him to be:

> The conversation was quite intellectual in substance. Not a single political slogan came out of his mouth during the three hours I was there with him. This was unheard of – to speak with a communist chief and not hear anything political, nothing whatsoever [...] My wife and I discussed it later, because she was present as well. As we were making our way home, our reaction was, 'How odd! He said nothing about communism, absolutely nothing.' Nor did he mention the party, the revolution and such things. The only topics were Gjirokastra and Moscow. When I left, he gave me some books as a present – a copy of Zacharie Mayani's book on the origins of the Albanian language and the complete works of Balzac.[2]

His relations with Kadare were among the most complicated the dictator had with anyone of note living under his dictatorship. However, the meeting of March 1971 was the first and the last between them. To the day he died, in April 1985, Hoxha never had another one-to-one encounter with the writer.

The novel on Albanian–Soviet relations came out early in 1973 under the title *Dimri i vetmisë së madhe* (The winter of great solitude). It had a strange fate. No sooner had it been published than a vociferous campaign of criticism was unleashed against it. Kadare was accused of defeatism and, even worse, of making Enver Hoxha appear side by side with some very unsavoury characters, such as street thugs, women of loose morals and so on. And of describing Albania as 'solitary', which was simply unforgivable. Kadare's condemnation seemed a done deal. In communist societies, such campaigns were invariably prologues to much more sinister punishment. The first step was already taken: the novel was banned, withdrawn from circulation and all unsold copies were 'turned into cardboard'. But as people were waiting for the inevitable, the

tide turned. At a plenary party meeting in Elbasan in May 1973, exactly two
months after the campaign against Kadare had been unleashed, Enver Hoxha
rose in Kadare's defence. This was completely unexpected. Hoxha called the
novel 'problematic' but not so problematic as to be totally rejected. He said
Kadare was a talented writer and that the book just needed some revising to
be improved. Hoxha had thrown Kadare a lifeline. Kadare's revised version
was published a year and a half later, with minor changes and a new title,
Dimri i madh (The great winter).

Between 1975 and 1985, the year of Hoxha's death, Kadare had many other
ups and downs. One thing remained constant – he was considered to be a
bourgeois and probably a French agent, an assumption based only on the fact
that his books were popular in the West. These were not just casual rumours
discussed by people over coffee. Bashkim Shehu, the son of Mehmet Shehu,
prime minister of Albania at the time, recalls how his father had told him in
no uncertain terms not to be seen in Kadare's company because Kadare was
a 'prejudiced man and an agent of the bourgeoisie':

> Kadare was suspected to be an agent. When I was arrested, they asked me
> about him in one of my interrogation sessions, namely whether my father
> had established links with the West through Kadare. Kadare used to travel
> to the West. They got nothing out of me with this line of questioning
> and eventually gave up. But the Sigurimi knew that Kadare was against
> the regime; I could feel that clearly in the interrogation room. They were
> virtually certain that he would end up in prison. Later I met one of my
> interrogators and asked him why they insisted so much on Kadare at the
> time. He said that proceedings had been initiated to lock him up, but then
> the case was either closed or suspended.[3]

An eventual arrest was in all likelihood stopped by Hoxha himself. Kadare's
Sigurimi file had no less than 1,280 pages in four volumes, by far the bulki-
est of any public figure in Albania. It was full of trivial information, mainly
tip-offs by Kadare's colleagues, criticisms of his writing style or reports of
conversations between friends, in which Stalin or some of the Albanian party
leaders had allegedly been made fun of.

In her memoirs, Nexhmije Hoxha described how her husband lost his temper with Kadare on several occasions and often said that the writer was 'throwing a wrench in the works' of the party, but he still came to Kadare's defence at critical times. Of course, in the final analysis, it must have been Hoxha who protected Kadare and the latter makes no attempt to deny it. However, in a TV interview he gave later, Kadare asked the obvious question 'Who did Hoxha protect me from?' and the answer was of course: 'From Hoxha himself.' Kadare did offer another possible explanation for Hoxha's ambivalence. The communist leader must have felt flattered by the way he was portrayed in *Dimri i vetmisë së madhe* and was reluctant to punish Kadare. By punishing Kadare, he would inevitably thwart the publicity he got from his cameo role in the novel, which, by all accounts, he seemed to have thoroughly enjoyed.

When asked about the issue by the author of the present book, Kadare explained: 'Relations between a great writer and a dictator are complex and difficult to fathom or explain. The reason is that both of them are tyrants in their own way, but in this confrontation, the dictator is the fake tyrant.'[4]

In his youth, Hoxha was known for his egotism and his desire to be the centre of attention all the time. This trait was invariably mentioned by people who knew him then, as was the other facet of his egotism – his lethal jealousy. The smallest and most trivial things could arouse his unforgiving wrath, which sometimes assumed frightening proportions. For instance, in one of his diary entries from the war, Hoxha lambasted Mustafa Gjinishi for being 'kowtowed to' by the English because he spoke the English language, while the others, 'who spoke French', were being ignored!

Aurel Plasari, one of the most distinguished personalities of Albanian culture today, had just finished his secondary studies at the time. Son of a family with a 'bad biography', he was not allowed to pursue his university studies after finishing secondary school. He had always stood out as a bright student who knew several foreign languages, although today he brushes off the suggestion that he was an 'excellent student'. He prefers to cite his school report, in which his teacher wrote: 'Aurel achieves maximum results with minimal effort.' But he had a major problem – his father, Anastas Plasari, a pioneer of the Albanian communist movement from the 1920s, had had

several brushes with Enver Hoxha during the war, which had led to the latter
issuing several consecutive orders for his liquidation. Although Aurel's father
managed to survive, his life under the regime was fraught with unending
hardships. After serving two years in prison between 1946 and 1948, he was
temporarily rehabilitated, only to get another conviction and revocation of his
civil rights, which led to his total exclusion from public life and condemned
him to the life of a manual labourer until his retirement. Aurel Plasari decided
he would fight for his right to go to university and started knocking on the
doors of various party officials. Although his father had committed no crime
and was largely the victim of the political intrigues of the 1940s – and was
even fully exonerated by the court – Aurel still had to declare in his school
application that his father was 'an enemy of the people'. The young man
decided to make a last-ditch attempt – he sent a letter to Hoxha complaining about the officials who were denying him the right to pursue higher
education. He was convinced he was entitled to it, firstly because he had the
required marks and ability, but also because he had already published three
or four major literary translations. At the time, Aurel Plasari had no idea that
Hoxha had once issued orders for his father's liquidation. Anastas Plasari's
children learned about this only after the Central State Archives decided to
make most of its documents available to the public. To everyone's surprise,
the dictator did respond, albeit not directly. In an interview many years later,
Aurel recalled the moment:

> It must have been 1980 or 1981. At the time I was a junior copy-reader
> for Spanish at the Mihal Duri publishing house. One day I made up my
> mind to write a letter to Enver Hoxha, 'Comrade Enver', to complain
> about being denied the right to pursue higher education, and especially
> to complain about the public officials who had so rudely slammed their
> doors in my face. I was young, but had already translated three or four
> books of world literature, which I still consider to be a modest achieve-
> ment, though at the time I overestimated their importance. I remember,
> for instance, that I complained about the deputy prime minister, Manush
> Myftiu, etc. My father knew nothing about this; in principle he was against
> anyone writing to Enver, he had made it very clear: no complaints and

no asking for any favours. We only learned about Enver Hoxha's orders to kill ('purge') Anastas Plasari in the 1990s, when the documents of the CPA were made public; by then my father was no longer alive. Father had never mentioned anything of the sort to us; he never let slip that his differences with Enver had reached such a point. Now I understand my father; he was being cautious and trying his best to protect us from harm. Had I known then what I know now, I would have never had the courage to write to the 'leader'. But I belonged to a generation born and bred in other times; I truly believed that injustices could be put right, that rights could eventually be won if one did not give up on them. I belonged to a family which had contributed to the liberation of the country; my father's sister had laid down her life during the war, in Korça, and two uncles were executed in a German concentration camp in Prishtina, etc. I thought it was a complete outrage that I was denied the right to pursue higher education![5]

Asked about whether the letter produced any results, Aurel Plasari explained:

There was no official response as such, of course, but my name did appear on the list of students admitted to the university. In 1982 I was working as a proofreader for the literary journal *Nëntori* when one of the heads of the Union of Writers and Artists summoned me to his office. 'I hear you wrote a letter to Comrade Enver,' he said. 'Yes,' I answered, and then, with the blissful innocence of youth I added: 'but I have not received a response yet.' He couldn't believe his ears. 'What response did you expect? Now you will either get to go to university or you won't... ever.' And then he added, 'A copy of your letter has come my way and Comrade Enver has written on the margin: 'This young man's father was our ideological opponent, but the party never said that his children should be treated this way.' I stood there, speechless, while he continued in a benevolent tone, 'Now you know how careful you have to be, you are a clever young man.' These last words and the manner in which they were uttered are imprinted in my brain. I realised that the future would be fraught with danger and that being extra cautious was a precondition for survival. I never forgot those words and I don't believe I ever will.[6]

What was it that made the dictator do what he did? According to Plasari:

> The only explanation I can think of – enlisting the help of Freud – lies
> in the pathological meanderings of the dictator's mind. The execution
> orders he had issued in the past were still lurking in the corners of his
> subconscious. He was probably thinking of the day of 'reckoning' when
> those orders would come back to haunt him. Who would believe that
> such orders ever existed if the son of the man himself would consider the
> dictator his 'benefactor'?[7]

Kristo Frashëri crossed paths with Hoxha again 20 years after he had been
sent off to the Peza partisan unit with the note, 'Dangerous individual, keep
an eye on him; at the least sign of wavering, execute him! Enver.' At the
time Hoxha and Frashëri were just two of the 200-odd founding members of a fledgling CPA, almost completely unknown among the people.
Twenty years later, the situation had changed radically. Expelled from the
party in 1942, Kristo Frashëri was lucky enough not to end up in prison and
managed to survive by keeping a low profile and becoming a historian. He
never discussed politics with anyone and had given up his youthful ideals
of 'equality for all'. Enver Hoxha was now Albania's uncontested leader – a
strong, ruthless leader revered like a demigod. The two men met quite by
chance, in a theatre foyer, one day, in spite of Kristo Frashëri's efforts to
remain in the shadows:

> My last encounter with [Enver] was in 1962, at a conference. Enver Hoxha
> gave his keynote speech in the 'People's Theatre'. During the break he
> came out to the foyer and began shaking hands with people. Hard as I
> tried not to catch his eye, he spotted me and began walking over to where
> I was standing. He asked me how I was. He must have sensed my unease,
> because he said, 'Come join us, do come!' And then he added, 'I have been
> following your work; history is perfect for you'. I knew better than to feel
> relieved by that remark – he was not to be trusted. It was not unusual for
> him to pat someone on the back and be nice and friendly to them on the
> eve of a deadly blow.[8]

Fortunately, nothing happened to Frashëri as a result of this encounter. In fact, Hoxha's words were construed as an endorsement that cemented his position as a historian and researcher. He never met Hoxha again and was never tempted to re-enter politics, not even after the 1990s, when the 'Hoxha threat' was removed by virtue of the dictator's death in 1985.

Like any other dictator, Hoxha had his whims and erratic moments. Those who were close to him described how, when travelling by car in Tirana or another town, he would peer through the window to see whether he could recognise anyone from his youth. In his memoirs Hoxha mentioned that he once saw Zef Mala, the purged leader of the Shkodra Communist Group, walking in the street. On another occasion he caught sight of Sejfi Vllamasi, a former prominent politician of the first half of the twentieth century, in Fier. A pioneer of Albanian independence, member of the assembly from 1921 to 1924, minister of industry and a staunch opponent of King Zog, Sejfi Vllamasi was forced by the latter to flee to Italy, France and Austria, before returning to Albania in 1939, when he collaborated with the Italians. Hoxha had some very scathing remarks to make about the 'shrivelled old man' who 'had managed to secure a pension after years of tending pigs'.

Hoxha could not resist putting down anyone who was anyone in the Albanian politics of his young days, and Vllamasi was one of them. In his book *Kur u hodhën themelet e Shqipërisë së re* (*Laying the Foundations of a New Albania*) he described how, while visiting the village of Gosa near Kavaja, he was taken to see the pigpen. An old man approached him and addressed him as 'Mr Hoxha'. This was Sejfi Vllamasi:

Near the road there were some buildings which looked like whitewashed sheds. I asked the farm manager: 'What are those sheds?'

'That is the pigpen,' he answered.

'Let's go and have a look,' I said […]

Our laughs attracted the attention of a shrivelled old man dressed in rags – apparently the watchman – who came and greeted me:

'How are you, Mr Hoxha?'

I turned to see… and who do you think it was? Sejfi Vllamasi! He was working as a watchman at the pigpen.

'In spite of everything,' I told him, 'the Communist Party gave you a job and now, for the first time ever, you are earning your living by the sweat of your brow.'

'Yes, sir, Mr Hoxha, but I'm getting too old to work now!'

'Well, of course you are old; these are the laws of nature. What can you do – you must feed yourself and, in order to feed yourself, you must work.'

'You are right, Mr Hoxha,' Sejfi answered, 'but if it pleases the government, would it be possible for me to get a pension?'

'A pension? What for? For not having ever done an honest day's work in your life? For being a member of the Fascist Council or for not being a patriot? Under Noli you voted for the reactionaries; then you spent your time gambling in exile while the people here were suffering, and then you returned with the Italians and became their henchman. Is that why you think you deserve a pension?'[9]

And a little further:

I saw him one other time, a few years later, on the roadside in Fier. He was almost bent double. I enquired about him and was told that he now received a small pension, after working as a watchman at the pen.[10]

Hoxha's narrative about this encounter and how he humiliated and tormented the broken elderly man contains at least two untruths. First, Vllamasi was not asking for an undeserved pension. On the day he met Hoxha, he was over 80 and still working, as the years of service before the advent of the communist regime did not count towards his pension. He had been 61 years old when the communists came to power – by then he had had a long career as an MP, government minister and medical doctor. When Vllamasi died in semi-internment, at 92 years of age, he was receiving a pitiful pension. Hoxha also lied when he said that he met Vllamasi by accident. Just before his visit to the village of Gosa, word had reached him that Sejfi Vllamasi had finished his memoirs – a voluminous work written over several decades. He had sent the manuscript to the Institute of History, with a short accompanying note: 'Please find enclosed my memoirs about events that happened and how I remember them. Keep them and use them if you wish. I did not want to die without giving them to you.'[11] After receiving a memo from Ramiz Alia on the matter, Hoxha became very curious. He asked to see a copy of the memoirs and after reading them he reportedly enquired about Vllamasi's whereabouts and what he did for a living. A few months later, he 'happened' to pass by the place where Vllamasi was working as a watchman. Vllamasi's memoirs, published in 1994, were very complimentary about King Zog. At an advanced age and with the benefit of hindsight, Vllamasi had revised his position on the king. This was probably what fuelled Hoxha's anger and prompted him to take the time and trouble to seek Vllamasi out and humiliate him in person.

Hoxha's eagerness to be in the loop about every minute detail of other people's lives was manifested in other ways as well, as his personal secretary, Haxhi Kroi, testifies. Known for his unquestioning loyalty to Hoxha, Kroi wrote voluminous memoirs himself, which were published only in part. Although of little documentary value, they do shed light on the way Hoxha operated. He would look through all the letters that were sent to him, whatever their subject matter – complaints, requests for favours or denunciations. Generally they contained nothing of real substance and took a considerable amount of his time; so, after his heart attack, his wife, possibly in agreement with Ramiz Alia, decided to limit the number of letters that were passed on to him. Hoxha immediately noticed that the volume of letters he received had decreased considerably and was told that this was done to spare him any unnecessary strain. He ordered that things be returned to the way they were, that is, that everything addressed to him be seen by him personally. Reading about the trivialities, jealousies, quarrels, passions, and trials and tribulations of other people seems to have been one of his favourite pastimes.

Hoxha's moments of whimsical magnanimity were often made known by his collaborators. These stories became urban myths and helped create the image of a kind and generous man who would spare a thought for anyone and who inspired love and understanding. Bashkim Shehu, son of former prime minister Mehmet Shehu, is probably the man who made the most interesting observation about this aspect of the dictator's behaviour. A smiling and liberal Hoxha made a much more favourable impression on a young

and naive Bashkim Shehu than his own father, whom he regarded as a strict
and rather intransigent figure:

> Up until a certain age I looked up to [Enver Hoxha]; he was a man of
> such great charm and a very good communicator, always very witty and
> pleasant. He had a lot of charisma, especially in the eyes of a child like me
> who had no notion of what power was. When I was 16 or 17, I was acutely
> aware of the differences between him and my father. I always thought that
> my father was old-fashioned; yes, he had the right ideas, but at the same
> time he was very conservative because he belonged to a different genera-
> tion, whereas [Hoxha] seemed more open-minded, more enlightened.
> My first major disappointment with Enver Hoxha was at my father's
> sixtieth birthday party. There was a dinner party to which members of the
> Politburo and some figures from the Presidium of the People's Assembly
> were invited. The speech that Hoxha gave at the dinner was a forewarning
> of the witch-hunt that would follow after the fourth plenary meeting. I
> was distraught and disappointed by it, and was not able to sleep all night.[12]

Thus, there was another side to Hoxha, his true dictatorial self which was
capable of sending chills down other people's spines. This is what Bashkim
Shehu said in his 2004 interview:

> I felt scared every time I saw the man. I did not trust his eyes, it felt like
> they pierced my soul – I was afraid that he would somehow manage to
> penetrate my thoughts. I tried to change them, but felt that no matter
> how hard I tried to suppress them, he would still manage to get into
> them somehow.[13]

Todi Lubonja describes a similar feeling in the following extract from his
book *Nën peshën e dhunës* (Under the weight of violence):

> Enver Hoxha would sit at the head of the table, like a pasha. He always
> reminded me of Ali Pasha – as I had seen the latter portrayed in a con-
> temporaneous etching – smoking his hookah. Now and then Hoxha's

mind would wander off. He seemed oblivious to his surroundings; his mind was on other things, probably on one of the evil plans that his diabolical mind was forever hatching [...] He would usually discuss major power-related issues in the Politburo and plenary meetings, after he had mulled them over in his mind. In those meetings he was totally alert, all eyes and ears, and ready to strike ruthlessly. He would hurl outrageous accusations, products of his evil and unbridled imagination. [Hoxha's] thinking was guided solely by hatred and total disregard for the truth. As far as he was concerned, the truth was his prerogative and served one purpose only, to accuse.

Of the speeches and reports written by Hoxha between 1956 and 26 June 1973, not a single one ever impressed me for the right reasons. I remember some formidably aggressive speeches, which he would give every time someone was to be expelled from the party. It was there that he unleashed his entire arsenal as an omnipotent leader: rhetoric, intrigue, insinuations, psychological pressure, intimidation, provocation and, invariably, some filthy language for good measure. On these occasions he would appear as the man of many faces that he was – at one moment he would play the part of a father who suffered for his prodigal son, and his eyes would well up in tears; the next he would loom as a henchman wielding an axe.[14]

This two-faced behaviour was Hoxha's trademark – often bordering on the schizophrenic, at times winsome, but almost always deadly.

Another story that circulated in Fier and Vlora in the 1960s is illustrative of his character and ruling style. Isuf Hysenbegasi was an otorhinologist who had been Hoxha's schoolmate at the Korça *lycée* and later went to university in Italy. They were close at school, after which their paths parted. Hysenbegasi was an outstanding student and returned to Albania with a degree in medicine, soon becoming one of the best-known physicians in his field. But he was not allowed to exercise his profession for long. In the wake of the war he was arrested and sentenced to ten years in prison. The only charge made against him was that he originated from a wealthy family in southern Albania. His Italian wife and daughter were sent back to Italy while the doctor spent many years in forced labour camps. According to documents made available in recent years, his punishment was ordered by Enver Hoxha and carried out by Koçi Xoxe. Dr Hysenbegasi himself knew this, or at least had guessed as much. He could not think of any reason why, other than Hoxha's jealousy of his academic success, or perhaps an old grudge about some youthful remark. One day in 1960, when he had been called to work at Fier hospital, he heard that Enver Hoxha had come to the hospital for a visit. Hysenbegasi decided to leave the building by the rear entrance to avoid any chance of running into Hoxha. But it was not meant to be. For security reasons, Hoxha entered the building through the rear entrance. The two former schoolmates suddenly found themselves face to face: one a former political prisoner with no residence permit for that town and practically homeless, the other the all-powerful leader of the country. The doctor froze in his tracks. Years later he told how he was lamed with fear, his knees were trembling and scenes of labour camps and prison cells began flashing before his eyes. He did not know how Hoxha would react, but he knew that he had spent ten years in prison because of him. What happened next surprised everyone. Hoxha recognised him and uttered one of those phrases that people close to him knew so well: 'Why, look who we have here, Dr Isuf! How are you, doctor?' Then Hoxha did something that took everyone by surprise – he put his arm round his old 'friend's' shoulders and started asking him about his life. He did not mention the prison, and the doctor, now almost numb with astonishment, did not say anything about it either. The local authorities observed the scene in amazement. Normally the doctor was not allowed to work at the hospital – he had been called in to help with treating the wounded after a recent earthquake in town. In normal circumstances he would be working on a farm, like many other former prisoners. Noticing the surprise of the people around him, Hoxha added: 'The doctor was not on our side, he was not in favour of the communists, but I can assure you, this man always loved and will always love Albania.' Dr Hysenbegasi said that Hoxha welled up, as if he were pining for the good old days. Before leaving, he stopped once again and said: 'Doctor, you know my address; any problem or difficulty, you know you can write to me.'

Dr Hysenbegasi never did. But this chance encounter that could have been fatal to him proved to be his salvation. On his return to Vlora, he was asked to report to the local party offices, where he was told that he would now be allowed to exercise his profession and was handed the keys to a small flat in the centre of town. To the day he died in the late 1980s, he was at a complete loss as to the reason behind Hoxha's dramatic change of heart and goodwill gesture, or Hoxha's motives for destroying his life in the earlier years.

Equally inexplicable is the story of Jusuf Vrioni, another distinguished Albanian intellectual, whom Hoxha had never met in person. Vrioni, son of a former prime minister and foreign minister of royal Albania, scion of one of the wealthiest Albanian families, and a former tennis and ice-hockey champion, went to school in Paris and lived in Paris, London and Rome, before returning to Albania in 1944. In fact, he was only visiting Albania for a few days, after which he intended to join his family in Italy and then go back to France. But during his visit the war ended and the borders were closed so that Vrioni was unable to leave the country. His social life consisted of dinners with members of the French and British missions in Tirana. This was a strong enough reason to arrest and sentence him to 13 years in prison. After serving the sentence he was offered a job as an Albanian-to-French translator. His translations of the novels of Ismail Kadare were received well in France, which led to him being transferred to the department for the translation of Hoxha's works. One day he found on his desk a copy of one of his translations of Hoxha's works, signed by Hoxha himself under a short 'thank you' note. Vrioni felt flattered, but his moment of glory did not last long. The same evening he was summoned to attend a party meeting where 'Comrade Vrioni' was reminded not to forget his background and the fact that he had served 13 years in prison.

Vedat Kokona, Hoxha's old friend from Korça, Paris and their teaching years at the *lycée*, had a similar story to tell. Kokona's life under the communist regime was full of trials and tribulations. In addition to being banished from Tirana several times, he was also dismissed from his job as a teacher for 'incompetence'. He managed to find a job as a translator at a publishing house where he had also published a novel, after years of being banned from creative writing. Kokona was at a meeting of the Union of Writers and Artists when he found himself face to face with Hoxha, as he recalls below:

During a break between the sessions of a long meeting, I saw [Hoxha] coming in my direction, shaking people's hands on the way. I was right in the corner, behind Shadan Toptani and Vehbi Skënderi. My fear was that he would pass by and ignore my presence, which would have had horrible consequences for me. I rejoiced like a child when he exclaimed, 'Why, look who we have here, Vedat!' He shook my hand (what a great honour for me) and congratulated me on the novel I had written. At that moment, the faces of his 'courtiers' – who hated my guts – beamed. On 7 August 1963, my fiftieth birthday, I even received a card from the Union of Writers and Artists.[15]

Numerous such stories illustrate Hoxha's duality of character – they all follow the same pattern of him meeting old friends and remembering old times, after which he would become nostalgic and benevolent for old times' sake – quite a departure from the heartless character he was known to be. He could afford to be nice to people who were no longer a threat. To him they were all losers who were resigned to their fates and who recognised his triumph, and instead of shouting 'off with their heads', he suddenly became magnanimous. He 'pardoned' them and was generous enough to let them exist on the stretch of land where he was the sun. Had they threatened his power or authority in any way, they would have gone the way of all the others who were purged in the mid-1970s.

19

The Medical Team

Dr Fejzi Hoxha reported to Enver Hoxha's adjutant, a colonel, only a few minutes after the latter had sent word to him via an officer of the national guard. It was August 1948 and the problem was not Hoxha but his mother, Gjyle, or Aneja, as everyone used to call her. The two Hoxhas had been friends since their youth and during the prewar years, and had kept their friendship even later. There is some speculation that they were distant cousins, but this has been denied by the two respective families. In his youth Fejzi Hoxha was also briefly involved in politics, but not on the side of the communists. His name was on the list of the participants of the Mukja meeting, but at the end of the war he appears to have joined partisan forces. It is not known how Enver Hoxha 'forgave' him for this, but apparently he did, and Fejzi became the dictator's doctor of choice and the two would even spend time together. Fejzi Hoxha was Enver Hoxha's personal physician for many years, after which he became part of the team of physicians that treated the dictator until the day of his death. He was probably the only doctor with whom Enver Hoxha had normal conversations, almost like a close family member.

On that August day in 1948, the doctor, who had been called on a completely unrelated emergency, was let in on some disturbing information about the prime minister's health. Nexhmije Hoxha told the doctor that her husband was always thirsty, drinking water all the time, and was constantly craving for sweets. She also said that he had gained a lot of weight in the past few months and his excessive thirst was accompanied by frequent urination. Dr Hoxha immediately recognised the symptoms – his childhood friend and prime minister of the country, by now a semi-obese 40-year-old, was suffering from advanced diabetes.

This was Hoxha's first major health problem. In the 41 years he ruled the country he was treated for many other related conditions, including heart problems. His sedentary lifestyle, his chain-smoking of up to 50–60 cigarettes a day, and the daily stress and pressures he suffered, greatly undermined his health. According to Dr Isuf Kalo, a clinical specialist in diabetes and Hoxha's personal physician for many years, Hoxha received treatment for his diabetes in several Eastern European countries:

> He went to the Soviet Union, to the Kremlin. It was normal practice at the time that leaders from other countries visiting Moscow would go for a check-up at the Kremlin clinic. I think he also went to Czechoslovakia. One of the physicians who treated Enver Hoxha was a certain Dr Pogroszewski, a distinguished Russian physician who applied the most up-to-date treatment methods.[1]

The Soviets were very willing to help – they sent one of their best physicians and a nurse to take care of the Albanian communist chief. In the meantime, Albanian physicians were trained and an Albanian nurse was attached to the Russian team in a sort of internship programme. Dr Fejzi Hoxha, formerly a general practitioner, also specialised in the treatment of diabetes and monitored his patient closely. After the break with the Soviet Union, Hoxha could not be treated in Eastern European clinics any longer, so the Central Committee decreed the establishment of a so-called 'Special Clinic', which was set up in the Bllok. The best physicians in the country were called to work there and Dr Paul Milliez would often travel to Albania from France for consultations. Dr Isuf Kalo remembers:

> Milliez was a well-known consultant to many world personalities – well known not only in France, but also internationally. His first contacts with Albania had nothing to do with Enver Hoxha's health. As a friend of Albania, he had contacts with the Albanian embassy in Paris. He had also treated Fiqirete Shehu and was close to the Shehus. We

consulted him, discussed the medical history and symptoms with him, but that was it; Hoxha was never seen by Milliez. They did meet, of course, but not as doctor and patient, although Milliez was aware of his medical history.[2]

Dr Milliez was chairman of the Franco-Albanian Friendship Association. An old friend of de Gaulle, renowned member of the French resistance and state secretary for health, Milliez was a distinguished political figure. From 1967 he became part of Hoxha's medical team and visited Albania regularly until 1985, when the Albanian leader died. It was Milliez who recommended which consultants should be engaged in the treatment of Hoxha and the other senior leaders, such as Mehmet Shehu and Hysni Kapo. In his memoirs, published in Paris after Hoxha's death, Milliez responded to comments about his involvement with the regime:

I was only exercising my profession. I knew that the regime there was a Stalinist one; I knew Enver Hoxha was a dictator. But I was not able to change the political regime of that country. What I could do was treat some of its leaders. This was my duty as a physician. I never thought of it as moral [endorsement] of a totalitarian regime.[3]

Of course, the local medical staff played the key role in Hoxha's treatment. Dr Isuf Kalo explained later that Hoxha had a devoted nurse, who took care of him 24 hours a day and seven days a week:

He had an excellent nurse, Kostandina Naumi; I am sure I have never seen a nurse with such total devotion and dedication. She carried her duties out rigorously – diabetes requires a strict regime and monitoring of the health, nutrition and medication of the patient, which she did in the best way possible.[4]

Kostandina Naumi's role, although not publicly acknowledged, must have been decisive in maintaining the dictator's health. It is not known how she became so close to the Hoxhas, but the fact is that she was one of the three people outside Hoxha's family whom Hoxha trusted most in his life, the other two being Sulo Gradeci, head of the dictator's security detail, and Fahri Bufi, his male nurse. In a 2007 interview, cardiologist Ylli Popa described how important and tricky it was to make decisions about the treatment and medication of such a high-profile patient. Every batch of medicine was prescribed only after thorough consultations among various physicians. The medicines were purchased by trusted agents of the Sigurimi working in Western countries, and then locked in the family's private pharmacy. They could only be removed from the cabinet with the authorisation of nurse Kostandina:

> The medical team decided what medication would be administered. The drugs were purchased by a different group of people, which included members of the Sigurimi who then brought them into the country. The drugs were immediately stored in the family pharmacy. The family had a very capable and trusted nurse who was completely devoted to Enver – and she was the only one who had the keys to the pharmacy. Her name was Kostandina. It was she who gave the shift nurse the drugs to be administered to Enver. She had everything under her strict control.[5]

After the Special Clinic was set up and staffed, a special medical team was set up to look after Hoxha and his health. He was the first of the leaders to set the trend of 'personal doctors'. Isuf Kalo, a specialist in diabetes, trained in China and France, who worked at the Special Clinic, was called by Hysni Kapo one day in late 1960:

> Hysni Kapo summoned me to his office. When I arrived, Dr Fejzi Hoxha was also there. He said, 'The party has decided to entrust you with an extremely important task. You will be personally responsible for the health of Comrade Enver and his family. Listen, you must work honestly and to the best of your ability, and the party and people will reward you for it.' At the time, I was only 31 and was stunned. I felt like a mountain had just landed on my shoulders.[6]

According to Ylli Popa, who became a member of the dictator's medical team in the mid-1970s, the entire team did not have more than ten members at any one time. The majority of them were cardiologists:

> Fejzi Hoxha was the head of the team. Then there was Nikolla Shurbani, a cardiologist and head of the department of cardiology at the hospital, who was on the team for as long as I can remember. Isuf Kalo was the family doctor. Then there were others who joined.[7]

Nikolla Shurbani, a former founding member of the CPA and a friend of Qemal Stafa, had known Enver Hoxha since 1941.

After 1960, Hoxha was occasionally seen by Chinese doctors, for example in 1973, when he had a heart attack. His medical record was also examined by some of the best French doctors. Whenever his medical record was sent to foreign consultants, it never included the real name and age of the patient, as seen in this report from autumn 1973:

> The 65-year-old patient has been suffering from diabetes mellitus for 26 years. Height 184 cm. Average weight until about 3–4 years ago: 87–8 kg. In the past 2–3 years: 84–5 kg. Smokes about 50 cigarettes a day and leads a very sedentary life. Does not have any symptoms or problems with his cardiovascular system, but a 1967 ECG Double Test (incomplete) revealed coronary insufficiency, with over 2 mm depression in the left precordials; ECG at rest had normal readings. Until early 1968 he was on insulin therapy between 40 and 60 ml.
>
> In the summer of 1967 the patient suffered a haemorrhage caused by diabetic retinopathy, which led to loss of sight in one eye for a few days. The haemorrhage was reabsorbed within a short period of time; traces of retinal microaneurysms and occasional microhaemorrhages. A second haemorrhagic episode led to temporary loss of sight in one eye in 1968. From that time, in addition to the therapy for diabetes, the patient was treated with eye drops and occasionally with citrus flavonoids. In mid-August of the present year, during an after-lunch stroll, he felt epigastric and retrosternal pain, which forced him to sit down for a few minutes.

One August afternoon, as he was strolling in the garden, he felt a light retrosternal pain which subsided by itself; no medication was administered. On the same day, around 1 a.m., while reading in bed, he felt retrosternal pain in the form of a contraction, which lasted for 1–2 minutes, accompanied by some sweating and an accelerated pulse rate up to 82 BPM. On 16 October 1972 the patient had long tiring meetings all day and had to take trinitrine twice, because of a feeling of pressure in his chest. On 17 October 1972 he felt tired and was slightly pale.

On 18 October 1972, as he was lying in bed, the patient reported feeling epigastric and chest discomfort, but then felt better when he stood up.[8]

Enver Hoxha's health improved temporarily, but in October 1973 he suffered a major heart attack on his birthday. Earlier, he had felt some chest discomfort after midnight, as he was lying in bed in his summer house in Durrës. The doctor who attended to the emergency after 13.00 realised that the stomach discomfort and nausea were not symptoms of a problem with his digestive system, but of a serious heart condition.

After the heart attack, the medical team expanded to include some of the best clinicians in the country – not only those who worked at the Special Clinic, but consultants from the university hospitals as well. Ylli Popa, a cardiologist who had graduated in Romania and had received further training in the Soviet Union, was immediately brought in as a consultant. Later on, he spoke about his first meeting with the Special Clinic team, also attended by Nexhmije Hoxha, the dictator's wife:

I was told to go to the Special Clinic and Nexhmije Hoxha briefed me on Enver's health. I remember that she always used to refer to him as 'Comrade Enver'. I thought it strange for a wife to address her husband like that, as if she were a household employee. I was part of the team for 12 years; I started after he suffered the heart attack – a really serious one. Myocardial infarction is always dangerous in its early stages. Enver's condition was slow to improve. At that time he was living in Villa No. 4, a governmental residence, next to the Republican Guards. The family had moved there temporarily while the new house was being built. The whole medical team would stay there 24 hours a day.[9]

A team of doctors was also brought in from China, sent by Mao Zedong, including Chairman Mao's and Ho Chi Minh's cardiologist, who had graduated in the United States. It is said that Hoxha viewed the Chinese team with a measure of distrust. Eventually the Chinese team left and Hoxha's health was entrusted to Dr Milliez from France and to the Albanian team of cardiologists. The medical team continued to stay at government Villa No. 4, next to the Palace of Brigades, until a day in April 1974 when Hoxha stepped out of his house for the first time after the heart attack. In the previous four months he had been housebound and received only his closest friends and collaborators; all other communication went through his wife. Her husband's heart attack was a turning point in Mrs Hoxha's life and her role in the family. From that time on she wielded much more power and influence, not only on her husband, but also on the Albanian political scene.

To be the dictator's physician was anything but easy – it was like walking a tightrope every minute of the day. What happened to Stalin must have added to Hoxha's paranoia and lack of trust in doctors. Ylli Popa, who was Hoxha's cardiologist for 12 years, related an incident which shook him profoundly and filled him with fear and distrust of others. Many years later, in response to a question as to whether it was scary being Hoxha's physician and if he ever felt frightened, Popa replied:

> I was terrified. Once, as he was having one of his episodes, we decided to check his heart functions on the ECG and placed the electrodes on his chest. Every heartbeat was recorded and displayed on the monitor. We were not in the same room with him; the wires were long enough to be hooked to the monitor in the next room to his. I liked that arrangement – when Enver was asleep, I could see from the monitor that he was calm in his sleep and I followed his coronary activity closely. The room where we had set up camp happened to be his library, and there were some wonderful books there. Usually, after the machine was hooked up, we would sit by the monitor all night. There were some apples on a plate and a thermos

with hot coffee, to help keep us awake. I liked looking at the books in the
library. One night I was the only one on duty and was browsing the shelves
when a title in French – the memoirs of Lavrentiy Beria, the former Soviet
interior minister – caught my eye. When I started leafing through the
pages, the book opened at a heavily underlined page towards the middle
of the book. I became curious – I wanted to see what sort of things Hoxha
found interesting. What I was about to read came as a total shock to me.
Skimming through the lines, my eye caught the name of Lukomsky, my
former professor in Moscow. I started reading more carefully. This was
Beria speaking: 'I asked professor Lukomsky to come to my office and
told him that this was an extremely confidential matter which he could
not discuss with anyone. I also told him that from the moment he left my
office, his every move would be under close supervision and he would be
followed everywhere. Lukomsky looked frightened, he became extremely
pale and sweaty – a natural reaction.' Beria had asked the doctor, 'Do you
know of a drug that can cause a surge of blood pressure?' Stalin was known
to suffer from hypertension. 'This is not something I want from you now,'
Beria added. 'Come back in a week, and bring that drug, if it exists.' And he
reminded the doctor once again that he would be under close surveillance
all the time. Lukomsky had no choice but to give him the drug. And he
did. In the period after World War II, Stalin and the other members of
the Politburo would gather around a large table and have dinner together,
watch World War II movies, listen to music, talk about the war and the
battles, etc. 'One night,' Beria continued, 'I was sitting next to Stalin, on
his right. Molotov was on his left. His wine glass had been barely touched.
[Stalin] excused himself to go to the bathroom, I think. I looked around,'
Beria continued, 'and when no one was looking, I took the phial out and
poured the contents into the glass. Stalin came back, sat down and raised
his glass, saying: Let's drink!' At a certain moment, he turned to Beria and
asked, 'Did you put something in this?' Beria was terrified, but kept his
composure and said, 'No, Comrade Stalin, how could I do such a thing?'
Then Stalin said, 'I was just kidding,' and drank the wine in one go. When
the maid went to give him the medicine the next morning, Stalin was
lying on the floor, next to his bed, already in a coma.[10]

This chilling discovery was too much for Ylli Popa to keep to himself. The next morning he told his colleague, cardiologist Petrit Gaçe. The latter was equally terrified: 'Oh my God, we are in real danger.'[11]

Hoxha's personal physician, Isuf Kalo, revealed the following in a 2010 interview given to the monthly magazine *ONE*:

> At university we were taught how to care for patients who were ordinary people. The Bllok inhabitants were not a normal species. Within the Bllok, the Hoxhas were even more special and delicate, while our main patient was a veritable god, an *Übermensch*. Nothing we learned at school could prepare my colleagues and me for treating an *Übermensch*. Physically, the Bllok people were just like everybody else – they would get sick and need treatment, but exercising one's profession with them occurred in a bewildering environment, full of unknowns and surprises.[12]

Fortunately, neither Ylli Popa nor any of Hoxha's other physicians suffered any consequences, although, as another member of the team noted, they were in a state of constant fear.

Hoxha kept regular notes about his health and his relations with the physicians. An entry for 21 August 1981 says: 'I'm not feeling that well. The doctors are getting on my nerves; they won't let up, as if I've got a thousand diseases. It's they who are sick, not me. They are overzealous.' Four days later, on 25 August 1981, he wrote:

> During the night everything was calm after Dr Isuf's visit.
> At 11.00, everything was fine, no concerns.
> At 17.00 I went out for a walk and I did not feel any discomfort. My pulse was normal, 63–4.
> At 19.30 I felt a bit unwell, but nothing to be worried about. Pulse rate: 61.

Hoxha was adamant that no one outside his close circle was to know about his health, not unlike many other political leaders in the world. His personal assistants took special care that Dr Kalo, who accompanied Hoxha everywhere, would not be seen by the public and arouse curiosity. When Hoxha became seriously ill and was dying, the public was not informed. The few people who happened to learn that Hoxha was in a coma, and were careless enough not to keep it to themselves, were arrested. One of them was an officer who had learned about Hoxha's condition from a Bllok chauffeur. The officer was arrested, brought before the court and sentenced to ten years in prison for the crime of 'agitation and propaganda against the people's power'. By the time he was sentenced, in 1986, Hoxha had been dead for several months.

The Special Clinic, established in the early 1960s, was kept under close supervision. No one, except a handful of authorised people, had access to the medical records of Hoxha, Shehu and Kapo. Isuf Kalo recalls: 'Hoxha's medical records were considered top secret. They were dealt with in the strictest confidence; the Special Clinic was created specifically for that purpose.'[13]

In the State Archives there is another 'top secret' document of the Sigurimi. This is a letter bearing no date or protocol number, probably written by a senior communist leader. It deals with the strict security measures taken in relation to an operation Enver Hoxha was to undergo on his arm, probably in the late 1970s. The letter said the operation was 'top secret' and a foreign surgeon – no name provided – would come from abroad to perform it. It was to take place at the Special Clinic, and measures were to be taken for it to be cleaner and better sterilised than ever and for the purchase of special equipment from Western countries, a list of which was attached. The list was in French, which leads one to think that it was requested by the French orthopaedist who was to perform the operation.

Among other things, the file for the operation contained a letter sent by the Central Committee to the minister of the interior. It suggested the names of two French surgeons and demanded information about them. The minister responded with a letter which approved only one of the names. After authorisation by the Politburo, possibly by Hoxha himself, the doctor was contacted by the Albanian authorities for arm surgery, and no other information was provided about the name or position of the patient. The surgeon was offered a handsome remuneration, travel fare and all expenses paid for his three-day stay in Tirana. The surgeon set off for Tirana 48 hours after agreeing, and thereafter was under constant surveillance by the Sigurimi.

From a memo sent by Sigurimi agents to the interior minister, we learn that the doctor worked at the Pitié-Salpêtrière Hospital in Paris. The doctor, who had come to France from one of the French colonies, seemed to be a reliable man, with no political affiliations, and was married. He had one small defect: he was reportedly having an affair with a nurse working at the same hospital. The name of the doctor is not disclosed. There is no further information as to how the operation went and what became of the said surgeon. All that is known is that such practices were common during the communist years.

20

The Great Purges

In March 1973 a group of young people from Lushnja sent an open letter to the daily newspaper *Zëri i rinisë* (The voice of youth) expressing their profound dismay at the eleventh RTSH National Song Festival held in Tirana in December 1972. The festival was in fact a great success and was received with unprecedented enthusiasm in the capital, especially by young people. Organised in a new and more liberal atmosphere, different from anything seen until then in Albania, the festival was welcomed as a breath of fresh air in a country where everything was squeezed into the straitjacket of communist ideology. Everything about it was different this time: the lively and rhythmic songs emulated Western pop tunes and the presenters and singers appeared on stage in trendy, Western-looking outfits. The festival was not an isolated attempt at modernisation. In the couple of years leading up to it, Tirana and Albania had been giving off signals of a more liberalised society. People in the capital were now allowed to watch Italian TV channels. Men with long hair were 'tolerated'. Bands and singers playing in bars and restaurants were more daring with what they chose to play. A wind of change had begun to thaw the big freeze of the Chinese Cultural Revolution.

But all the hopes and expectations for an eventual opening to the West were brutally thwarted. The open letter to *Zëri i rinisë* was the first sign of the vicious campaign that was to follow. Todi Lubonja, Fadil Paçrami and a number of other liberal communist officials were swiftly dismissed from their positions and arrested. In Todi Lubonja's words:

Liberalism became something to be avoided like the plague. The first to raise their voices against any sort of liberalism were the traditionalists, mouldy conservatives, forsaken talentless people ready to stifle anything remotely novel or unfamiliar, but also the odd talented individual who jumped on the same bandwagon arguing that 'no one, no matter how talented and distinguished, can ever escape from the yoke of the political regime they live in'.[1]

The fourth plenary meeting of the Central Committee, held at the Palace of Brigades (the former Royal Palace), heralded the bone-chilling drama that was to follow. It was by far the most terrifying of all meetings in the series of plenary sessions that were held over the years to follow, with punishments to match. In his memoirs, Todi Lubonja recalled Hoxha's thundering speech and the accusations raised against him:

> The very palace was reverberating with the sound of his bellowing voice. It was as if he were speaking to an empty conference room. All the other Politburo members were bent over their desks, taking assiduous note of everything he was saying, yet not knowing what exactly it was that they were writing. Those who had spoken earlier in the meeting were trembling with fear – their speeches had been anaemic by comparison to the thundering anathemas Enver Hoxha was hurling at us. He was howling: 'You cosmopolitans, anti-nationalists, anti-socialists, anti-this, anti-that, anti…! You worms, you lowlifes! You belong in Moscow and Leningrad. Or in Paris, with the bourgeoisie and the capitalists! Or in Belgrade! We will crush you like worms; you are the dregs of society, the lowest of the low!'[2]

Lubonja and Paçrami ended up in prison, as did their families. Their punishment seemed extreme, but what happened to other protagonists of Albanian politics in the next few years was far more cruel and shocking.

In July 1974 the main leaders of the army – defence minister Beqir Balluku, army chief of staff Petrit Dume and another senior military figure, Hito Çako – were arrested. An expeditious trial was staged, at the end of which they were found guilty of participation in a coup d'état and sentenced

to death as 'putschists'. To this day no one knows what sins they had committed to deserve such punishment. They had always been known for their
unquestioning and unending loyalty to Enver Hoxha.

One curious thing about the execution of all the 'enemies from the ranks of
the military' is Hoxha's exemplary determination to keep the places they were
buried a secret. In his trial in 1983, former interior minister Kadri Hazbiu was
asked whether he knew where Beqir Balluku, Hito Çako and Petrit Dume
had been buried. He answered: 'I know the general area, but not the exact
place. I'm sure about this because it was I who gave instructions that their
remains should never be found, because these were the instructions I had
received myself.'³ Later on, when asked by the investigating judge whether he
had made any enquiries about the whereabouts of the graves of the 'putschists'
and 'saboteurs', Kadri Hazbiu responded:

> I remember I did. After the suicide of the traitor Mehmet Shehu, when I
> was defence minister, I spoke on the phone with the traitor Feçor Shehu
> and told him to go and see whether the bodies of the traitors executed
> in 1975 had decomposed yet. Sometime later, the traitor Feçor Shehu
> reported to me that they had opened the graves of two of the saboteurs
> that had been executed and buried in the Tirana area, and found that they
> had not decomposed yet. He told me that they had poured chlorine or
> acid – I can't remember exactly what it was – into the graves, to accelerate
> decomposition. We decided that their graves had to be reopened again
> after a certain period of time. This was because I wanted to exhume and
> rebury their remains after the flesh had decomposed, so that no one would
> be able to recognise them – that was the order I had received.⁴

This was neither the first nor the last of the macabre acts committed by the
communist regime and Hoxha personally. On at least two occasions, Hoxha
himself gave strict orders for measures to be taken so that Mehmet Shehu's
remains would never be found. The former prime minister was buried,
exhumed and reburied three times on Hoxha's orders. His hatred and obses-
sions, that extended even to the remains of the people he had executed, are
among the most incomprehensible aspects of those years of terror.

A total of 461 professional soldiers were arrested at the same time as Balluku, including 54 officers – the Albanian People's Army, a force most loyal to Enver Hoxha, received the most deadly blow it had suffered since its foundation in July 1943. Campaigns against the army and the Ministry of the Interior continued in the years to come. In 1974, several other arrests were made: Lieutenant General Muhamet Prodani and Major General Halim Ramohito were interned in Roskovec; Lieutenant General Sadik Bekteshi was interned in Sheqëz near Berat; and Major General Abaz Fejzo was sent for 'physical re-education' to a farm-machinery-repair workshop in Gramsh.

The campaign against the military showed no signs of abating. In May 1975 another wave of arrests followed. This time the targets were 'saboteurs of the socialist economy', including deputy prime minister Abdyl Këllezi and ministers Koço Theodhosi and Kiço Ngjela. The first two were sentenced to death and executed that same year, while Kiço Ngjela was sentenced to imprisonment and only released in 1991.

The next of kin of the convicted 'enemies' were banished to remote places; their adult sons were also imprisoned. Other relatives were either dismissed from their jobs or demoted, depending on what positions they held. Some decided to denounce their disgraced relatives publicly, in order to save themselves and their children from any further repercussions. Following the arrest and conviction of their spouses, many women and men were indeed forced to seek a divorce and publicly denounce the father or mother of their children as an enemy.

Between 1976 and 1978 the political situation seemed to calm down somewhat. Hysni Kapo and Mehmet Shehu remained the two most important people after Hoxha. It was clear that one or the other would be the dictator's successor – at least that was what people believed until the summer of 1979, when Hysni Kapo, who was holidaying in Pogradec at the time, was suddenly taken ill with severe pains in his back and stomach. As the doctors failed to agree on a diagnosis, Enver Hoxha decided that Kapo be sent to Paris for tests and treatment. Hoxha was not known to be particularly in favour of any senior leaders travelling abroad for treatment, but on this occasion a feeling of foreboding prompted him to make that decision.

Hysni Kapo travelled to Paris, where he was diagnosed with pancreatic cancer. Enver Hoxha was still in his villa in Pogradec when he received the secret message informing him of Kapo's condition and the grim prognosis. Kapo did not have long to live. People close to Hoxha remember how, upon receiving the message, Hoxha walked out of the house, visibly upset and agitated. He probably needed some air. Or maybe he wanted to reflect on how a death announcement might disturb the balance of power in Tirana.

Enver Hoxha never saw Hysni Kapo again. All efforts to treat him, including a difficult operation in Paris, failed, and the third most important man of the regime died on 23 September 1979, at a clinic in Paris.

After Kapo's death, a swathe of rumours and speculations circulated that he had been poisoned or eliminated by the Sigurimi, on Hoxha's orders. These rumours seem to have reached Hoxha as well. His diary entry of 27 September 1982 describes a meeting with Vito Kapo, Hysni Kapo's widow:

Monday, 27 September 1982

I spoke to Vito Kapo and drew her attention to the fact that rumours were circulating in the country that Comrade Hysni Kapo did not die of cancer, but was liquidated. I told her, 'I am giving you a formal warning, because it was you who first came to me with the suspicion that Hysni might have been liquidated. I told you, on that occasion, that the causes of the cancer have not been discovered yet and there is no treatment for it – the best scientists in the world are working on finding a cure. All facts lead to the conclusion that Hysni was suffering from an incurable form of cancer.'

After the 1990s, rumours that Hysni Kapo had been liquidated began to circulate again. Dossiers were compiled and names mentioned, but they were not based on any solid evidence. What was published in the press and presented as 'evidence' was little more than speculation and rumour. The most likely, indeed, the only plausible version is that Kapo simply died of pancreatic cancer, which was diagnosed at an advanced stage and led to his swift demise. Hoxha played no role in it.

Hysni Kapo's death left a void in the Albanian political scene. Now Mehmet Shehu was the only successor in line. Prime minister of the country, senior member of the Politburo, a man fiercely loyal to Hoxha and known for his hard-line views and heavy-handedness in dealing with people, Shehu's position in the communist hierarchy seemed solid and secure. In 1980 he had more functions than at any other time in his career. The next in line after Shehu – Ramiz Alia, 14 years his junior and 17 years Hoxha's junior – was generally not taken as seriously. However, Alia had a secret weapon that consolidated his position considerably – his niece was married to Hoxha's eldest son.

The last time Hoxha and Shehu appeared in public together was on the podium of the 1981 May Day Parade. Cameras captured them in a comradely embrace, greeting people with their locked hands held high. The prime minister's precipitous end would be seen only a few months later, in early September 1981.

Demise of a Prime Minister

One day in August 1981, Mehmet Shehu was in his office at home when his son Skënder went to see him and announced that he was in love with a young woman whom he intended to marry. Skënder was the prime minister's middle and, by many accounts, favourite son. At the time, he was still studying in Sweden and the fact that he had not yet found someone to settle down with had reportedly been a bit of a worry for his father. Now he seemed to have finally made his choice. The object of his affections was a pretty young volleyball player on the first Dinamo team, several times champions of Albania. Her name was Silva Turdiu, daughter of Qazim Turdiu, a university professor who had graduated in France and was a well-known figure in Albanian academic circles. The Turdius had had it rough under the communist regime, as had many other families from Tirana who were traditionally anti-communist. Silva Turdiu's mother was a close relation of Arshi Pipa, a former political prisoner *célèbre* who had fled Albania after his release in 1956 and settled in the United States. Unlike other former political prisoners who fled the country, Pipa never stopped denouncing the Albanian communist regime in the West. He attended conferences and was often invited to speak in political programmes on Western radio stations, including Radio Free Europe and the Voice of America. Pipa worked as a professor at the University of Minnesota and published a number of articles and books on communism in Albania.

Mehmet Shehu was at a loss as to how to react to the news. He was really perturbed by what Skënder said about the girl's family and the words just came out: 'Of all people, did you really have to go and get involved with them?' Fiqirete Shehu, the prime minister's wife, had reacted in exactly the same way: 'Oh dear, why did you have to get involved with them?!'[1]

Mehmet Shehu did not give his blessing immediately. The next morning he asked interior minister Feçor Shehu for a detailed report on the young woman's family, including her behaviour and morals. The report was on his desk that same afternoon. In essence, there was nothing there that Skënder had not told him already. In fact Qazim Turdiu, the young woman's father, had himself written a letter with all of the same information and given it to the prime minister's son. The interior minister added that the girl's behaviour was impeccable, that she was a volleyball player on the Dinamo team and also on the national team. The interior minister himself had recommended her to the coach. The report went on to say that many eligible young men in the Bllok had an eye on her, including Kadri Hazbiu's son. This was the first time in his life that Shehu did not think of asking Hoxha's opinion. 'What would you do if you were me?' he asked the minister. 'I would come to you and ask you what to do,' was the answer.

Mehmet Shehu made his decision. In his auto-critique at the Politburo meeting he explained that he decided not to ask Hoxha because he did not want to disturb him while on holiday in Pogradec. According to the memoirs of Bashkim Shehu, Mehmet Shehu's youngest son, in his eagerness to see his middle son finally settle down, Mehmet Shehu, prime minister of Albania for 27 years, decided to announce the engagement that same week. Just a few months earlier, Skënder Shehu, by then in love with Silva Turdiu, had turned down a proposal for an arranged marriage to one of Nexhmije Hoxha's nieces. But this was water under the bridge now – and Mehmet Shehu decided to give his blessing to the union. Silva's father, Qazim Turdiu, paid a visit to the Shehus and the engagement became official on the last day of August.

No one knows why Shehu did not ask Hoxha's opinion on his son's engagement. Why did he rush things and go ahead with the engagement ceremony? Had someone else done the same thing, Shehu would have been the first to condemn the act. The explanation is probably very simple – although known for his political intransigence and heavy-handedness towards others, Shehu's weakness as a parent predominated over his political beliefs.

Nexhmije and Enver Hoxha were the first to go round to the Shehu's to pay a congratulatory visit. In his diary entry of Thursday, 3 September 1981, Hoxha wrote: 'Paid a visit to Mehmet and Fiqirete, to congratulate them on Neli's [Skënder's] engagement.' Bashkim Shehu, the prime minister's youngest son, who was there when the dictator and his wife arrived, reproduced the conversation in his book *Vjeshta e ankthit* (Autumn of angst) 12 years later:

> 'I know your father, Professor Turdiu,' Enver Hoxha said to Silva slowly, in his deep voice. 'He is a respectable man. Give my regards to him. I'm very happy that Mehmet went ahead with this engagement.'
>
> 'I, too, know your mother very well,' Nexhmije added. 'We went to the same school during the war. Give her my regards!'[2]

Seated between the two, little did the pretty young woman know that she had just manoeuvred herself into the eye of a terrible political storm. The engagement marked the start of a witch-hunt that was to lead to one of the most notorious crimes of the communist regime, against an entire Bllok family, and the liquidation of the prime minister of the time.

At Hoxha's insistence, the engagement was called off only eight days later. The two main leaders of the country, the dictator and his designated successor, met for three hours in Hoxha's study at his home. No record exists of what was said exactly, but part of the conversation can be reconstructed based on what Bashkim Shehu and Nexhmije Hoxha recounted in their memoirs. One of Hoxha's security staff, who was on duty that day, testified that Hoxha's unmarried sister, Sano, had said to some of the serving staff: 'How can Enver not be bitter, when even his closest friends want to take advantage of him?'[3] This passing comment, made shortly after the three-hour conversation between the two most powerful men in Albania, reveals a deep-seated resentment. Hoxha had perceived the engagement as an affront, or even worse, as a betrayal.

According to Isuf Kalo, Hoxha's family doctor, when the couple returned from their visit to the Shehus on 3 September 1981, a relative told Nexhmije Hoxha that the engagement had caused a lot of stir in town. The woman added that all this was because of the young woman's background. Nexhmije

Hoxha immediately called Sulo Gradeci and asked him to gather information about Silva Turdiu. By that evening the information was on her desk, together with a note that this was the same file that Mehmet Shehu had received from the interior minister a few days earlier.

Enver Hoxha must have been very surprised by the interior minister's notes and Shehu's course of action. He probably tried to make sense of what was going on. No one knows how sincere Hoxha's personal diary from those days is, but it does shed some light on his escalating anger against Shehu and the role other communist leaders played in fuelling it:

Tuesday, 8 September 1981

I spoke to Comrade Ramiz. He had learned about the engagement of Mehmet's son to Turdiu's daughter and told me about the many enemies [of the regime] that come from both sides of the family, the Turdius and the Pipas.

Friday, 11 September 1981

I called Mehmet from Korça to ask him about his son's engagement to a young woman from a family teeming with war criminals, some of whom were executed and others of whom had fled the country. The entire city is buzzing with the news, and I only learned this from other sources. Mehmet was fully cognisant of the facts when he gave his approval. This is a grave political error on his part. The transcript of my conversation with him is in my safe.

Saturday, 12 September 1981

Spoke to Mehmet about the tangled issue of his son's engagement. The transcript of my conversation with him is in my safe.

I called a meeting with the secretaries of the Central Committee, comrades Ramiz Alia, Hekuran Isai and Simon Stefani, to inform them of Comrade Mehmet's grave political error in allowing his son's engagement to a girl from the Turdiu family, and asked their opinion about the matter. Simon could not come, Hekuran condemned the act, as did Ramiz [...] I called Kadri and asked him whether he was aware of what Mehmet had done. He said that he had learned about it and added that there were a lot of things he could say about Mehmet's other son, Bashkim, and his wife, whose behaviour left much to be desired. People spoke ill of them.

Sunday, 13 September 1981

Spoke to Mehmet and Fiqirete about their son. Nexhmije was also present. The transcript of the conversation is in my safe.

Thursday, 24 September 1981

Spoke to Mehmet about the improper behaviour of his other son, Bashkim, and his wife, Marjeta, in public. These were reported to me by interior minister Feçor Shehu. Mehmet was shaken, of course, because of all these grave things happening in his family, and said that he would take measures.

Why did Shehu so eagerly rush to do Hoxha's bidding by calling the engagement off? It is difficult to say. The two men took the secret of their *tête-à-tête* meeting of 11 September 1981 to their graves. The transcripts that Hoxha mentions in his diary were not found in the Central State Archives, or in Hoxha's or Shehu's personal archives. They were probably removed from the safe by Nexhmije Hoxha after her husband's death. The conversation that holds the key to Mehmet Shehu's elimination and the rise of Ramiz Alia was never made public.

Recent revelations, however, have provided insight into what was discussed at that meeting and Mehmet's subsequent unease. Asked by his two sons why he decided to call the engagement off when he had been aware of Turdiu's background much earlier, Mehmet Shehu responded: 'But now this matter of Arshi Pipa has come up! It was not exactly how we thought it to be.'

What was it that Mehmet Shehu did not know about Arshi Pipa and what had he been told or shown? It was probably some document that lay at the heart of Hoxha's rancour and Shehu's demise. In 1973, as Hoxha was slowly recovering from his heart attack, Arshi Pipa published a satirical biography of the dictator, in which he alluded to the latter's homosexuality, as illustrated by these lines: 'Glory to your ass, oh dandy, / This is what explains it all.'[4]

Of course, the leaflet, which was readily available to all Albanian émigrés, must eventually have reached the counter-intelligence department of the Sigurimi. It is likely that they did not dare to give it to Hoxha. Or if they did, he did not pay much attention to it. But on 3 September 1981, as he was paying his visit to the Shehus, Arshi Pipa's file was retrieved from the archive of the Ministry of the Interior, 'at the request of the great one', as the Sigurimi used to refer to Enver Hoxha. This version of events could provide an explanation for Hoxha's growing bitterness towards his deputy.

By allowing his son's dubious engagement in complete contravention of communist norms and without the prior approval of the 'great one', and by allowing this rapprochement with a family of 'enemies' whose close relative had the audacity to attack Hoxha personally, Shehu had taken some liberties which could assume more threatening proportions if and when he became Albania's number one. It is not clear whether the engagement was the true reason or just a pretext for eliminating Shehu. But one thing that it did was to help reinforce the dictator's perception of Shehu as lacking loyalty. The covert animosity between Nexhmije Hoxha and Fiqirete Shehu, which sometimes would spill out into an all-out conflict between the families' security and serving staff, did not make things any easier for Shehu. If anything, it helped cement the perception that Shehu was in such a hurry to become number one that he was behaving as such while Hoxha was still alive.

One day in late September 1981, Enver Hoxha asked Isuf Kalo, his personal physician, to stay a bit longer after the routine morning check. It was just to give him the following instruction: 'If there's something about my health that you need to ask about or discuss with anyone, contact Ramiz! Understood?' The doctor's reply was: 'Of course, understood!'[5] After Hysni Kapo's death and until that day, his instructions were to speak to Nexhmije Hoxha and Mehmet Shehu. Now Mehmet Shehu 'ceased to be' and Hoxha placed his trust in Ramiz Alia. The latter corroborated the doctor's account in his book *Enveri ynë* (Our Enver).

The doctor, who by now was familiar with the way things worked in the Bllok, understood the message perfectly. From that moment, Mehmet Shehu ceased to be the designated successor and the slow, but steady, campaign for his elimination began to take its course. Shehu himself seemed unaware of the

enormity of what was going on around him. He who had been both a witness
and protagonist in the liquidation of many other former 'comrades' failed to
read the signs when his turn came. Or maybe he did, but was powerless to
act against the flow of events, as Bashkim Shehu, his son, wrote in his book:

> In the course of three and a half months, from early September to 18
> December 1981, Mehmet Shehu's career nosedived. He did nothing to
> fight the decline. What he did was the opposite of what he should have
> done: self-blame and constant self-criticism, total surrender to the will
> of his friend, torturer and murderer, Enver Hoxha.[6]

Shehu's decline in those autumn months of 1981 was painfully played out in
the public eye. Hoxha kept playing the diabolical cat-and-mouse games he was
so good at. By the end of September, the prime minister noticed for the first
time that his subordinates, until then unquestioningly and humbly obedient,
had become rebellious and disrespectful. TV reports of public events which
he attended, such as the Korça party conference, edited him out. Hoxha had
not spoken to him for days.

On 16 October 1981, the day of Hoxha's birthday, Mehmet Shehu was
told that his wife Fiqirete need not visit the leader as part of the Politburo
delegation as she had always done; she could go as part of the delegation of
the Central Committee of the PLA. As he was climbing the stairs of Hoxha's
house, Shehu noticed that Hysni Kapo's widow was there with the members
of the Politburo, the same thing she had done for years. But his worries were
soon dispelled by the way Hoxha welcomed him. An official recording of
the birthday party, which was not broadcast at the time, shows Hoxha being
extremely friendly and gracious to Shehu – there was a warm embrace and
Shehu was invited to sit next to the dictator, who often referred to him as
'my comrade-in-arms'. When Shehu made the birthday greeting 'May you
live long for the sake of the party', Hoxha replied: 'Both of us, together, dear
Mehmet. You too! And do take care of yourself. We are not as young as we
used to be and the party needs you today and in the days to come.'[7]

Shehu must have felt extremely relieved that day. Viewing the footage
30 years later and with the benefit of hindsight, one can feel the chilling

undercurrents whirling under the surface of the jovial party atmosphere. In the
space of just a few months, 12 people who were warmly embraced by Hoxha
that day were given extreme punishments: four were executed, one committed
suicide and the remaining seven would serve long prison terms. For many
of them this was their last encounter with the dictator, who saw them off
at the gate, with a smile on his face, even looking a bit sad to see them go.[8]

The documentary on Hoxha's birthday was never shown for the simple
reason that, by the time it left the cutting room, Mehmet Shehu had killed
himself and many of those present were either standing trial or already serving sentences. Hoxha could not be shown embracing people who became his
victims a few months later.

The prime minister's youngest son, who survived the ordeal, provides
insight into the events. Mehmet Shehu was being openly ostracised by his
comrades, which could mean only one thing – his fate had been sealed. At
the same time, Ramiz Alia, whom Shehu had hardly considered a rival in the
past, was being propelled into prominence. While he was shunning Shehu,
Hoxha was increasingly being seen in the company of Ramiz Alia, both in
the streets of the Bllok and in Vlora. In the midst of this atmosphere fraught
with angst for the Shehus, Hoxha made one of the surprising moves that
he was so well known for. At a time when Mehmet Shehu was practically
isolated and pressure was brought to bear on him to own up to and apologise
for his failures in front of the grass roots of the party and, to add insult to
injury, his subordinates were openly disrespecting him, Hoxha asked to see
Shehu's eldest son, Vladimir. For two hours Hoxha lectured Vladimir on his
father's contributions to the National Liberation War and the construction of
socialism. In the end, Hoxha asked Shehu's son to stay close to his father at
this difficult time – his father was tired and not getting any younger. Hoxha
wrote the following note in his diary:

Friday, 25 September 1981.
    I asked Mehmet's eldest son, Vladimir, to come and see me. I told him
that it was best if he did not move out and continued to live in a separate
flat under the same roof as his parents. There was nothing wrong with
moving out, of course, but considering Mehmet's condition and the grave

situation created in their family, I told him, 'It is best if you stay close
to him at this time of need; both you and we must help him overcome
this situation.' Vladimir replied that he would tell his father he was not
going to move out.

The message Vladimir took home gave rise to a sigh of relief in the Shehu
family, but this was nothing more than one of the games the dictator liked
to play with his future victims. Sources close to the Hoxhas say that he had
learned that Shehu's eldest son had had an argument with his mother and
he and his wife had moved out in protest. Hoxha was probably trying to give
the Shehus the false hope that his anger was directed at the culprit rather
than at the whole family.

Mehmet Shehu's decline was slow, not because Hoxha had any qualms
about striking at his friend, but because he was afraid of the power that the
prime minister had accumulated over the years. After the four-hour conversation they had at his house, Hoxha did not feel at ease in Shehu's presence
and security was stepped up. All other meetings between the two were held
in the office. At this time Hoxha's health problems resurfaced. His physicians
recall he had numerous problems related to stress during that time.

The frosty relations between the two men became evident for all to see at
the Eighth Congress of the PLA. On 17 December Hoxha called a meeting
of the Politburo to discuss Mehmet Shehu's case. On 16 December Mehmet
Shehu sought to speak to Hoxha on the phone but was not put through. He
wanted to seek Hoxha's assurance that the latter would help him 'rectify' the
error and that their relations would return to normal. Hoxha did not come to
the phone. Shehu was told that Hoxha was resting and he could try calling
back the next morning.

In fact, Hoxha was not at home when Mehmet Shehu called. On the
evening of 16 December 1981, the rest of the Politburo members were called
to attend an informal meeting at the Palace of Brigades. This only became
known 29 years later, in the summer of 2010, when a note made by a Sigurimi
agent was found, describing the extra security measures at the former Royal
Palace that night. It is likely that Ramiz Alia, Hoxha's future successor, had
a pivotal role to play in arranging that meeting. Only one member was not

present: Mehmet Shehu, the prime minister, who would be tried at a meeting the next day.

The sound recording of the 17 December meeting was found and played 20 years later. The minutes of the meeting, which circulated during the years of the communist regime and were eventually published in 1992, had been heavily redacted. The attacks on Shehu were fierce. They were mostly voiced by people of no significant political weight who rose to prominence at the Eighth Congress of the party – people the prime minister probably did not even know existed. Late at night, right before Hoxha was scheduled to take the floor, the meeting was adjourned to the next day. Shehu and Hoxha barely exchanged any words with each other and Hoxha left the meeting in the company of Ramiz Alia. 'Reflect on the criticism,' he told Shehu coldly.

These were the last words exchanged between the two men whose working relationship and personal friendship dated back to 1944. After serving 27 years as prime minister of Albania, Mehmet Shehu committed suicide in his bedroom that night. On the side table there was a letter with this note: 'To be opened by Comrade Enver Hoxha only.'⁹ The contents of the letter, very similar to the last letters written to Hoxha by Xoxe and others, remained unknown for over 22 years. Speculation abounded. Parts of the letter were read at the meetings of the Politburo and Central Committee the next day. The letter was reportedly full of accusations against Ramiz Alia and Kadri Hazbiu, but the full text was thought to have been lost. It was found in the archives of the Central Committee of the PLA and published in the press in 2003. Thirty years after Shehu's death, the letter clearly reveals a man who had decided to leave this world of his own accord:

Comrade Enver,

When you gave me your book *Kur lindi Partia* [When the party was born], the dedication written in your own hand read: 'Dear Mehmet, you were and are one of the glorious leaders of the party, always at the frontline of the battle, always ready to come to the defence of the people, our socialist homeland and the party that brought us up as revolutionary leaders, staunch communist fighters and dedicated servants of the people. The party and the people will be forever grateful for what you have done for them. Your closest friend in times of trouble and victory, Enver, 11 June 1981.'

I, your closest friend in times of trouble and victory, committed a political and ideological error recently by allowing the engagement of my son, Skënder, to the daughter of Qazim Turdiu, which I broke off after your just intervention. I explained the reasons that led to that error in my 39-page auto-critique of 12 November. I would not remove a single comma from that statement, because it is absolutely sincere. However, that statement was rejected by all who were present at the Politburo meeting of 17 November, and you called it an 'alibi' and asked me to reflect on all the criticism made by the Politburo members and to radically revise my statement, which you called an 'alibi', i.e. a lie and deceit.

Your note of 28 October 1981, in response to the draft auto-critique that I sent you to read, said that I should analyse my negative character traits, which would help me discover the true reason behind the error of my ways. You called them 'some negative traits of (my) character, which sometimes seep through the good work I do for the party, which I love and for which I would readily lay down my life'. Yes, Comrade Enver, I was always willing to give my life for the party if need be. And this is what I, your closest friend in times of trouble and victory, as you rightly called me, am doing now as a last resort, to give you, my teacher, my comrade, my brother, a chance to learn the truth.

I am giving my life for the party without hesitation and in full conviction that there is no other way left for me to defend the party. From whom? From that snake in the grass Iago and the Khrushchevs who managed, unfortunately for the party, to get close to you and pull you away from me, your friend in times of trouble and victory. Who are they (Iago and the Albanian Khrushchev)? It is for you to find out – they are known by all.

I won't remove a single comma from what I wrote and said to you, my comrade and Marxist–Leninist teacher and brother. But now that I am departing, I would like to tell you what I have not been able to tell you until now, because you never gave me the chance to tell you the truth about them. I am not killing myself; I am being killed by the scheming Iago, Koçi Xoxe's henchman and disciple, with his filthy intrigues and alliance with Khrushchev, whom you regard as 'sincere'. Both of them are working to dig a grave for socialist Albania. What Beqir Balluku and his gang were not able to do, will be achieved tomorrow by our Khrushchev, the man whom I heard with my own ears say, when we broke up with Moscow, 'Why, is it only we who are Marxist–Leninists?' Meaning that he did not agree with our break-up with the Khrushchevite revisionists. You might not believe me – that is up to you – but, as I was not given a chance before to tell you about the Iago–Khrushchev plot, I decided to do this now. Today they claim to be 'pure' communists, but if you are not around tomorrow, Khrushchev will turn his eyes to Khrushchevite Moscow [...] Comrade Enver, I made those errors for the reasons I presented in my auto-critique, and I do have shortcomings, but the allegations that I tried to 'rival' you, to put myself before the party, or other allegations that were made against me are not true. I never did that – that is a monstrous accusation I will never accept. In addition, my auto-critique was not an 'alibi', it was a frank statement. I worked all my life for the party, the people, and never for a 'position', 'fame' or as a 'strategist', nor was my intention to upstage Enver Hoxha, or to gain personal privileges. The gravest accusation made by Iago, Khrushchev and the others incited by them is that I made those errors because I put myself first, because I cultivated a personality cult, and because I wanted to gain prominence at the expense of the party. How can the battles we waged together against internal and external enemies be so easily forgotten? It was not you who called me an enemy; it was Iago, Khrushchev and the others, who accused me of putting myself before the party, practically calling me an enemy.

But, no, comrade Enver, I am not the enemy – the enemy is Iago. Do you remember when we were discussing Skënder's engagement in your study, where I came to get your advice about the political error I had made? I told you that the enemy has always tried to drive a wedge between us, and I mentioned to you Koçi Xoxe, Liri Belishova and Zhou Enlai? They never achieved their aim. Beqir Balluku tried to do the same, but his plot failed. But Iago has managed to do it this time. You can call me whatever you want, I cannot stop you! But I am giving my life for the party. My last wish is: protect the party and socialism from Iago and Khrushchev because if you do not, the country will be run by the Khrushchevites and that will be the end of socialism. If you disregard what I'm telling you about our Iago and Khrushchev, then it will not be my fault, my dear Enver, the responsibility will be entirely yours. I have done my duty in the only way that has been left to me – by killing myself.

Once again: protect the party from Iago and Khrushchev! Our party has quite a few other cadres who are loyal to it.

Long live our glorious party and its Marxist–Leninist course! Long live you, to ensure that the party will not be harmed by Iago and Khrushchev, two of the most dangerous plotters of all time!

Down with imperialism – especially American imperialism! Down with revisionism, especially social-imperialism (and Chinese revisionism)! Long live communism! Down with the reactionaries!

My last wish – take care of Fiqirete, my sons (including Skënder and Bashkim), their children and wives! You can say that Mehmet died 'accidentally' while handling his guns, if you think that it would be better for the party, or make up any other story you like. Even if you call me an enemy, I believe that time will reveal everything. The truth never dies.

I'm dying an innocent man. Albania's Iago killed me!

Mehmet Shehu
17 December 1981[10]

Shehu was obviously concerned about the fate of his family after his death, hence his last request to Hoxha, as his closest friend, to take care of them. None of that happened. Shehu's family was interned. His wife and two of his sons were arrested. The eldest son electrocuted himself, or was killed. The reaction to Mehmet Shehu's last will came on 23 December 1981, when Manush Myftiu, head of the Committee for Internments, and interior minister Feçor Shehu prepared a top-secret memo ordering the exile of the Shehu family to Belsh, near Elbasan. The initial internment term was for five years, to be reviewed at the end of that period, and contained the following conditions: they had no right to leave the area; they had to report to the police station twice a day; and they had to engage in forced labour in agriculture.

The memo appears to be quite lenient compared to another document discovered only recently. This was a list of questions given to the investigators conducting the interrogation of Fiqirete Shehu. The list was compiled by Enver Hoxha himself; it was even in his own handwriting. In fact, it was Hoxha who was conducting the interrogation from his villa in Pogradec. He did not seem to have any pangs of remorse whatsoever, although Fiqirete and her husband had been among his closest associates for many years. Indeed, the interrogation and torture sessions were even filmed, and Enver and his wife watched them in the evening on their VCR, as their daughter-in-law, Liljana Hoxha, revealed in an interview in 2007:

> On the day that Shehu went on trial we were in Pogradec. Everybody else, sons and wives, returned to Tirana to follow the trial from there. I couldn't bear those things. I mean, I was on Enver's side, but I did not condone the killing, I could not bear the thought of people being killed. I did not feel like watching the trial. I was alone that afternoon and I went to see Enver Hoxha, for whom I had great affection and respect. As I passed through the back door to enter the living room, I saw Nexhmije Hoxha sitting in her usual chair. Of course, Enver must have been there, too, but I couldn't see him. It would be a lie to say that he wasn't there, but I couldn't see him. On the TV screen I saw someone I recognised. It was Fiqirete Shehu speaking. I did not expect that and was horrified. I hid behind the wall – I was in complete shock. They were watching her trial. I was in tears. In the evening he asked to see me and I gave him the silent treatment. He asked me why I had been crying, and I replied it was because Sokol had left me there on my own and said he wasn't taking the whole family with him.[11]

Liljana Hoxha is the only one who has shed some light on the life of the Hoxhas in the days and weeks after the elimination of Mehmet Shehu and his family. In her account, 29 years after those events, she noted:

> I remember Mehmet Shehu's death; it's not that such things happened every day. The suicide story was not that convincing. I had my doubts,

but I could see that the others in my family were not affected much by it. Indeed, Nexhmije Hoxha went to her office as usual, left Enver alone at home, while Ilir and Pranvera and their spouses, who had never set foot in my apartment before, came over to me that day, to give me the great news that Mehmet Shehu had killed himself. It was absurd – they were smiling. Enver Hoxha hung his head low and never looked anyone in the eye for an entire year.[12]

No one can explain how Nexhmije Hoxha could bear to see her old friend being tortured or how Enver Hoxha could look at photos of Mehmet Shehu's dead son, whom he had held on his lap as a child. Hoxha had expressly asked the interior minister to send him the photos, which he later ordered to be archived.

In 1992 Fatos Lubonja was released from prison after serving a 17-year term. He had been jailed in 1974 and his father followed him to prison a little later. Lubonja's daughters, who were toddlers when he went to prison, were 20-year-olds by the time he was released. After the fall of the dictatorship, on one of his routine visits to Tirana prison as a member of the Albanian Helsinki Committee, he came face to face with Nexhmije Hoxha. She had been arrested in December 1991 and was still awaiting trial at the time. That day he asked Nexhmije Hoxha: 'I can understand what you did to your political opponents, or to your former collaborators, but why all the hatred against their children, whom you once held in your arms like your own?' Nexhmije Hoxha's only answer was: 'I did not know you were in prison.'[13]

22

The Final Purges

I t was around 08.30, and Enver Hoxha was having breakfast at home when Ramiz Alia arrived at his house. The date was 18 December 1981. A little earlier Alia had received a call from Ali Çeno, head of the prime minister's security detail, with the news that Mehmet Shehu had been found dead in his bedroom. It looked like he had shot himself with a Makarov pistol. The officer said that a letter, addressed to Enver Hoxha, was still lying on the night table beside his bed. The letter was folded up and a handwritten note on its back said it was to be given to Comrade Enver. Ramiz Alia had told the officer to inform the Ministry of the Interior immediately and not to let anyone touch the body. In all his interviews with the press in the years that followed, Ramiz Alia, the man who succeeded Hoxha as leader of the PLA, always presented the same version of events. According to him, it was Hoxha who spoke first:

> 'Let's conclude the meeting today. We'll hear what Mehmet has to say, and I agree with what you proposed.'
>
> We had proposed that he be given a warning.
>
> 'There's nothing to conclude. He shot himself,' I said.
>
> Enver froze. This took him completely by surprise.
>
> 'Why did he kill himself? What came over him?' he asked.
>
> He did not expect that; there had been nothing at the meeting to warrant it. All the comrades present expressed their opinions. Of course, he was criticised, but the conclusion reached was that he would only be given a warning.[1]

To the service staff on duty that day Hoxha did not seem surprised; if anything he seemed very edgy.[2] Subsequent events lead one to think that, if Hoxha was not Shehu's executioner, he must have known that Shehu would be eliminated that day. He immediately authorised the start of investigations. Defence minister Kadri Hazbiu arrived at the deceased prime minister's house 30 minutes after receiving Hoxha's call. His task was to retrieve the letter that the prime minister had left for Hoxha. At that early stage, when no one yet knew how the whole affair would be dealt with, Hazbiu had this to say to Shehu's family: 'His is a condemnable act.'[3]

Less than a year later, his visit to Mehmet Shehu's home, on Hoxha's instructions, would feature as one of the counts of the indictment raised against Hazbiu himself. According to the indictment, Hazbiu's visit to Shehu's house that morning was part of his attempts to hide the traces of a saboteur group they were both part of.

The Politburo meeting reconvened and proceeded normally, as if nothing had happened and Mehmet Shehu were still alive, until the early hours of the evening. Clips from the meeting were publicly aired for the first time in 2010. They showed the members of the Politburo sitting around a table, listening to Hoxha's recorded speech, when Hoxha entered the room. It was his shadow that appeared first, followed by a pale, death-like Hoxha wearing a light coloured suit and a heavy smile. The tape recorder was stopped and all those present in the room stood up and started clapping and cheering in unison: 'Enver Hoxha! Enver Hoxha!' He greeted them with the question: 'Who was speaking?' No one dared to speak. They were numb with fear and were probably wondering whose turn it would be next after the prime minister. Then Ramiz Alia's voice was heard: 'It was Comrade Simon.' Enver Hoxha made a nondescript gesture and began to speak slowly. It did not seem like an impromptu speech, nor was it one of those grand orations that he was known to burst into on similar occasions. He began to elaborate on his thesis that Mehmet Shehu had been an enemy of the regime and a dangerous agent all along, and that his suicide was a result of his failure to eliminate Hoxha himself. How did Hoxha learn, in those six to seven hours after Shehu's death, that Shehu was an enemy and an agent? How could one draw such a conclusion when the investigation was yet to take place? Why did Hoxha choose this meeting to divulge documents he had been keeping in his safe since 1964, which purported to show that Shehu had been an agent of the British Secret Intelligence Service (SIS) during the war? None of these questions ever received an answer. The reason is simple: the process of Shehu's liquidation had in fact started in mid-September and the whole affair unfolded as the chronicle of a death foretold. Mehmet Shehu was publicly condemned as a traitor and agent of several foreign countries, including the British SIS, the German Gestapo, the Italian ORVA, the French intelligence services, the Yugoslav UDBA and the Soviet KGB, followed by a campaign of *damnatio memoriae* of the dangerous 'multiple agent'.

On 18 December 1981, around midday, two Sigurimi officers knocked at the door of Behgjet Pacolli's room in Hotel Dajti, where he was staying. Pacolli, who would briefly become president of Kosovo in 2011, was in Tirana on a business trip as the representative of a Swiss textile firm. He had an important meeting at Tekno Import that afternoon, but the meeting was cancelled. The officers told Pacolli, in no uncertain terms, that he had to leave Albania immediately and go to Yugoslavia. He packed up his things quickly and went downstairs to pay for the room. There he noticed that the hotel was being emptied of all its guests. All foreigners who were on Albanian territory were given until 20.00 hours to leave the country. Only when he arrived in Titograd did Pacolli learn the reason behind his unceremonious expulsion – Albanian State Television had by then announced the news of the suicide of the Albanian prime minister. The news item consisted of a brief announcement: 'Prime minister Mehmet Shehu shot himself last night following a nervous breakdown,' after which a short obituary was read. The regular programme schedule followed, with an episode of *The Good Soldier Švejk*.[4]

The news of the prime minister's death came as a shock to all Albanians. If the dry manner in which the news was announced was anything to go by, it was clear that no one had heard the end of it yet. On 19 December defence minister Kadri Hazbiu sent an order to all military units instructing them to remove all photos of Mehmet Shehu from walls. In addition, all citations from his works had to be removed from walls and military training centres and any literature referring to him destroyed.

No one knows whether Mehmet Shehu really shot himself, or was shot by someone. It is unlikely that the question will ever receive a definite answer. Yevtushenko's saying about there being no such thing as suicide, only homicide, has a ring of truth to it. The only two people who could shed light on what happened to Shehu, Nexhmije Hoxha and Ramiz Alia, never spoke about it. The third, Kadri Hazbiu, suffered the same fate as Mehmet Shehu one year later, and took the secret with him to the grave.

On 14 January 1982, Enver Hoxha went to his office and sat at his desk for the first time after the prime minister's suicide. He did not call any of his secretaries to record his daily messages, diary entries or other notes. He probably did not want anyone to know what he was going to write down. With a shaky hand he began putting his thoughts on paper under the title: 'Some reflections on Kadri Hazbiu (notes to myself, as an aide-memoire)'.

In a matter of a few hours he filled some 25 pages, which can be summed up in the following key paragraphs:

Kadri Hazbiu is an upright man; I trust him. He is loyal to the party and has shown his loyalty at work and in his everyday life. He is kind and unassuming. I would like, however, to make the following notes about him.

[Hazbiu] did not like Mehmet Shehu and denounced him as an enemy, as we all did. Even as a member of the government, he used to stand up to Mehmet when he thought something was not right. He told me several times that he did not agree with some of Mehmet's decisions [...] It was Kadri who came up to tell me that Mehmet and Fiqirete had told the guards at the Durrës beach compound to leave their posts and Fiqirete had openly invited other holidaymakers to enter the no-go area. Kadri was against it and had told Mehmet what he thought about it: 'You cannot go around breaching Politburo decisions,' he said. Mehmet's answer was, 'OK, OK, but let's not exaggerate!' [...] He never liked Fiqirete much either; often not making the slightest effort to hide his feeling [...] Kadri was open, honest and kind to the comrades; if he had any criticism to make, he would make it openly. He had valid opinions and knew how to present them properly. When we decided to arrest Feçor Shehu, he hesitated a bit in the presence of Ramiz and Hekuran, saying,

'We need to be careful, we mustn't let Fiqirete Shehu lead us up a blind alley.' [...] He told me, 'We must keep an eye on Hekuran to make sure that he does not rush things. After all that's happened, the morale of the Sigurimi officers has taken a bit of a bashing.' I told Kadri that Hekuran is fair and prudent and that he always consulted me, and him, and Ramiz [...] Kadri's suspicions are unfounded; he has no evidence, no facts. Why is he doing this?! [...] Kadri told me that he had an uneasy conscience for having proposed Feçor [Shehu] for the post of interior minister, for not being vigilant, and for not uncovering any putschists while he was interior minister himself [...] I have always (three times) tried to reassure and encourage him by saying that his career at the interior ministry was long and fruitful, and people do sometimes make mistakes at work [...] I told him clearly that he should not lose any sleep over it: 'The party, the country and I trust you. It's time to roll up your sleeves as there is a lot of work to be done and the enemy may strike at any moment. We must be united.' The next day, Kadri came and told me that he wanted to hand his auto-critique in writing to me. I told him there was no need. He would not listen: 'Please, I want to read it to you.' He insisted and I listened as he read. 'O K,' I said, 'but I don't see any reason why you should read it out to the Central Committee.' There was nothing special in that auto-critique. Kadri is a good and hard-working comrade. I wrote all these things as an aide-memoire for myself.[5]

It is not known whether Hoxha retrieved his notes on Kadri Hazbiu in the autumn of the same year, or whether he added further notes to his file. The way events unfolded seems to point to the fact that Kadri Hazbiu had been targeted for arrest early in 1982, or even shortly after Shehu's suicide in December 1981.

Kadri Hazbiu was charged with being a member of Mehmet Shehu's 'anti-party' group. He was arrested in September 1982, right after a group of Albanian exiles led by Xhevdet Mustafa landed on Albanian territory from the sea. An eight-hour stand-off between Mustafa and Albanian security forces ensued in an area only 80 kilometres south of Tirana. It was claimed that Mustafa's mission was to liquidate Hoxha and that, not only was Hazbiu aware of it, but he was in fact the one who had commissioned Mustafa for the job. In addition, it was claimed that Hazbiu had been at Mehmet Shehu's house on the evening of 17 December 1981, before Shehu committed suicide, and that he went back to the scene the next morning, to destroy anything that could compromise their organisation. Hazbiu's protest that after the Politburo meeting of 17 December he had attended a birthday party together with 30 other people, who could certainly vouch for him, went unheeded. He also tried to explain that on the morning of 18 December he had gone to Shehu's house on Hoxha's strict personal order, to collect the suicide note – but that also fell on deaf ears. The defence minister explained that he had handed the note to Enver Hoxha in person. Hazbiu denied any involvement with Feçor Shehu's alleged 'enemy group'. However, Fiqirete Shehu was said to have confessed under duress that Mehmet Shehu, Feçor Shehu, Kadri Hazbiu and she were members of the same 'anti-party' organisation.

The charges in Hazbiu's indictment concerned things that went back as far as World War II. They included his relations with the Yugoslavs and the Soviets, and lesser charges, such as wiretapping his office at the Ministry of Defence.

Recordings from the plenary meeting of the Central Committee of the PLA which convened to condemn his activity contain dialogues like the following:

'Kadri, do you remember when you came to report to me, at the Dajti villa?'
　'Do I remember what, Comrade Enver?'
'Remember what year it was?'
'I can't remember exactly, probably 1967, or 1968?'
'Did I summon you, or did you ask to see me?'
'I don't remember, Comrade Enver!'
'Yes, you do; of course you do.'
'I really don't remember Comrade Enver.'
'This is the problem. That is the essence of your hostile activities!'[6]

Kadri Hazbiu was arrested and made to stand public trial. As with the others who were charged before him, little is known about the real reasons behind his fall. There was some speculation that after Shehu's death, Hazbiu was the Politburo member with the most superiority after Hoxha, and hence, an obstacle to Ramiz Alia's climb to the top. It was also noted that he had been at the head of the Ministry of the Interior – or the 'tenebrous power', as it was often called – for 30 long years. Whatever the reason, Hazbiu would indeed be an obstacle to Ramiz Alia's ascent to the top and that is probably why he ended up being executed by firing squad in 1983, alongside interior minister Feçor Shehu, health minister Llambi Ziçishti and a senior Sigurimi official, Llambi Peçini.

The reasons behind the execution of the health minister are equally obscure – he was not by any means what one would consider a prominent figure in the Albanian political establishment. Some alleged that he was sentenced to death for having expressed his surprise that no autopsy was conducted on Mehmet Shehu's body. According to others, he had looked at the body and said that everything pointed to a typical murder and not a suicide. However, these are only speculation and no one has been able to provide a reliable explanation, including Ramiz Alia, Hoxha's successor. When asked about it at an interview, he said simply: 'That was how things were done at that time, no one knows for sure!'[7]

Feçor Shehu's appearance before the bench was dramatic. The former interior minister and Sigurimi officer for over 40 years declared that he had been savagely tortured and forced to admit the charges, which he now denied. Aranit Çela, the presiding judge, only exclaimed sarcastically: 'You don't say! Really?' The judge's next caustic remark left Feçor Shehu at a loss for words: 'Are you trying to say you were unaware that torture is used in prison?' Feçor Shehu was charged with conspiracy against the regime as part of the same organisation as Kadri Hazbiu. The entire indictment against the man who had been interior minister for two years and a key Sigurimi figure for 30-odd years was contained in little more than half a page, compiled by general prosecutor Rapi Mino:

This enemy, with the cynicism of a mafioso, was actively involved in the preparation of all sorts of terrorist acts. His activities culminated on 16 December 1981 when, in his capacity as a Yugoslav UDBA agent, he

transmitted to super-agent Mehmet Shehu the order for the physical
liquidation of the first secretary of the Central Committee with a firearm.
Why exactly 16 December? It has been explained that Mehmet Shehu,
in collusion with his foreign masters, the UDBA and the CIA, took
the decision in December 1981 because at that time the Kosovo issue was
becoming too unwieldy for the Titoites to handle and the Yugoslavs were
left completely exposed before public opinion. In those circumstances, the
the proponents of Greater Serbia and the Yugoslav UDBA decided to
divert attention by causing trouble in Albania. Pursuant to orders issued
in Belgrade on the eve of the Politburo meeting, the Yugoslav embassy
in Tirana instructed Feçor Shehu, its agent and liaison person, to meet
Mehmet Shehu and convey to him the UDBA order that Enver Hoxha
had to be liquidated at all costs, even if he had to do it at the [Politburo]
meeting and then kill himself. Such was the pressure the UDBA was under
vis-à-vis the situation in Kosovo, that they decided to 'burn' their best card,
super-agent Mehmet Shehu. This is the reason why the defendant Feçor
Shehu went to see Mehmet Shehu at his home on 16 December 1981 to
convey to him the said orders from headquarters. He claims that on 16
December 1981 he never went to Mehmet Shehu's home. There is ample
evidence to the contrary. Defendant Xhavit Ismailaga handed him the
message containing the Yugoslav order, and the visit that terrorist Feçor
Shehu paid to the house of traitor Mehmet Shehu on 16 December 1981
was witnessed by another member of their organisation, Ali Çeno, and
independently corroborated by evidence provided by Besnik Kasa, Nikolla
Londo and Astrit Veliu. In addition, Nesti Nase testified that Feçor Shehu
and Llambi Ziçishti talked in his presence about the physical elimination
of Comrade Enver.[8]

Feçor Shehu and Kadri Hazbiu were executed together. With them, Mehmet
Shehu, who shot himself a year earlier, and Koçi Xoxe, who was executed
in 1949, Enver Hoxha had eliminated every interior minister that held the
ill-fated post between 28 November 1944 and 1982 – a record almost equal
to Stalin's.

23

The Years of Solitude

E arly in 1983, a new book by Enver Hoxha appeared in all the bookshops of the capital – *Titistët* (*The Titoites*), which focused on Albanian–Yugoslav relations. It was the latest in a series of 13 volumes of memoirs that Hoxha published in the last seven years of his life – an average of two books a year. With a total of 68 works published in his lifetime, he set a record that any prolific writer in the world would envy.

By this time, Enver Hoxha was the only remaining first-generation communist still standing at the helm of power. The rest of the founding members of the CPA had disappeared from the political scene; most of them had been executed or locked up in dank prison cells, victims of a regime they themselves helped build. Several others were interned in remote labour camps together with their families. Now and again Hoxha would enquire about them, as shown in the numerous Sigurimi records containing the note 'Files made available to the leadership'. He also received regular reports on the conversations his latest victims were having with other inmates in prison.

The dictator led a quiet and uneventful existence in his mansion in the Bllok, surrounded by his close family. His life had taken on a leisurely rhythm – he was wont to spend the winters in Tirana and the summers in his villa in Pogradec. The area in the Bllok where the Hoxhas lived had become more out of bounds than ever. The family had outgrown the one-time home of the Italian civil engineer Belloni, so they moved into a much larger, newly built residence next to it, designed by architect Sokrat Mosko and his young assistant Klement Kolaneci. The latter would soon become Hoxha's son-in-law. The new residence could be described as large, spacious and perhaps

functional, but not attractive, probably due to Mrs Hoxha's constant med-
dling in the project. The construction of the house was completed in 1973.
Although all furnishings and appliances were purchased and imported from
abroad – nothing produced in Albania at the time was up to standard – all
those who had a chance to look at the house after 1991 were disappointed by
the rather tasteless and modest interior. The apartments were laid with plain,
run-of-the-mill carpets bought from Standa, one of the lowest-end Italian
supermarket chains, a far cry from the Persian rugs of their former house
(confiscated from wealthy homes at the end of the war), or the hand-made
carpets produced in Albania. It is likely the latter were not even considered as
an option simply because they were 'made in Albania' and featured traditional,
'unfashionable' folk patterns. There was nothing remarkable about the other
aspects of the interior design either. The armchairs, comfortable-looking but
quite jarring compared to the rest of the furniture, were by no means the best
furniture money could buy at the time.

The only impressive objects in the entire house were the bookcases that
housed Hoxha's huge personal library. Built on-site by Albanian carpenters
in a 1930s style, and made of veneer shelving, they were a fine specimen of
Albanian workmanship. They contained Hoxha's numerous books – a wonder-
ful, albeit eclectic collection. Hoxha loved his books and every year he would
order new ones from the annual catalogues sent out by French publishers. In
addition, the French government had reportedly allocated a fund of several
thousand French francs to buying books for Enver Hoxha and three other
senior communist leaders in Albania. This was confirmed later by people
who had worked for the Albanian Committee for Cultural Relations with
Foreign Countries, although no corroborating documents to this effect have
ever been found.

Though he was reportedly able to communicate in Italian and understand
some Russian, French remained Hoxha's strongest foreign language. French
was thus his main source of information and contact with the rest of the
world. One can only truly appreciate the significance of this if one consid-
ers that the first and last time Hoxha visited a Western country as a head
of state was in 1946, and the last time he ever crossed the Albanian border
was in December 1960. His favourite newspapers were *Le Monde* and the

International Herald Tribune. Given that for many years there was only one flight a week to Tirana airport, by the time the newspapers reached him, the news would have been well out of date.

Records show that Hoxha's library boasted nearly 22,000 books. Most of them were on history, or biographies and memoirs of the world's greatest figures. He had also a number of autographed books, by writers like Paul Éluard or Louis Aragon, or political figures like Mao Zedong and Dolores Ibárruri. A closer look at Hoxha's book inventory, now preserved at the National Library, reveals a couple of curious facts.

Firstly, many of the books he owned were banned for the wider Albanian public, such as religious volumes and biographies of popes and saints. A second category, equally prohibited to the public, included books on secret cabals and plots against political figures, such as conspiracy theories on the assassination of President Kennedy, assassination attempts against Hitler, and so on. Their underlined passages indicate that Hoxha had more than a passing interest in such events. The third and rather more curious group was that of vampire stories. No one knows what gave rise to his fascination with vampires – he was probably exposed to them as a child in his home town of Gjirokastra. Another curious collection is that of detective fiction, consisting mainly of Agatha Christie murder mysteries.[1]

That Hoxha was a *lecteur assidu* is not in any doubt. Dr Ylli Popa, who was able to browse through the dictator's books during his long night shifts as the dictator's physician, has testified to this. On more than one occasion Hoxha's medical log contained entries that confirmed his love of reading: 'Complained of a contractive retrosternal stricture at around 1 a.m., as he was reading in bed.' The head of his security detail described an occasion when the family raised the alarm that 'Enver had disappeared'. Later that night he was found in the basement of the old house, where many of his old books were kept. Apparently Hoxha had lost track of time and continued reading well into the small hours of the morning, with a blanket wrapped around his shoulders.[2] (The security officers were probably baffled by these late-night escapades spent over what they thought were 'old and, by the look of them, worthless books'.) Judging by the great number of novels in his library, Hoxha seems to have had a strong penchant for fiction as well. Ismail

Kadare was convinced that Hoxha was very knowledgeable about fiction. However, for all the reading he did, Hoxha's own writing remained mediocre and unrefined throughout, lacking both in expression and style. This raises the academic question of whether the amount of reading one does has any direct bearing on one's own writing. In Hoxha's case there seems to have been no correlation. Liri Belishova, one of Hoxha's collaborators between 1949 and 1960 and a former member of the Politburo, recalled an occasion when they travelled together to Moscow by boat. According to her, each day Hoxha appeared on deck with a different book in his hand. She became curious and asked him how he was able to read so fast. Hoxha reportedly answered: 'Come on, Liri, who has time to read every page of every book! You get the gist by reading a few pages from the beginning, some from the middle, and then the ending.' No one can say whether Hoxha was speaking in jest or in earnest. Was it just a joke or was this indeed how he read his books? Whatever the case, he seems to have had a special relationship with books and they remained his second-greatest passion after politics. Perhaps the only other passion.

In 1983, Enver Hoxha's grip on power seemed stronger and more unquestioned than ever. He lived in his new house with his wife and two sons, Ilir, who had married Ramiz Alia's niece, and Sokol, who had married a secondary-school teacher, a clever young woman whose family was not otherwise related to members of the communist leadership. Hoxha's architect daughter, Pranvera, and her husband, himself an architect and son of a senior communist leader, also lived under the same roof. None of the children showed any interest in pursuing a political career. No one knows why Hoxha chose not to push them in that direction. Perhaps it helped him sleep better at night. By this time the dictator had several grandsons and granddaughters and he liked to go out for leisurely walks with them around the Bllok gardens, where other inhabitants of the exclusive neighbourhood were rarely seen.

His was a rather sad and solitary existence – there was no one he could discuss things with or pay a visit to. A few years earlier, long discussions over coffee at Mehmet Shehu's or Hysni Kapo's house were a regular evening ritual. But Kapo was now dead and Shehu had been eliminated. After the purge of his old comrades, the only one remaining from the 'old guard' was

Ramiz Alia, a full 17 years his junior and too young to share memories or recall the good old times when Hoxha came to power. Hoxha also missed the get-togethers at the Party House, the discussions, the jokes and the games of billiards he was so good at.

Nexhmije Hoxha, too, led a very lonely life. None of her former school friends and communist activists from the Queen Mother Pedagogical Institute were around any more. Liri Gega had been executed in 1956; Fiqirete Sanxhaktari (Shehu) was in prison; Drita Kosturi, Liri Belishova and Naxhije Dume were all interned in godforsaken corners of Albania, ostracised by the local communities and under strict reporting conditions. It was as if the memories of her youth had also ended up in prison cells and internment camps. Nexhmije Hoxha was completely alone.

However, the couple found a way to overcome their solitude. By this time Hoxha had grown completely uninterested in matters of state and country, and was focusing solely on his past. Understandably the past held much more appeal for him than the future. With Nexhmije as the main editor of his works, he embarked upon a major writing project, the outcome of which was a curious legacy of no less than 13 books of memoirs, including: *Vite të vegjëlise* (The childhood years), *Vite të rinisë* (The youth years), *Kur lindi Partia* (When the party was born), *Kur u hodhën themelet e Shqipërisë së re* (published in English as *Laying the Foundations of a New Albania*), *Rreziku anglo-amerikan për Shqipërinë* (published in English as *The Anglo-American Threat to Albania*), *Titistët* (published in English as *The Titoites*), *Hrushovianët* (The Khrushchevites), *Shënime për Kinën* (published in English as *Reflections on China*), *Dy popuj miq* (published in English as *Two Friendly Peoples*) and *Me Stalinin* (published in English as *With Stalin*). No other dictator in the world and certainly no other communist leader in the Eastern bloc ever wrote as many books as he did. Some leaders never even bothered to write their memoirs.

Hoxha was a unique case. His copious body of work was an attempt to impose his own version of history – a version rigged with untruths, but which no one dared to challenge at the time. Today in the Central State Archives one can find sheets from Hoxha's original manuscripts, with dense handwritten notes on the margins made by his wife. At the time, Nexhmije Hoxha was the director of the Institute of Marxist–Leninist Studies, an institution set up precisely for the purpose of publishing Hoxha's works. Some of her notes were rather curious. In some cases she demanded that the names of certain convicted people be redacted or 'skipped'. When this was not possible, as in the case of a letter addressed to partisan commander Mehmet Shehu at the time of the battle for the liberation of Tirana, the name was deleted and the new addressee became Hysni Kapo. The publication of Hoxha's works was a large-scale operation, involving a dedicated team of writers and many translators who translated his works into several foreign languages. Millions of dollars were spent on printing his works in foreign languages and in distributing them throughout the world. None of his books ever went to press without receiving Nexhmije Hoxha's seal of approval. In some cases, she also wrote the prefaces to them.

At the time of their publication, the only challenges to the version of events Hoxha presented came from abroad. On the one hand there were the Yugoslavs, who started publishing their wartime archival documents, and on the other there were the writings of former British officers who had served in missions to Albania during the war. Both sources contradicted many of Hoxha's claims and questioned his honesty; indeed, in many cases they held that Hoxha's versions of events were nothing but downright fabrications.

Around that time, the second TV channel in Yugoslavia began broadcasting a new history series with interviews of World War II protagonists who had known and collaborated with Hoxha during the war. In addition, they published documents from the Archives of the Central Committee of the CPY, including Nako Spiru's fateful letter on Hoxha, and letters that Enver Hoxha and Nexhmije Xhuglini had sent to Dušan Mugoša. It became clear that these documents were very different from the versions of the same letters published in Hoxha's memoirs.

Of the young British officers who had been to Albania during World War II, several went on to have impressive political careers. Among them was Julian Amery, who held a number of ministerial posts in Conservative governments. Many of those who had published their memoirs shortly after the war dismissed Hoxha's memoirs as ridiculous and presented a version much different from his, amply supported by Foreign Office documents.

Nonetheless, Hoxha did not care about what the rest of the world thought or said. He lived in his own gilded cage, revered as a god – an all-powerful and ruthless tyrant. The print runs of his books ran into hundreds of thousands of copies. School pupils and university students were forced to study them, and factory workers were obliged to attend additional classes where they read excerpts from the works. The opinions of people beyond Albania's borders did nothing to deter him. If anything, Hoxha's accusations against the Yugoslavs became even more vicious. Tito, his greatest rival, had died several years earlier, in May 1980, but the Albanian dictator still bore a grudge against him. People who were close to Hoxha at the time remember that for decades he was jealous of the popularity Tito enjoyed among the international community. The fact that Tito's funeral was attended by major world leaders was perceived by Hoxha as a personal insult.

By 1984 he must have felt the weight of the growing solitude and silence around him. Clips from privately filmed videos discovered 25 years after his death show a frail and solitary figure in the back of a Mercedes-Benz being driven around the streets of Tirana, followed by a camera car and a security vehicle. The stately car moved slowly through the streets of the rundown capital allowing him time to catch a glimpse of places he used to frequent as a young man. Then the car turned back onto the main boulevard and returned to his lonely den in the Bllok, from where he had ruled with an iron fist since November 1944.

While he was leading this dull existence, Albania was going through some extremely tough times. The country was totally isolated. Its entire border was draped with barbed wire and, in places, electric fences. Sixty-four per cent of the coast was declared a 'military zone' and was completely out of bounds. People who attempted to flee the country were usually killed on the spot. In the eyes of the regime, those who fled deserved to be killed. Anyone captured alive was charged with treason and given a prison sentence ranging from ten years to life imprisonment. In 45 years, only 6,000 people managed to get over the border. Some 1,200 people were killed, 94 per cent of whom were under the age of 30. Powerful jamming devices known as *zhurmues* (noise-makers) were installed all around the country to prevent Italian and Yugoslav radio and TV stations from penetrating into Albanian territory.

In 1984 Albania was the third-poorest country in the world, with an average per capita income of 15 US dollars a month and a population subsisting on meagre food rations. In some towns, a family of four would get no more than one kilogram of meat per month. Private property and private initiative were illegal. Peasants were not allowed to keep their own sheep or cattle and, from 1982, they were not even allowed to keep any 'private' chickens. Things got so absurd that, in 1989, when the regime acknowledged that collectivisation had got out of hand, it took three major plenary meetings of the PLA to discuss and decide whether to allow peasants one kid or one lamb per family. Large numbers of people in the countryside were on the verge of starvation and children and adults alike were suffering from malnutrition-related diseases. In the poorest villages, people were living on a diet of cornbread seasoned with a few drops of olive oil and a sprinkle of salt, or garnished with sugar sprinkled with water to make the sugar stick to the bread.

Tirana was the poorest capital in Europe. Its inhabitants lived in small flats, four to ten people to a flat of 50-odd square metres, barely fit for two. There were only 1,265 cars in the entire country. Franz Josef Strauss, then prime minister of Bavaria, was the first Western politician to visit communist Albania, in 1984. Strauss was on his way to Greece, accompanied by his two sons and a couple of friends, when he decided to request a transit visa to travel through Albania. Initially he was flatly refused, only to receive a polite invitation from the Albanian authorities the next day. Strauss entered Albania, where, contrary to his expectations, he was afforded a very warm welcome. This was the time when Albania was under a lot of economic strain and had been sending some subtle signals of a willingness to 'open up'. According to Sofokli Lazri, a foreign-policy advisor at the time, Hoxha considered West Germany to be Albania's best bet at establishing trade relations with a Western country – he was probably prepared to go as far as to accept some sort of economic protectorate. Given that France was known to support Yugoslavia, and Britain supported Greece, Germany remained the best option for Albania. However, Hoxha's vision of economic cooperation between the two countries was a one-way flow of unconditional economic aid to the country and no political concessions made by the regime. As these matters were being discussed in party circles, Strauss and his party were travelling from Shkodra to Tirana. Max Strauss, Franz Josef Strauss's son, still remembers the trip to Albania and Tirana as a sort of surreal nightmare:

> We reached Tirana on the third day. As we entered the town, we noticed a rather dramatic difference. At night, the town was in total darkness. There were no cars. We saw only a few trucks, most of them broken down. Some people were trying to repair them. They were East German trucks. There were no Western trucks at all. The roads were in a sorry state. I remember seeing statues of Stalin and Lenin. We went to a place where they had an exhibition of Albanian technology. When we entered, we saw an Enver Hoxha tractor. Our friend from Mercedes-Benz had a look at it and said, 'Yes, yes. We used to make these back in 1920.' The technology on display there was indeed from the 1920s. There were still manual telephone switchboards and the like.[3]

By mid-1984 Enver Hoxha's health took a turn for the worse. In fact, he had not been well since 1982. This is how Liljana Hoxha describes the last three years of his life:

> He would barely speak. For a year it was as if he was not there at all. He was always sitting with his head down, in total silence. On May Day 1982 he had his picture taken – it was such a lovely photograph, he looked so optimistic in it, but he was in a terrible state. It was his last May Day picture. He was practically carried to the podium. His condition worsened visibly day after day, until he died.[4]

The last time Enver Hoxha appeared before the public was on 29 November 1984, exactly 40 years after he first climbed onto a similar podium as the new leader of Albania and as head of the Provisional Government formed in Berat. It was the fortieth anniversary of the communist regime in Albania, by which time Hoxha had ruled the country for over half of its existence as an independent state. Given the state of his health, few people were expecting Hoxha to attend the festivities, but he did. A special lift got him up onto the podium and the camouflaged railings prevented him from falling over. TV and film crews were given special instructions not to take close-up shots. Hoxha gave his last speech, which, as it later transpired, had been pre-recorded. He just mimed the words. It was a short, exalted speech, laden with figures of speech and marked nationalist tones, a reflection of his policies over the years. Surprisingly, this time he did not dwell long on any of the ideological myths and dogmas he had force-fed to the Albanians in the 40 years of his rule. His speech ended with a message that could be considered his last political will and testament:

> In all the years under the leadership of the party, our most beloved Albania has been radically transformed; it has enjoyed so many achievements, such rejuvenation and all-round development as never before in the course of history. Let us safeguard all that we have achieved like the apple of our eye and take these achievements even further, so that future generations will inherit a stronger Albania, a Red Albania, red like the eternal fire burning in partisan and communist hearts and ideals, an Albania that will live and prosper for centuries to come.[5]

As Hoxha was reading out these lofty lines, he looked like a ghostly shadow of his former self, someone whom the Grim Reaper had forgotten, or perhaps someone who had been allowed to hang around for just a bit longer so that he could give this final speech. Across from the podium, on the pavement, on the streets and at home in front of their TV sets, there must have been people who had seen him 40 years earlier, on that momentous midday of 28 November 1944. But this time, none of them were enthusiastic or given to cheering. The Albania Hoxha had promised 40 years earlier did not exist. It was never achieved. What the Albanian people were left with was best described as a nightmarish caricature of Stalin's Soviet Union, a carbon copy of Stalinist oppression crammed within the borders of a small country of 3 million people. To add insult to injury, the hungry and humiliated Albanians were forced to endure slogans like: 'We'd rather feed on grass than betray the principles of Marxism–Leninism!' In fact, there were no principles to talk about any more. Empty slogans of this sort were simply an expression of the age-old instinct of political survival, a means of holding on to power.

More than anyone else around him, Hoxha himself must have been aware that death was lurking round the corner. On the evening of 28 November 1984, exactly 40 years after the grand ball at Hotel Dajti where he first appeared with his then wife-to-be, Hoxha invited Dr Paul Milliez to his home for dinner. Of all the foreign delegations and dignitaries who attended the celebrations, Paul Milliez and his wife were the only ones who were invited to Hoxha's home. Also present was Ramiz Alia, Hoxha's protégé and next in line, who had never met Milliez before. According to Mrs Hoxha's memoirs, this is how Hoxha introduced Alia to the French doctor:

My friend, I'm getting old, and my health is not the best it could be. Younger comrades, like this one [Alia], will step in. There are still comrades in the leadership of the party who participated in the anti-fascist resistance movement when they were very young.[6]

This was the only time Hoxha explicitly indicated who his designated successor was.

Around this time he began to have his first mental aberrations. A clip from a Politburo meeting, first aired by the French TV station Planète+, showed a Hoxha completely at a loss as to where he was and why he was there. Vito Kapo, Hysni Kapo's widow and the then minister of light industry, was reporting to the Politburo. Only the transcript of the full dialogue reveals what really went on:

HOXHA: Vito, are you here? Have you come on your own?

VITO KAPO: Yes, I've come on my own.

HOXHA: Will you be able to cope?

VITO KAPO: Other comrades from the government are also here, Comrade Enver.

HOXHA: This situation... Are the comrades from the government, but above all, are you, minister of light industry, and are there, or are there not, and so on and so forth...

VITO KAPO: No, no, there will be others.

HOXHA: Has the new one been finished? It can work at double the present
    capacity, why does it not? Have there been any investments in 1955?

VITO KAPO: 1985.

HOXHA: Yes, 1985.

VITO KAPO: Very few.

HOXHA: Why?

VITO KAPO: There have been shortages recently, Comrade Enver, and it
    has not been possible to get the right supply of raw materials in order
    for the industry to run at full capacity.

HOXHA: How do you mean there is a shortage of raw materials?

VITO KAPO: Imports.

HOXHA: Uh-uh.

VITO KAPO: The 1984 investments were successful.

HOXHA: What about in 1985?

VITO KAPO: We believe so.

HOXHA: And the five-year plan quotas, will they remain the same, 300,000
    in 1958, 1985 rather, 300,000 in 1939, 300,000 in 1940?[7]

The meeting was held in February 1985: this was Hoxha's last attendance in
a meeting at the offices of the Central Committee of the PLA. For three
months, his health had gone daily from bad to worse. He could neither
stand nor speak. Isuf Kalo, his personal doctor, remembers: 'He never talked
about death. Although it was inevitable, it came unexpectedly. I think he
was quite balanced in the way he coped with his condition and eventually
with his death.'[8]

On the morning of 7 April, Hoxha asked to see his children and grandchildren. Film footage shows him sitting in his studio, wearing a dark-beige
suit and his hair properly combed; he looked in surprisingly good shape. He
was smiling and reacting normally – no one would have thought that there
was so little life left in him. The next clip shows him seated downstairs on
the tiled porch. It was a beautiful April day. Sulo Gradeci continued filming
and taking pictures – these were to be the last photographs of the whole
family together.

On 8 April 1985, around 11.00 hours, Nexhmije Hoxha called the male nurse and asked him to take Hoxha out into the garden. Sitting in his wheel-chair, his hair in disarray, he was a totally different person from the jovial man shown in the pictures of the previous day. As he was being wheeled out of the house and into a sunny corner in the garden, with his eyes hidden behind a pair of large sunglasses, Hoxha was a ghastly apparition. The film clips of the event, discovered only in 2010, show him being wheeled around in his chair. Now and then, the wheelchair stops and he feebly strokes the statues in the garden. These were Hoxha's last hours captured on film. Death, the great equaliser, was waiting to take him to the same place as thousands of his innocent victims.

24

Death and What Remained

On the morning of 9 April 1985 Sokol Hoxha, Enver Hoxha's younger son, was at the beach villa in Vlora when a security officer knocked at his door. His father was very ill and he was to return to Tirana immediately.

Enver Hoxha had lapsed into clinical death since 09.00 that morning, while the nurse was washing him, as Nexhmije Hoxha remembers:

> It was a little before nine when I entered the room with the newspaper *Zëri i popullit* in my hand [...] I was watching what the nurse was doing and waiting for him to finish, when all of a sudden Enver shuddered and his chin hit his chest [...] I jumped on my feet and cried 'Enver!' Then I frantically watched as the nurse laid Enver quickly on the floor and told me to call the doctors immediately, before he started mouth-to-mouth resuscitation. I pressed the bell hard and long and the doctors arrived promptly.[1]

The doctors were not able to do anything. They found Hoxha lying on the floor. Just before he fell, Hoxha had tried to take a couple of steps, pushed by one last surge of energy, but was not able to go any further. He collapsed to the floor with a thud, in a scene eerily reminiscent of the last moments of his idol, Josef Vissarionovich Stalin. The attempt to get his heart beating again seemed to work briefly, but he would not come round. The man who ruled Albania for 41 years had fallen into a coma from which he would never awake. The countdown had begun.

Enver Hoxha died at 02.10 hours on 11 April 1985. He departed from this world without leaving any last words or saying his goodbyes. All the

Politburo members gathered at his house, half dazed from lack of sleep and visibly concerned. No one knew what would happen next. Hoxha had indeed indicated who his successor would be, but no one could say what kind of leader Alia would turn out to be.

Two of the doctors, Ylli Popa and Petrit Gaçe, were in the room when the dictator drew his last breath. It fell to Gaçe to break the news to Ramiz Alia, who was in the next room with interior minister Hekuran Isai. This is how Ylli Popa remembers the conversation at that critical moment:

> We went into the next room. They were standing right behind the door and asked:
> 'How is he?'
> 'Comrade Enver passed away,' Petrit informed them.
> Hekuran Isai turned to Ramiz and said:
> 'Long live the party!'
> This was the formula used at the time. And then a couple of seconds later, he added:
> 'Long live you, Comrade Ramiz!'[2]

His survival instinct, honed over years of living under the dictatorship, led the interior minister to bow to the new leader now that Hoxha had ceased to be. *Le roi est mort, vive le roi!*

The body of the dictator was taken to the morgue that evening. The next day he lay in state in the main hall of the Presidential Office building at the southern end of the main boulevard. This edifice had been built in 1960 to house the Soviet embassy, but no Soviet diplomats ever got to work there. The deceased dictator was prepared for viewing by make-up artists from the New Albania film studio and dressed by the morticians in his favourite grey suit. In fact, after the 1950s he was never seen wearing dark suits in public – his favourite colours were beige and light grey. The catafalque was banked with cut flowers and wreaths; on a small table at one end, his medals and decorations were displayed in an orderly fashion on silk cushions. One of them caught attention in particular: the highest decoration of all – 'Hero of the People'!

At 07.00 that morning, prime minister Adil Çarçani made the official announcement to the Politburo. His words, taken out of context, sound a bit silly: 'In spite of enormous and infinite efforts made by the party and its Central Committee, Comrade Enver Hoxha has died.'[3] The members of the Politburo, many of them government ministers, began to wail loudly. The prime minister himself was constantly wiping his tears away and could hardly speak. Interior minister Hekuran Isai placed the Sigurimi and police force on high alert. Prison guards were reinforced, random checks in towns intensified and individuals who were perceived as troublemakers were detained. On 11 April, the Ministry of the Interior issued 45 security-related orders and mobilised over 8,000 extra people.

At 10.00 hours Radio Tirana read out the joint statement of the Politburo, the Central Committee of the PLA and other major bodies. A solemn voice told the Albanians that their immortal 'leader' was no longer alive. The statement was worded in such a way that the word 'death' was never used. Instead, phrases like 'the heart of the great leader of the party and the people has stopped beating' were used. Communists would not accept death.

At 13.00 Reuters spread the news throughout the world. The first comments began to arrive on the same afternoon. Agence France-Presse's Bertrand Rosenthal wrote the following:

> Enver Hoxha died today at the age of 76, after more than 40 years in power, during which he made no concessions at the head of a communist party whose ideological, economic and social orthodoxy has made Albania the only Stalinist and atheist country in the world.
>
> Emulating other historical communist leaders, Enver Hoxha, a tall, ever-smiling and elegant man as seen in images on Albanian TV, created a personality cult similar to that of Stalin, whose date of birth is still celebrated in Tirana.
>
> Enver Hoxha was an ally of the Yugoslav leader Josip Broz Tito in World War II, but turned against him and sided with Stalin during the first crisis of the communist world. At that time he pledged that he would 'settle accounts with Tito's clique', who had reportedly said about him: 'Poor Mr Hoxha, he doesn't know anything about Marxism beyond its name.'

The Albanian leader would also exploit all international unrest to rid himself of potential rivals in the party, accusing them of treason or plotting against him.

Among the first who commented on the death were the Soviets. A Tass article stated:

Moscow, 11 April – Enver Hoxha's death is not expected to lead to a speedy normalisation of Soviet–Albanian relations, which for over a quarter of a century have been reduced to invectives only, say diplomatic sources in Moscow. The Soviet press has refrained from making any further comments on the death of the man who used to be Khrushchev's comrade-in-arms before turning against him and calling him an 'adventurer', nor did he use any better terms for the latter's successors in the Kremlin.

In the next few days the world press described Hoxha as 'the strangest dictator in the world', and 'the man who set up the most isolated regime ever known', but commentaries were generally short and insignificant. The deceased dictator was already being forgotten.

Marxist and left-wing delegations from around the world were invited to attend the funeral. Militant Kosovar groups living in the West were also invited. Tirana declined the messages of condolence from Moscow and London, declaring that it wanted nothing to do with the respective countries. The United States kept silent.

Hoxha's death was treated as nothing short of a national calamity in Albania. The government announced seven days of national mourning during which all other activities were suspended. For three days, there were long queues of people forced to pay homage to the dictator and public displays of grief and hysteria, reminiscent of scenes from Mao Zedong's funeral nine years earlier. In the press and on radio and TV nothing else was discussed but the 'national calamity'. School children were instructed to write poems and essays about 'Comrade Enver', which were then bound together and sent to Nexhmije Hoxha. Factories set up display corners, with photos of him smiling and with quotations from his books. The word 'ENVER' appeared in huge letters on mountainsides. Prison commanders forced prisoners to send collective letters and telegrams of condolence to Nexhmije Hoxha. Those who refused to sign were punished with 30 days of solitary confinement, while 12 prisoners had their sentences extended by two to five years.

On 14 April, the day of the funeral, the Politburo decreed that over 34 collective farms and factories would be named after Enver Hoxha. The University of Tirana was also given his name in spite of the fact that Hoxha himself never managed to graduate from university. In addition, it was decided that three monuments would be erected in his honour in Gjirokastra, Korça and Tirana, the towns that were considered to be milestones in his life and political career. The monument in Gjirokastra was erected on a promontory in town; the one in Korça replaced the well-known *Luftëtari Kombëtar* (national fighter), a monument that had been a main feature of the town centre since 1938; the oversized statue in Tirana, placed across the square from the equestrian statue of Skanderbeg, remained there for just three years.

The funeral ceremony was perfectly organised. Hoxha was buried next to the Mother Albania Monument at the Cemetery of the Martyrs of the Nation. When the coffin was lowered into the grave and the red marble slab with the inscription 'Enver Hoxha 1908–1985' was placed over it, Ramiz Alia declared:

> There should be no date of death on this marble stone! It should only have '16 October 1908' on it. There is just one date for Enver Hoxha, his date of birth, and that is how it will always be, there is no death for him. Enver Hoxha is immortal.[4]

After these solemn words Alia bent over and kissed the plaque bearing the name of the former communist chief.

Hoxha's death marked the end of an era in the history of communist Albania. The day after the funeral, as dignitaries were paying visits of condolence to the house of the deceased, a distressed and tearful Nexhmije Hoxha was captured saying to Vito Kapo: 'He's left us, Vito; he's left us to join Hysni and the comrades!' This came as a surprise to many Albanians who heard it, for communists were not supposed to believe in God or in life after death.

Was Nexhmije Hoxha after all a believer in her heart of hearts? Or could it be that the deceased, the one-time Koran-school pupil, had been a believer himself? Nexhmije Hoxha had instinctively said something she no doubt really believed at that moment: Enver Hoxha had gone to join his friends! But which friends? Who was waiting for him on the other side? What kind of revenge would they exact on him for their lives cut short? For the families he had destroyed? For the children he had killed? For the torment and the tribulation he had caused? How many of them would hold him personally responsible for putting a ruthless end to their common dream? For creating an Albania that ended up the very opposite of what they had dreamed? In the great beyond they would all be equal. There, he could not execute anyone, he could not declare them traitors, criminals or unworthy ingrates. There, they would finally have the opportunity to sit him down and tell him what they really thought of him, something none of them had dared to do while he was alive, that Enver Hoxha had in fact died a long time ago, back in November 1944, when he destroyed all hopes for a better future by establishing a loathsome dictatorship, the scourge of at least three generations unlucky enough to live under it.

The communist regime crumbled five years later. In December 1990, the Albanians rose up in their numbers to start from scratch and resume their old European dream. They wanted to delete all memories of the man who destroyed their lives and to ensure that the 50-year-long nightmare was over and would never return.

It had been a nightmare of tragic dimensions: in his 46 years of rule, 5,037 men and 450 women were executed; 16,788 men and 7,367 women were convicted and sentenced to three to 35 years of imprisonment, terms which were often extended by reconvictions in jail; 70,000 people were interned; and 354 foreign nationals were executed by firing squad, of whom 95 were Albanians from Kosovo.

On 20 February 1991, over 100,000 inhabitants of Tirana gathered to topple the bronze statue of Enver Hoxha that loomed in Skanderbeg Square. The hulk was then dragged by a lorry through the streets of the capital up to the gates of the university campus, where the students had been on hunger strike for several days. Their main demand was for Enver Hoxha's name to be removed from the university. On the same evening, statues and busts of the dictator were also toppled or discreetly removed throughout the country.

In May 1992, Enver Hoxha's remains were transferred to the Tirana municipal cemetery. At the same time, many of those who had been executed under his rule because they had aspired to a free society were reburied at the Cemetery of the Martyrs of the Nation. Finding the remains of the majority of Hoxha's former comrades and collaborators proved a very difficult task; in fact many of the executed communists and anti-communists were never found. The Albanian soil still keeps them in its bosom – testament to an era of collective absurdity, suffering and trauma.

Chronology of the Life of Enver Hoxha

1908	16 October: Hoxha is born in Gjirokastra.
1927	Hoxha begins attending the French *lycée* in Korça.
1930	Hoxha receives an Albanian government scholarship to study in Montpellier in France.
1934	March: Hoxha's scholarship is terminated by minister of education Marash Ivanaj. Hoxha moves to Paris and then Brussels.
1935	Hoxha works in Brussels.
1936	Hoxha returns to Albania and makes his living as a teaching assistant.
1939	7 April: Italian forces invade Albania. King Zog and the royal family flee to Greece.
1941	8 November: foundation of the CPA.
1942	25 August: Hoxha edits the first edition of communist newspaper *Zëri i popullit* (The people's voice).
	16 September: Peza Conference.
1943	Hoxha is made general secretary of the CPA.
	8 September: Italy capitulates, and German troops occupy Albania.
1944	24–8 May: Hoxha is appointed chairman of the Anti-Fascist National Liberation Council at the Congress of Përmet.
	28 November: communist forces under Enver Hoxha take control of Tirana and assume political power in Albania.
1946	11 January: formal establishment of the People's Republic of Albania.
	23 June–2 July: Hoxha pays an official visit to Yugoslavia.
1947	14–26 July: Hoxha visits Moscow, where he meets Stalin for the first time.

1948   Beginning of the alliance with the Soviet Union, which lasts until 1961.
        3 October: purge of Koçi Xoxe.

1949   21 March–11 April: second meeting with Stalin.
        26 November: third meeting with Stalin.

1950   5 January: fourth meeting with Stalin.

1951   19 February: bomb explodes outside the Soviet legation in Tirana
        and results in a wave of arrests and executions.
        2 April: fifth meeting with Stalin.

1955   18 July: unofficial meeting with Nikita Khrushchev.

1956   October: Hoxha and Mehmet Shehu visit China.

1959   25 May–4 June: Nikita Khrushchev visits Albania.

1960   16 November: Hoxha denounces Khrushchev's policies at the meet-
        ing of the 81 communist parties in Moscow.

1961   Beginning of the alliance with the People's Republic of China, which
        lasts until 1978.

1964   10–17 January: visit to Albania by Chinese prime minister Zhou
        Enlai.

1966   March: Cultural Revolution in Albania.

1967   6 February: beginning of the campaign against religion.

1968   13 September: Albania withdraws from the Warsaw Pact.

1973   26–8 June: fourth plenary session; purge of the so-called liberals and
        condemnation of Todi Lubonja and Fadil Paçrami.

1974   July–August: purge of Beqir Balluku, Petrit Dume, Hito Çako and
        the military.

1975   26–9 May: purge of Abdyl Këllezi, Koço Theodhosi and Kiço Ngjela
        at the Seventh Congress of the Central Committee.

1978   29 July: rupture of the alliance with China.

1981   18 December: purge and mysterious death of Mehmet Shehu.

1985   11 April: Hoxha dies in Tirana and is succeeded by Ramiz Alia.

1990   11 December: introduction of political pluralism and the end of the
        communist dictatorship.

1991   20 February: the statue of Enver Hoxha is toppled by angry crowds
        in Skanderbeg Square in Tirana.

Glossary of Key Figures

ALIA, RAMIZ
(1925–2011)

Political figure and last head of state of communist Albania. His niece married Enver Hoxha's son Ilir. On the death of Enver Hoxha in 1985, Alia took over the party leadership until the end of the dictatorship in 1991.

AMERY, JULIAN
(1919–96)

British military officer and writer who was in Albania during World War II as a member of the Special Operations Executive.

ANDONI, VASIL
(1901–94)

Political figure of World War II. Leading figure of the anti-communist resistance movement Balli Kombëtar.

ANDROPOV, YURI
(1914–84)

Soviet political figure. He was general secretary of the CPSU from 1982 to 1984.

ARBNORI, PJETËR
(1935–2006)

Affiliated with the nascent Social Democratic Party of Albania, he was imprisoned for 28 years (1961–89). After the fall of the dictatorship, he was head of the Democratic Party and speaker of the Albanian parliament.

BAJRAKTARI,
MUHARREM
(1896–1989)

Anti-communist guerrilla fighter in World War II. He escaped abroad in 1946 and died in Belgium.

BAKALLI, MAHMUT
(1936–2006)

Kosovo Albanian political figure. Head of the Central Committee of the communist party in Kosovo from 1971 to 1981.

BALLUKU, BEQIR
(1917–75)

Political and military figure of the communist period. He served as minister of defence from July 1953 to July 1974, and was chairman of the People's Assembly from 1957 to 1974. Balluku was a member of the CPA/PLA's Central Committee and the Politburo from 1948 to 1974. In August 1974, he was suddenly arrested and accused of organising a military coup d'état with two other military figures, Petrit Dume and Hito Çako. General Balluku was found guilty of high treason and executed on 5 November 1975.

BEJA, SHEFQET
(D.1947)

MP who was arrested in May 1947 and executed.

BEKTESHI, SADIK (1920–2000)

High-ranking military official of the communist period. As a lieutenant general, he was purged in 1974. He was interned near Berat, and was released in 1990.

BELISHOVA, LIRI (B.1923)

Political figure of the early communist period. She was married to Nako Spiru. Belishova was expelled from the party in 1960 as pro-Soviet and spent the next 31 years in internment (1960–91).

BIÇAKÇIU, IBRAHIM (1905–77)

Political figure of the 1930s and 1940s. Son of a wealthy landowner. Last prime minister of pre-communist Albania (September–October 1944), under the German occupation. He was arrested in December 1944 and imprisoned until 1962.

BIRÇE, QEMAL

Sigurimi officer in the 1980s.

BOGDO, SULO (D.1944)

Figure of the World War II period. He took part in the conference of Mukja in 1943. He was a lawyer, in whose house the newspaper *Bashkimi* (Unity) was edited. He was shot in 1944.

BOJAXHIU, LAZËR (1908–71)

Brother of Mother Teresa and one-time artillery captain in the army of King Zog.

BREZHNEV, LEONID (1906–82)

Soviet political figure. General secretary of the CPSU from 1964 to 1982.

BUDA, ALEKS (1910–93)

Representative historian of the communist period and founding member of the Albanian Academy of Sciences, of which he was president from 1973 onwards.

BUFI, FAHRI

Male nurse who attended to Enver Hoxha.

BULLATI, PETRO (D.1956)

Military figure. He was purged and shot with Liri Gega and Dali Ndreu.

BUSHATI, SULÇE BEG (D.1945)

Anti-communist figure during World War II. He was captured and shot by the communists in March 1945.

CACHIN, MARCEL (1869–1958)

French political figure. One of the founders of the French Communist Party in 1920 and editor of the communist newspaper *l'Humanité* (1918–58).

ÇAÇI, JAHJA

Military figure of the World War II period.

ÇAJUPI, ANTON ZAKO (1866–1930)

Southern Albanian poet who lived mostly in Egypt.

ÇAKO, HITO (1923–75)

Political and military figure of the communist period. In 1974, when he was deputy minister of defence, he was arrested in a purge and was sentenced to death for high treason as a putschist.

CAKRANI, KADRI (1903–72)

Military figure during World War II. He was a commander of the anti-communist resistance movement Balli Kombëtar. At the end of the war, he escaped abroad and died in the United States.

CANCO, DHIMITËR

Public figure of the 1930s. He founded the Cinema Gloria in Tirana.

ÇARÇANI, ADIL (1922–97)

Political figure of the late communist period. He was prime minister of Albania from 1982 to 1990.

ÇELA, ARANIT (B.1923)

Aranit Çela served as prosecutor in the postwar witch trials that took place in Albania in the late 1940s. In July 1954, he was made president of the Supreme Court. In the 1970s and 1980s, in this capacity and as a member of the so-called Central Expulsion and Deportation Commission, he was one of the most powerful figures of the regime, and one of the most hated. He is reputed to have sent hundreds of people to their deaths. In July 1996, Çela was sentenced to death himself for crimes against humanity. His sentence was then commuted to 25 years in prison, but he was pardoned the following year in view of his age.

ÇITAKU, RAMADAN (1914–90)

Founding member of the CPA in 1941 and Albanian ambassador to Yugoslavia in 1947–8. He was purged in November 1948 but not imprisoned.

ÇOBA, NDOC (1865–1945)

Catholic political figure from Shkodra. He was minister of finance in the 1920 government of Sulejman bey Delvina. During World War II, he was elected as head of the National Liberation Council at the Peza Conference.

COT, PIERRE (1895–1977)

French left-wing politician and leading figure of the Popular Front government of the 1930s.

COUVE DE MURVILLE, MAURICE (1907–99)

French political figure. He served as minister of foreign affairs from 1958 to 1968 and as prime minister from 1968 to 1969.

ÇUPI, FRROK

Journalist, writer and public figure of the 1990s.

DANI, RIZA (1887–1947)

Political figure from Shkodra. He was arrested in May 1947 and was executed.

DAVIES, EDMUND FRANK (1900–51)

British military officer and writer, who was in Albania during World War II as a member of the Special Operations Executive.

DEDA, NIKOLL

Catholic priest, who was executed in March 1948.

DEDIJER, VLADIMIR (1914–90)

Serbian partisan fighter, communist political figure and biographer of Tito. He was author of the book *Jugoslovensko–albanski odnosi (1939–1948)* (Yugoslav–Albanian relations 1939–1948).

DE RADA, GIROLAMO (1814–1903)

Italo-Albanian poet and figure of the early nationalist movement.

DERVISHI, KASTRIOT (B.1972)

Publisher and historian. He is currently head of the archives of the Albanian Ministry of the Interior and has published several books about the communist period, based on archival material.

DISHNICA, ESAT

Uncle of Ymer Dishnica.

DISHNICA, YMER (1912–98)

Political figure of the World War II and early communist periods, and nephew of Esat Dishnica. He was minister of health and chairman of the People's Assembly (1946–7). He was purged in 1947 but not imprisoned.

DODA, XHEVDET (1906–45)
Kosovo Albanian military figure who fought for the communist NLA during World War II. He is said to have been caught in Prizren in September 1944 and sent to Mauthausen, where he died.

DOSTI, HASAN (1895–1991)
Political figure of the World War II period. Dosti was a leading member of the anti-communist resistance movement Balli Kombëtar, and fled to Italy in October 1944. He died in Los Angeles.

DUBČEK, ALEXANDER (1921–92)
Czechoslovak political figure. He was general secretary of the Communist Party of Czechoslovakia from 1968 to 1969, and leader of the reform movement of 1968.

DUME, NAXHIJE (1921–2008)
Political figure. As minister of education in 1948, she was the first female minister in Albanian history. She was married to Nesti Kerenxhi and was purged with him as pro-Yugoslav. She lived in internment until the end of the dictatorship.

DUME, PETRIT (1920–75)
Military and political figure of the communist period. Dume was reported to be a fanatical communist of unstable temperament. In November 1974, as a high-ranking military officer, he was suspended from duty during the purge of the army, and was arrested in December of that year. Although seemingly innocent like many other military figures of the period, Dume was sentenced to death for high treason and was shot on 5 November 1975.

DURAKU, EMIN (1918–42)
Kosovo Albanian partisan, captured by fascist forces near Lipjan in late 1942.

DURAKU, REXHEP
Kosovo Albanian figure. Father of Emin Duraku.

EKMEKÇIU, FETAH
Activist in the Zogist resistance during World War II.

ERMENJI, ABAZ (1913–2003)
Political figure of the World War II period. He was a leading member of the anti-communist resistance movement Balli Kombëtar. Ermenji returned to Albania after the dictatorship in 1991.

FALLO, DHIMITËR
Political figure of the World War II period. He was a member of the anti-communist resistance movement Balli Kombëtar.

FEJZO, ABAZ (1925–87)
High-ranking military official of the communist period. As a major general, he was arrested in 1982, and died in prison.

FILIPOVIĆ, SAFET
Yugoslav political figure.

FRASHËRI, ABDYL (1839–92)
Political figure of the 'Rilindja' (Revival) period. He was a leading figure of the League of Prizren in 1878, and was the brother of Sami and Naim Frashëri.

FRASHËRI, KRISTO (B.1920)
Scholar and historian. He was an early member of the CPA, but was expelled in 1942. He later became a leading historian.

FRASHËRI, MEHDI (1872–1963)
Political figure, publisher and writer, and cousin of Mid'hat Frashëri. He was prime minister of Albania (1935–6) and a member of the High Regency Council during the German occupation. Frashëri fled abroad in 1944 and died in Rome.

FRASHËRI, MID'HAT (1880–1949)	Political figure, publisher and prose writer (under the pen name Lumo Skëndo), and cousin of Mehdi Frashëri. He was head of the anti-communist resistance movement Balli Kombëtar from 1942 onwards. He fled to Italy in 1944 and died in New York.
FRASHËRI, NAIM (1846–1900)	Poet and nationalist figure of the Rilindja period, and brother of Abdyl and Sami Frashëri. He is considered by many as the 'national poet' of Albania.
FRASHËRI, SAMI (1850–1904)	Writer, publisher and ideologist of the Rilindja period, and brother of Abdyl and Naim Frashëri.
FRATARI, RAIF	Military figure of the World War II period. He was a major in 1943 when he signed the Mukja Agreement on behalf of Balli Kombëtar.
FROWICK, ROBERT HOLMES (D.2007)	US diplomat who was active in the Balkans in the 1990s and thereafter.
FULTZ, HARRY T. (1888–1980)	US educator. He was founder of the influential American Vocational School of Tirana in 1922, which he managed until 1931.
FUNDO, LLAZAR (1899–1944)	Communist political figure. He was an arch-enemy of Enver Hoxha, who had him beaten to death in September 1944.
GAÇE, PETRIT (1927–96)	Surgeon and physician of Enver Hoxha, who was present at his death.
GEGA, LIRI (D.1956)	Political figure of the communist period. She was married to General Dali Ndreu and was purged and executed with him in November 1956.
GJEBREA, RAMIZE (1923–44)	First wife of Nako Spiru. She was shot by partisans in 1944.
GJINI, FRANO PJETËR (1886–1948)	Catholic priest who was executed in March 1948.
GJINISHI, MUSTAFA (1912–44)	Communist figure of the World War II period. He was a potential rival of Enver Hoxha, and was killed at the latter's behest in August 1944.
GOMULKA, WLADISLAW (1905–82)	Polish political figure of the communist period. He was the leader of Poland from 1945 to 1948 and was general secretary of the Polish United Workers Party from 1956 to 1970.
GORBACHEV, MIKHAIL (B.1931)	Soviet political figure. He was general secretary of the CPSU from 1985 to 1991 and the last head of state of the Soviet Union.
GRADECI, SULO (B.1922)	Bodyguard of Enver Hoxha. He was arrested in 1992.
HARAPI, ANTON (1888–1946)	Catholic writer and political figure. He was a member of the High Regency Council during the German occupation, was arrested in June 1945 and shot.
HAZBIU, KADRI (1922–83)	Political figure of the communist period. He was minister of the interior and head of the notorious Sigurimi from 1954 to 1980. Hazbiu was purged in 1982 and executed soon thereafter.

HAZNEDARI, NEVZAT (1920–84)	Notorious legal figure of the early communist period. He was state prosecutor in many political trials.
HENDERSON, GEORGE D.	US diplomatic figure. He was head of the American diplomatic mission to Albania in 1945.
HERRI, XHEMAL	Supported by dictator Ahmet Zogu, he was made chief of police in 1926. During World War II, he was a representative of the Legaliteti resistance movement.
HODGSON, D. E. P.	British general and head of the British mission in Albania in 1945.
HOXHA, ENVER (1908–85)	Political figure and leader of communist Albania from the partisan victory in 1944 until his death in 1985.
HOXHA, FADIL (1916–2001)	Kosovo Albanian political figure of the communist period.
HOXHA, FEJZI	Personal physician of Enver Hoxha.
HOXHA, ILIR (B.1949)	Elder son of Enver Hoxha.
HOXHA, LILJANA	Wife of Sokol Hoxha and thus daughter-in-law of the dictator.
HOXHA, NEXHMIJE, NÉE NEXHMIJE XHUGLINI (B.1921)	Political figure of the communist period. Wife and close collaborator of dictator Enver Hoxha. After the dictatorship, she was imprisoned for six years (1991–7).
HOXHA, PRANVERA (B.1954)	Daughter of Enver Hoxha. She was married to Klement Kolaneci.
HOXHA, SOKOL (B.1957)	Second son of Enver Hoxha.
HURSHITI, JAVER (1880–1945)	Political and military figure of the 1930s and 1940s. He was minister of justice in 1943, and was sentenced to death in April 1945.
HYSENBEGASI, ISUF	Schoolmate of Enver Hoxha in Korça. He later studied in Italy and became a physician, but was sentenced to ten years in prison for stemming from a wealthy family.
ISAI, HEKURAN (1933–2008)	Political figure of the communist period. After the elimination of Mehmet Shehu, he served from January 1982 to February 1989 as minister of the interior, and, from July 1990 to February 1991, both as minister of the interior and deputy prime minister. Hekuran Isai was a powerful figure in the PLA hierarchy throughout the 1980s.
IVANAJ, MIRASH (1891–1953)	Political figure of the Zogist period. He was minister of education from 1933 to 1935. He fled to Greece in 1939, but returned to Albania in 1945. Ivanaj was arrested in May 1947 and died in prison.
JAKOVA, TUK (1914–59)	Founding member of the CPA in 1941. He held several ministerial posts from 1946 to 1953, including deputy prime minister. He was purged in June 1955 and died in prison.
KADARE, ISMAIL (B.1936)	Leading Albanian prose writer and poet.

KALO, ISUF	Personal physician of Enver Hoxha.
KAPO, HYSNI (1915–79)	High-ranking political figure throughout the communist period; member of the Politburo and the Central Committee until his death in Paris. He played a major role in Hoxha's clash with Nikita Khrushchev in 1960–1.
KAPO, VITO (B.1922)	Political figure of the communist period. She was the wife of Hysni Kapo and held numerous political positions.
KARDELJ, EDVARD (1910–79)	Yugoslav political figure from Slovenia. An early member of the CPY, he was a close ally of Tito and served as foreign minister of Yugoslavia (1948–53) and president of the Yugoslav parliament (1963–7).
KASIMATI, SABIHA	Teacher of biology. She was executed during repression in the wake of the bombing incident at the Soviet embassy in Tirana in 1951.
KÇIRA, PIERIN	Sigurimi officer in northern Albania in the late 1940s.
KËLCYRA, ALI (1891–1963)	Political figure of the anti-communist resistance movement Balli Kombëtar. He fled to Italy in October 1944, and died in Rome.
KËLLEZI, ABDYL (1919–77)	Political official of the communist period, and head of the state planning commission in the early 1970s. Together with Koço Theodhosi and Kiço Ngjela, he fell victim to the purge at the Seventh Congress of the Central Committee in May 1975, allegedly for grave revisionist mistakes and sabotage of the economy. He was swiftly relieved of his posts, expelled from the party, arrested and executed.
KELMENDI, ALI (1900–39)	Early figure of the Albanian communist movement. In 1930 he was sent by Moscow to Albania, where he founded some clandestine communist groups, in particular the Korça Group, and took part in communist agitation. He died of tuberculosis in Paris.
KERENXHI, NESTI (B.1920)	Military figure. In 1947, he represented Albania at the Security Council of the United Nations, and was briefly minister of the interior. Kerenxhi was married to Naxhije Dume. He was purged with her as pro-Yugoslav, and interned.
KHRUSHCHEV, NIKITA (1894–1971)	Soviet political figure. First secretary of the CPSU from 1953 to 1964.
KLISSURA, HANA	Daughter of Ali Këlcyra (Klissura) and niece of Ekrem bey Vlora. She emigrated to Italy with her father after World War II and lives in Vienna.
KOKALARI, HAMIT (1909–89)	Writer and translator, and brother of Musine Kokalari. Author of *Kosova, djepi i shqiptarizmit* (Kosovo, the cradle of Albanianism).
KOKALARI, MUNTAZ (D.1944)	Brother of Musine Kokalari.
KOKALARI, MUSINE (1917–83)	Prose writer and political figure associated in the 1940s with the Social Democratic Party. She was arrested in January 1946 and sentenced to 25 years in prison. She died in internment in Rrëshen.

KOKONA, NEDIN | Brother of Vedat Kokona. Arrested after World War II and sentenced to prison.

KOKONA, VEDAT (1913–98) | Writer and lexicographer. He was acquainted with Enver Hoxha in his youth and was later author of noted French–Albanian and Albanian–French dictionaries.

KOKOSHI, GJERGJ (1904–50) | Political figure of the early communist period. He was the first communist minister of education in October 1944, though he was more closely associated with the nascent Social Democratic Party. Kokoshi was arrested in January 1946, and died in Burrel prison of tuberculosis.

KOLANECI, KLEMENT | Assistant architect of Enver Hoxha's villa in the Bllok. He became the dictator's son-in-law, when he married Pranvera Hoxha.

KOLECI, VASKË | Sigurimi officer and deputy minister of the interior. He was purged with Koçi Xoxe in 1948 for being pro-Yugoslav.

KOLEKA, SPIRO (1908–2001) | Political figure of the communist period. As a member of the Central Committee from 1948 to June 1991 and of the Politburo from 1948 to 1981, he was a leading figure of the communist hierarchy right to the end of the dictatorship.

KOLIQI, ERNEST (1903–75) | Public figure, scholar and prose writer. He was head of the chair of Albanian language and literature at the University of Rome from 1939, Albanian minister of education in 1939–41 and president of the Albanian parliament in 1943. He fled to Italy in November 1944.

KOLLI, REXHEP | Member of the Central Committee of the CPA in the 1970s and minister of the interior.

KOMATINA, MILAN | Yugoslav political and diplomatic figure. He was secretary of the Yugoslav embassy in Vienna in the mid-1950s.

KONDI, ALQI | Political figure of the 1940s. He was an activist of the Anti-Fascist Youth of Albania, and was the brother of Vito Kapo.

KONOMI, MANOL (1910–2002) | He was general secretary at the Albanian Ministry of Foreign Affairs in 1946 and later minister of justice. He was relieved of his post as minister of justice in March 1951.

KOSTURI, DRITA (B.1920) | Resistance fighter during World War II.

KOTA, KOÇO (1889–1949) | Also known as Kostaq Kotta. Political figure of the 1920s and 1930s who served as a minister under Ahmet Zogu. He fled to Greece at the end of 1944, but was kidnapped by communist agents, taken back to Albania and sentenced to prison, where he died.

KRISTO, PANDI (B.1914) | Political figure of the early postwar period, member of the Politburo and head of the state control commission. He was a close associate of Koçi Xoxe, with whom he was purged.

KROI, HAXHI | Personal secretary of Enver Hoxha.

KRYEZIU, CENO
BEY (1895–1927)

Kosovo Albanian political figure. He was the brother of Gani, Hasan and Said Kryeziu, and the brother-in-law of Ahmet Zogu. Ceno bey Kryeziu was Albanian minister of the interior in 1925, and ambassador to Yugoslavia in 1926–7. He was assassinated in Prague, no doubt by an agent of Zogu.

KRYEZIU, GANI
(1900–52)

Kosovo Albanian anti-communist resistance fighter during World War II, and brother of Ceno, Hasan and Said Kryeziu. He was captured by communist partisans in January 1945 and sentenced to prison.

KRYEZIU, HASAN

Kosovo Albanian political figure of the World War II period, and brother of Ceno, Gani and Said Kryeziu.

KRYEZIU, SAID
(1911–93)

Kosovo Albanian anti-communist resistance fighter of the World War II period, and brother of Ceno, Gani and Hasan Kryeziu. He fled via Greece to Italy in November 1944 and emigrated to the United States in 1959.

KUPI, ABAZ
(1892–1976)

Political figure and resistance fighter of the World War II period, also known as Bazi i Canës. He was head of the monarchist resistance movement Legaliteti. He fled to Italy in October 1944 and died in New York.

KUQALI, KOL

An MP who was arrested in May 1947 and probably executed.

KURTI, SHTJEFËN
(c.1898–1972)

Catholic religious figure in Shkodra in the 1940s.

KUSHI, VOJO
(1918–42)

Communist partisan figure of the World War II period. He died in Tirana in a spectacular shootout at his house with the Italian police and was made a hero of the communist cause.

LAZRI, SOFOKLI
(1924–2002)

Journalist and, later, foreign-policy advisor in the final years of the communist regime.

LEPENICA, HYSNI
(1900–43)

Military figure of the World War II period. From August 1943 he was commander of all Balli Kombëtar forces in southern Albania. He was killed by Italian troops near Gjirokastra.

LIBOHOVA, EQREM
BEY (1882–1948)

Political figure of the Zogist and World War II periods, and the brother of Mufit bey Libohova. On 19 January 1943, he formed an Albanian government. However, his service as prime minister and minister of the interior lasted for a mere three weeks. He fled to Rome in July 1943.

LIBOHOVA, MUFIT
BEY (1876–1927)

Political figure of the early independence period, and brother of Eqrem bey Libohova. In 1925, Ahmet Zogu made him minister of justice and finance and later, minister of foreign affairs.

LLESHI, AQIF
(1894–1983)

Activist from Dibra before and during World War II. Uncle of Haxhi Lleshi.

LLESHI, HAXHI
(1913–98)

Political figure of the communist period. In August 1953, he was elected to the post of chairman of the Presidium of the People's Assembly and was thus formally head of state of Albania until November 1982. After the dictatorship, he was convicted of crimes against humanity in May 1996.

LUBONJA, FATOS
(B.1951)

Publicist, writer and one-time political prisoner. Son of Todi Lubonja.

LUBONJA, TODI
(1923–2005)

Public figure of the communist period. He was first secretary of the party youth organisation and became a close colleague and friend of Ramiz Alia. From 1964 to 1968, he served as editor-in-chief of the daily newspaper *Zëri i popullit* (The people's voice), and was then director of Albanian radio and TV. Lubonja was purged in 1973 and sent to prison for 13 years.

LULO, ANASTAS
(D.1943)

Also known as Anastas Lula. He was a founding member of the CPA in 1941 and was executed by a communist firing squad.

LUZAJ, JUSUF
(1913–2000)

Political figure, poet and scholar. He was associated with the anti-communist resistance movement Balli Kombëtar. After the communist takeover, he escaped to Italy and died in Chicago.

MCLEAN, BILLY
(1918–86)

British military officer in Albania during World War II.

MALA, ZEF
(1915–79)

Early communist figure. He was head of the Shkodra Communist Group. After World War II, he was director of the Central State Archives until his arrest. He then spent 27 years in prison.

MALËSHOVA,
SEJFULLAH
(1901–71)

Political figure and poet of the communist period. He joined the CPSU (1930–2), but was subsequently expelled as a Bukharinist. Malëshova was minister of culture in the first communist-controlled Provisional Government after World War II. He was purged in February 1946 under his arch-rival Koçi Xoxe and was interned in Fier, where he died.

MALINOVSKY,
RODION
(1898–1967)

Soviet military commander and minister of defence from 1957 to 1967.

MALO, JAVER
(1919–97)

Diplomat and writer of the communist period. He was Albanian ambassador to France from 1967 to 1975 and one of the country's best-known diplomatic figures abroad.

MARKU, GJIN
(1918–86)

General and early member of the politburo of the Albanian communist party. He was purged in 1948.

MARUBI, PJETËR
(1834–1903)

Italian photographer, also known as Pietro Marubbi, who settled in Shkodra and is now considered the father of Albanian photography. His business was taken up by Kel Marubi (1870–1940) and later by Geg Marubi (1909–84).

MËNIKU, HALIL
(D.1967)

Member of the anti-communist resistance movement Balli Kombëtar during World War II. He was mayor of Tirana in 1943–44.

MIKOYAN, ANASTAS
(1895–1978)

Soviet political figure from Armenia. He served as Soviet minister of foreign trade (1953–4), deputy chairman of the council of ministers (1955–64) and chairman of the presidium of the Supreme Soviet (1964–5).

MILLIEZ, PAUL (1912–94)	French physician and international specialist in arterial hypertension, who treated Enver Hoxha in Tirana up to the latter's death in 1985.
MINO, RAPI	General prosecutor of the communist regime in the early 1980s and a member of the Central Expulsion and Deportation Commission. He was arrested and sentenced to five years in prison in July 1996.
MITROVICA, REXHEP (1887–1967)	Kosovo Albanian historical and political figure of the World War II period. Prime minister of Albania from November 1943 to July 1944.
MOISIU, ALFRED (B.1929)	President of Albania from July 2002 to July 2007. He is the son of army general Spiro Moisiu.
MOISIU, SPIRO (1900–81)	Military figure. He was commander of the NLA in World War II. Moisiu was purged in 1946 but was not imprisoned. He was the father of Alfred Moisiu.
MOSKO, SOKRAT	Architect who was responsible for Enver Hoxha's villa in the Bllok.
MUÇO, SKËNDER (1904–44)	Leading figure of the anti-communist resistance movement Balli Kombëtar during World War II.
MUGOŠA, DUŠAN (1914–73)	Kosovo Montenegrin communist political figure, and founding member of the CPA in 1941. He was later a hardliner in the communist hierarchy in Kosovo, both as secretary of the provincial committee for Kosovo (1956–65) and as president of the assembly of Kosovo (1960–3).
MULLETI, QAZIM (1893–1956)	Governor of Tirana, who was denounced by Enver Hoxha as a traitor for collaboration with the fascists.
MÜNZENBERG, WILLI (1889–1940)	German political figure. In 1924, he was a member of the Reichstag for the German Communist Party and later 'Moscow's propaganda tsar'.
MUSTAFA, XHEVDET (D.1982)	Albanian-American figure who lived in Staten Island, New York, where he was known as an anti-communist. He landed in Albania secretly by boat on 25 September 1982 in an alleged plot to assassinate Enver Hoxha and restore the monarchy. His small group was soon captured and he was killed. It has been alleged that his plot was in fact instigated by the Sigurimi.
MYFTIU, MANUSH (1919–97)	Political figure of the communist period. After World War II, he was a protégé of Mehmet Shehu and was thus immune from Enver Hoxha's many purges. Myftiu was deputy prime minister from 1976 to July 1990. After the fall of the dictatorship, he was sentenced to five years of prison for abuse of power, but was released on bail in view of his advanced age.
NAUMI, KOSTANDINA	Nurse who attended to Enver Hoxha.
NDREU, DALI (1912–56)	Military figure in the communist period. He was married to Liri Gega, and was purged and executed with her in November 1956.

NGJELA, KIÇO
(1917–2002)

Political figure of the communist period. Kiço Ngjela was minister of trade in the 1970s and was purged in May 1975 for grave revisionist mistakes. He was subsequently imprisoned, and only released at the end of the dictatorship, in February 1991. Father of Spartak Ngjela.

NGJELA, SPARTAK
(B.1948)

Lawyer, writer and political figure since the fall of the dictatorship. The son of Kiço Ngjela, he spent many years in Burrel prison for 'agitation and propaganda'.

NIMANI, ELHAMI
(D.1998)

Kosovo Albanian political figure. He was a founding member of the CPA in Tirana in 1941. He later served as Yugoslav ambassador to various countries.

NISHANI, OMER
(1887–1954)

Political figure of the early communist period. He was Albanian head of state from March 1945 until he was purged and forced into retirement in July 1953. He is said to have committed suicide in May 1954.

NOLI, FAN
(1882–1965)

Political figure, Orthodox Church leader, writer, poet and translator. Fan Noli was an early figure of the Albanian Autocephalous Orthodox Church and was prime minister of Albania in 1924. Toppled by Ahmet Zogu, he fled to Italy at the end of that year, and eventually moved to Boston (1930), where he headed the Albanian Orthodox Church in exile.

NUSHI, GOGO
(1913–70)

Political figure of the communist period. Gogo Nushi was a member of the Central Committee from 1948 and was one of the rare communist leaders of the period to have survived all the purges unscathed.

OHRI, IRFAN
(B.1884)

A commander of the anti-communist resistance movement Balli Kombëtar during World War II.

OMARI, BAHRI
(1889–1945)

Political figure of the World War II period. In late 1943, Bahri Omari served as foreign minister in the cabinet of Rexhep Mitrovica, and was a member of the executive board of Balli Kombëtar. He was married to Fahrije Hoxha, the sister of Enver Hoxha. Nonetheless, in April 1945, he was sentenced to death at the communist Special Court for war criminals and enemies of the people, and was executed.

OROLLOGAJ,
THOMA
(1888–1947)

Political and legal figure of the 1930s and 1940s. He was a major leader of the anti-communist resistance movement Balli Kombëtar. As such, he was arrested by the communists in early 1947 and died in prison in November of that year.

PACOLLI, BEHGJET
(B.1951)

Kosovo Albanian businessman and later political figure.

PAÇRAMI, FADIL
(1922–2008)

Political figure and dramatist of the communist period. In June 1973, he and Todi Lubonja, head of Albanian radio and TV, were singled out by Enver Hoxha in a drive against liberal and foreign influence in Albanian culture. Relieved of all his positions, he was arrested in October 1975, convicted of sabotage in the field of culture and sentenced to 25 years in prison.

PALAJ, BERNARDIN
(1894–1946)

Catholic priest, folklorist and poet. He was arrested in 1946, tortured by the Sigurimi and died in prison of tetanus.

PALMER, C. A. S. British military figure during World War II. He was a lieutenant colonel and a member of the British military mission in Albania in April 1945.

PAUKER, ANA (1893–1960) Romanian communist leader after World War II who was purged in 1952.

PEÇI, SHEFQET (1906–95) Political figure of the communist period. He played an active role in the communist resistance movement in World War II. After the war he was promoted to the rank of major general (1949), and served in various ministerial posts including vice chairman of the People's Assembly (1970–82). He was sent to prison in 1995 after the fall of the dictatorship, and died there.

PEÇINI, LLAMBI (D.1983) Senior official of the Sigurimi. He was purged with Kadri Hazbiu in 1982 and executed the following year.

PENG, DEHUAI (1898–1974) Communist Chinese minister of defence from 1954 to 1959.

PERISTERI, PILO (1909–2009) Political figure of the communist period and founding member of the CPA in 1941. He was a member of the Central Committee from 1948 to 1991 and a candidate member of the Politburo from 1952 to 1981. Peristeri was the only founding member of the CPA to have survived all the purges under Enver Hoxha.

PESHKËPIJA, NEXHAT (1908–70) Anti-communist figure during World War II. He was a member of the Free Albania (Shqypnija e Lirë) Committee in exile and died in Dearborn, Michigan.

PETRELA, ISMAIL (D.1944) Leader of a guerrilla group during World War II. He was executed by the communists in 1944.

PEZA, MYSLIM (1897–1984) Resistance fighter of the World War II period. In March 1945, he was nominated as deputy chairman of the Presidium of the People's Assembly, a post he held until 1982.

PIJADE, MOŠA (1890–1957) Yugoslav communist political figure and close collaborator of Tito during and after World War II.

PIPA, ARSHI (1920–97) Scholar, writer and public figure. Pipa was arrested in April 1946 and imprisoned for ten years. After his release in 1956, he escaped to Yugoslavia and emigrated to the United States two years later. He held teaching posts at various American universities and, until his retirement, was professor of Italian at the University of Minnesota in Minneapolis.

PLASARI, ANASTAS (B.1903) Also known as Nastas Plasari. Communist figure of the Zogist and World War II periods. He was a member of the Zjarri (Fire) communist group, and was imprisoned for two years after the war. He was the father of Aurel Plasari.

PLASARI, AUREL (B.1956) Writer, scholar and public figure. He served as director of the National Library of Albania.

PLLUMI, ZEF
(1924–2007)

Catholic priest and writer. He spent 28 years in prison and internment camps. After the fall of the dictatorship, he was made rector of the Franciscan Church of Shkodra.

POPA, AGIM
(B.1927)

Under the communist regime, he was professor of Marxist philosophy and was editor-in-chief of the daily newspaper *Zëri i popullit*.

POPA, YLLI
(B.1930)

Physician and cardiologist. From 1997 to 2007, he was head of the Albanian Academy of Sciences.

POPOVIĆ, MILADIN
(1910–45)

Montenegrin political figure of the communist period and founding member of the CPA in 1941. It was Popović who groomed Enver Hoxha to take over the leadership of the party. He returned to Kosovo in September 1944 where he was assassinated in March 1945.

PREMTJA, SADIK
(1914–91)

Communist figure of the World War II period. During World War II, Sadik Premtja, also known as Sadik Premte, who was associated with Llazar Fundo, became a rival and arch-enemy of Enver Hoxha, who spoke with disgust of him. He fled to Italy in 1944 and from there to France. The Sigurimi is said to have made three attempts to assassinate him in Paris in the postwar years.

PRENDUSHI, MATI
(1881–1948)

Catholic priest who was executed in March 1948.

PRODANI,
MUHAMET
(1922–97)

Lieutenant general in the armed forces in the 1970s. He was purged in December 1974 and sent into internal exile. In 1980 he was sentenced to 14 years in prison and was only released in 1990.

QAMILI, HAXHI
(1876–1915)

Muslim rebel leader under the reign of Prince Wied in 1914. He was hanged by Esat Pasha Toptani in the summer of 1915.

QEMALI, ISMAIL
(1844–1919)

Political figure of the Ottoman and early independence periods. After a long and distinguished career in Ottoman service, Ismail Qemali, also called Ismail Qemal bey Vlora and Ismail Kemal bey Vlora, declared Albanian independence in Vlora in November 1912. He died in Perugia in Italy.

QENDRO, ARISTIDH

Early figure of the communist movement, in the Korça Group. He was denounced as a traitor by Enver Hoxha.

QUKU, FAIK
(1899–1963)

Military figure from Shkodra. In World War II, he took part in the anti-communist resistance movement Balli Kombëtar. He escaped from Albania at the end of the war, and died in New York.

RAMOHITO, HALIM
(1925–2013)

High-ranking military figure of the communist period. He was a major general in the armed forces until he was purged in December 1974. He was in prison from 1982 to 1988.

REXHA, ZEKERIA
(1910–72)

Kosovo Albanian writer and historian. He fought in World War II for the communists in Kosovo.

RINO, NDREKO
(B.1921)

Commander of a communist partisan unit in Libohova during World War II. Subsequently (1951–71) responsible for border defence in Albania. Author of several books.

SANXHAKTARI,
FIQIRETE

See Shehu, Fiqirete.

SEJKO, TEME
(1922–61)

Military figure of the communist period. He was given the rank of a rear admiral and was appointed commander of the Albanian navy (January 1958–July 1960). He was purged in 1960, arrested and accused by a military tribunal in May 1961 of planning a coup d'état by selling the Albanian navy to the American Sixth Fleet. Sejko was strangled to death during torture before he could be executed.

SELFO, SYRJA
(D.1948)

Minor political figure from Gjirokastra. He was originally a close collaborator of Enver Hoxha, but was purged with Koçi Xoxe in 1947 and executed.

SHANTO, VASIL
(1913–44)

As a member of the Shkodra Communist Group, he was a founding member of the CPA in 1941, and died in fighting in February 1944.

SHANTOJA, LAZËR
(1892–1945)

Catholic writer, poet and translator. After years as a priest in Austria and Switzerland, he returned to Albania in 1939. At the end of 1944, he was arrested by the new communist regime as a collaborator. He was mercilessly tortured in prison where his arms and legs were broken. In January 1945 he was condemned to death by a military court, and was then shot (by a female soldier) and buried in Tirana in a nameless grave.

SHEHU, BASHKIM
(B.1955)

Albanian writer and son of Mehmet Shehu. He was imprisoned after the death of his father in 1981 and only released at the end of the communist dictatorship.

SHEHU, FEÇOR
(D.1983)

Brutal minister of the interior in the 1970s. He was executed in September 1983.

SHEHU, FIQIRETE
(1919–88)

Wife of Mehmet Shehu and member of the Central Committee of the PLA from April 1952. She was imprisoned after the death of her husband in 1981, and died in internment.

SHEHU, MEHMET
(1913–81)

Political figure of the communist period. During World War II he was one of the best-known commanders of the National Liberation Movement. He was the number-two figure of the party and government leadership, after Enver Hoxha, until the end of his days. From 1954 to 1981, he served as prime minister and from 1974 to 1980 as minister of defence. After an apparent power struggle with Enver Hoxha, he committed suicide in his villa in Tirana. Hoxha subsequently accused him of having been a 'multiple agent' working for a wide range of foreign secret services.

SHTYLLA, MEDAR
(1907–63)

Political figure of the World War II and communist periods. He was minister of economics in 1945 and minister of health in 1953. From 1958 to 1963, he served as president of the People's Assembly.

SHUKRIA, ALI
(1919–2005)

Kosovo Albanian political figure of the communist period. Ali Shukria or Shukriu was Serbian minister of the interior and, in 1950, a member of the Serbian parliament. From 1963 to May 1967 he was chairman of the executive council of Kosovo, thus becoming virtual prime minister of Kosovo. He is remembered as a particularly pro-Serbian politician who served Yugoslavia loyally in the face of a rising Albanian nationalist movement. He lived in retirement in Belgrade until his death in January 2005.

SHURBANI, NIKOLLA	Physician and cardiologist, and a founding member of the CPA. He was a member of the medical team that treated Enver Hoxha.
SINISHTA, GJON (1930–95)	Catholic clergyman, writer and editor of the *Albanian Catholic Bulletin*. He lived in San Francisco.
SKANDERBEG (1405–68)	Also spelled Scanderbeg. Albanian national hero who resisted the Ottoman invasion.
SKËNDO, LUMO	*See* Frashëri, Mid'hat.
SMILEY, DAVID (1916–2009)	British military officer in Albania during World War II. He was sent to Albania in April 1943 with Billy McLean.
SPAHIU, BEDRI (1908–98)	Political figure of the early communist period. Spahiu was a member of the so-called Youth Group and was present at the creation of the CPA in November 1941. After the war, he served in various government posts, including state prosecutor and deputy prime minister. He was purged in 1955 on charges of being pro-Yugoslav and was sent to prison until November 1974. He was finally released from internment in May 1990.
SPAHIU, XHAFER (B.1923)	Political figure of the communist period. He held many high-ranking posts from the 1960s to the 1980s, such as secretary of the Central Committee (1966–70) and deputy prime minister under Mehmet Shehu (1970–6).
SPIRU, NAKO (1918–47)	Political figure of the early communist period. He joined the communist partisans after the Italian invasion of April 1939 and, as a member of the so-called Korça Group, he was present at the creation of the CPA in November 1941. During World War II, he was considered Enver Hoxha's right-hand man. After the war, he was minister of economics (1946–7), and was married to Liri Belishova. In 1947 he was purged and 'committed suicide'.
STAFA, QEMAL (1920–42)	Communist revolutionary figure of the World War II period and founding member of the CPA in 1941. He died in a shootout in Tirana and became a martyr to the communist cause.
STARAVECKA, XHELAL (1912–75)	Resistance fighter of the World War II period. He was initially with the communists and later with the nationalists. He escaped to Italy and died in France.
STEFAN, THOMAS	US military figure of Albanian origin. He was a commander of the field mission of the Office of Strategic Services (OSS) in Albania.
STEFANI, SIMON (1929–2000)	Political figure of the communist period. He was chairman of the People's Assembly from 1978 to 1982 and minister of the interior from 1989 to 1990. In 1994, after the dictatorship, he was sentenced to eight years in prison.
STËRMILLI, HAKI (1895–1953)	Public figure, prose writer and playwright. During World War II, Stërmilli joined the resistance movement, and after the communist takeover he was elected as an MP and then made director of the National Library.
STOJNIĆ, VELIMIR (1916–90)	Yugoslav military figure, and emissary of Tito during World War II.

SUSLOV, MIKHAIL (1902–82)
Soviet statesman during the period of the Cold War. He was chief ideologist of the party until his death.

TASHKO, KOÇO (1899–1984)
Nationalist and communist figure and founding member of the CPA in 1941. He was Albanian ambassador to the Soviet Union (1946–7), deputy foreign minister (1947–53), ambassador to Bulgaria (1954–5) and chairman of the central auditing commission. During the break with the Soviet Union in 1960, he was expelled from the party, deprived of his parliamentary immunity, denounced as an enemy of the people, imprisoned (1969–78) and interned.

TERESA, MOTHER (1910–97)
Catholic religious figure of Albanian descent. Born in Skopje as Agnes Gonxhe Bojaxhiu, she founded the order Missionaries of Charity in 1950 and was awarded the Nobel Peace Prize in 1979. She visited Albania in December 1990.

THEMELI, ZOI
Sigurimi head in Shkodra in the late 1940s.

THEMELKO, KRISTO (B.1915)
Founding member of the CPA in 1941, He was purged in November 1948, but was later a senior member of the Sigurimi. Author of the book *Tirana e përgjakur* (Bloodbath in Tirana).

THEODHOSI, KOÇO (1913–77)
Political official of the communist period, He was minister of industry and mines in the early 1970s. Together with Abdyl Këllezi and Kiço Ngjela, he fell victim to the purge at the Seventh Congress of the Central Committee on 26–29 May 1975, allegedly for grave revisionist mistakes and sabotage of the economy. He was swiftly relieved of his posts, expelled from the party, arrested and executed in the spring of 1977.

THOREZ, MAURICE (1900–64)
French political figure. He was general secretary of the French Communist Party from 1930 to 1964.

TILMAN, H. W.
Major in the British armed forces and a member of the British mission seconded to the General Staff of the NLA in Albania during World War II.

TITO, JOSIP BROZ (1892–1980)
Yugoslav political figure. President of Yugoslavia from 1953 to his death in 1980.

TOPTANI, ABDUL
Father of Ihsan Toptani.

TOPTANI, ESAT PASHA (1863–1920)
Political figure from a wealthy landowning family. He was active in Albanian politics and power struggles around the time of World War I, and was assassinated in June 1920 in Paris, where he was buried.

TOPTANI, IHSAN (1908–2001)
Historical and public figure who was the son of Abdul Toptani. During World War II, he played an important liaison role in efforts to unite the various resistance movements. In October 1944, he fled to Italy and in 1949 he moved to England, where he died.

TOPULLI, ÇERÇIZ (1880–1915)
Nationalist figure and guerrilla fighter from Gjirokastra.

TOTO, ET'HEM	Captain of the gendarmerie under King Zog and then minister of the interior (1935–6).
TOTO, ISMET (1908–37)	Writer and publisher. He was sentenced to death by King Zog and hanged in 1937 during the repression of anti-Zogist uprisings.
TOTO, SELAHUDIN (1914–47)	Writer and publisher. He took part in the communist resistance during World War II and was a member of the People's Assembly in 1945. He was arrested in May 1947 and executed.
TSALDARIS, KONSTANTINOS (1884–1970)	Greek conservative political figure and prime minister of Greece in 1946–7.
TUCI, MARIA	Catholic nun who was declared a martyr of Christianity after her death in Albania.
TURDIU, QAZIM (1917–99)	Professor of mathematics whose daughter Silva was engaged to Skënder Shehu, the son of Mehmet Shehu. The engagement served as a pretext for the downfall and death of Mehmet Shehu.
ULQINAKU, MUJO (1896–1939)	Military figure from Ulqin (Ulcinj, now in Montenegro). He took part in resisting the Italian invasion of Albania in April 1939, and was killed in the fighting.
VAILLANT-COUTURIER, MARIE-CLAUDE (1912–96)	Daughter of Lucien Vogel and member of the French resistance during World War II.
VAILLANT-COUTURIER, PAUL (1892–1937)	French writer, journalist and communist political figure.
VËRLACI, SHEFQET BEY (1877–1946)	Political figure of the World War II period. Prime minister of Albania under Italian occupation from April 1939 to December 1941.
VLLAMASI, SEJFI (1883–1975)	Political and nationalist figure of the Zogist and World War II periods. Vllamasi was a member of Balli Kombëtar in 1943 and was sentenced to prison by the communists in November 1944. After nine years in jail, he was released and sent into internment in Fier, where he worked as a lowly herdsman.
VOGEL, LUCIEN (1886–1954)	French art publisher, magazine editor and left-wing aesthete.
VOKSHI, ASIM (1909–37)	Kosovo Albanian military figure from Gjakova. He studied in Italy and served in the International Brigades during the Spanish Civil War.
VOKSHI, BIJE	The aunt of Asim Vokshi.
VRIONI, JUSUF (1916–2001)	Translator and public figure. Jusuf Vrioni lived in Paris from 1923 onwards, where his father, Iljaz bey Vrioni, was ambassador. He was arrested in 1947 and accused of spying for France and of playing tennis. After his release in 1958, he became a noted Albanian–French translator, in particular of the works of Ismail Kadare.

VUKMANOVIĆ, SVETOZAR ('TEMPO') 1912–2000)	Yugoslav political figure. Partisan commander during World War II and vice president of Yugoslavia in 1953–8.
VUKMIROVIĆ, BORKO BORO (1912–43)	Member of the Yugoslav communist movement, in particular in Kosovo.
VULLKANI, SOTIR	Founding member of the CPA in 1941.
VYSHINSKY, ANDREY (1883–1954)	Soviet political figure and diplomat who was Soviet foreign minister from 1949 to 1953.
WEXLER, MAX (1870–1917)	Also spelled Max Wechsler. Romanian Jewish Marxist theoretician, socialist activist and journalist.
WIED, WILHELM, PRINCE OF (1876–1945)	German prince and, briefly, monarch of Albania (1913–14). He left Albania at the start of World War I and never returned.
WILSON, HENRY MAITLAND (1881–1964)	British military figure. In 1944, he was supreme Allied commander in the Mediterranean.
XHAFERRI, QEMAL	Military figure.
XHELO, HALIM (1894–1937)	Left-wing figure from the Vlora region. As an anti-Zogist, he lived abroad in the 1920s and 1930s and died in Moscow.
XHUGLINI, NEXHMIJE	*See* Hoxha, Nexhmije.
XOXE, KOÇI (1911–49)	Political figure of the early communist period and founding member of the CPA in 1941. As a tinsmith, Xoxe was one of the very few communist leaders of Albania with a genuinely proletarian background. He was also one of the most ruthless. As deputy prime minister and minister of the interior, he was a major figure in the party hierarchy from early 1946 to October 1948, but was purged and executed in 1949.
ZAVALANI, TAJAR (1903–66)	Writer and left-wing public figure. He left Albania in 1939 and, joining the entourage of King Zog, moved to England in 1940. In 1941 he created an anti-Zogist organisation known as the 'Free Albania' movement.
ZAZANI, ENVER (D.1947)	Childhood friend of Enver Hoxha. As an MP, Enver Zazani, also known as Enver Sazani, was arrested in May 1947 and executed.
ZIÇISHTI, LLAMBI (1923–83)	Physician, professor and minister of health in the early 1980s. He was purged with Kadri Hazbiu in 1982 and executed the following year.
ZIÇISHTI, MIHALLAQ (1921–94)	Military figure on the communist side during World War II. He was a member of the Central Committee of the PLA from 1952 and held various high military and political posts. He was purged in 1982 as part of the 'hostile group' of Kadri Hazbiu and was sentenced to 25 years' imprisonment. He was released in 1990.

ZISI, ANDREA

Early figure of the Albanian communist movement. He lived in exile in Athens in the 1930s and was head of the Zjarri (Fire) communist group in 1937.

ZLATIĆ, SAVO
(1912–2007)

Partisan physician in Croatia and later Yugoslav envoy to Albania in the post-World War II period.

ZOGU, AHMET
(1895–1961)

Political figure and monarch of Albania, known then as King Zog. He overthrew the government of Fan Noli in 1924, and became the country's president and then king (1928–39). He fled Albania during the Italian invasion of April 1939 and settled in England and later in Egypt.

Notes

3. FROM GJIROKASTRA TO KORÇA

1 Interview with Ismail Kadare on the TV programme *Opinion*, broadcast on TV Klan, December 2003.

2 Enver Hoxha, *Kur u hodhën themelet e Shqipërisë së re: kujtime dhe shënime historike* (Tirana: 8 Nëntori, 1984).

3 Enver Hoxha, *Vite të rinisë: kujtime* (Tirana: 8 Nëntori, 1988). All quotations from Enver Hoxha's memoirs have been translated from the original for the purposes of this English edition. Published English-language translations of works by Hoxha listed in the bibliography have not been used.

4 Vedat Kokona, *Endur në tisin e kohes: kujtime* (Tirana: Botimet Kokona, 2005).

5 Ibid.

6 Enver Hoxha, *Vite të rinisë*.

7 Interview with Hana Klissura on the TV programme *Opinion Plus*, broadcast on TV Klan, November 2007.

4. FROM FRANCE TO BELGIUM: THE DROPOUT

1 Lazër Radi, *Mirash Ivanaj, kujtimet e një ministri* (Tirana: Lilo, 1996).

2 Enver Hoxha, *Vite të rinisë: kujtime* (Tirana: 8 Nëntori, 1988).

3 Enver Hoxha, letter to Anastas Plasari, 8 June 1943, Central State Archives.

4 Anastas Plasari, 'Takimet e mia me partite komuniste: kujtime historike' [manuscript, Plasari family archives].

5 Stéphane Courtois and Marc Lazar, *Histoire du Parti communiste français* (Paris: PUF, 2006). (In fact, Enver Hoxha was never a student at the Sorbonne.)

6 Enver Hoxha, *Eurokomunizmi është antikomunizëm* (Tirana: 8 Nëntori, 1980).

7 Arshi Pipa, *Albanian Stalinism: Ideo-Political Aspects*, East European Monographs 287 (New York: Columbia University Press, 1990).

8 Enver Hoxha, *Kur u hodhën themelet e Shqipërisë së re: kujtime dhe shënime historike* (Tirana: 8 Nëntori, 1984).

9 Interview with Hana Klissura on the TV programme *Opinion Plus*, broadcast on TV Klan, November 2007.

10 Ibid.

5. TEACHER OF MORAL EDUCATION

1 Enver Hoxha, *Vite të rinisë: kujtime* (Tirana: 8 Nëntori, 1988).
2 Vedat Kokona, *Endur në tisin e kohes: kujtime* (Tirana: Botimet Kokona, 2005).
3 Interview with Abaz Ermenji on the TV programme *E diela debat*, broadcast on TVSH, October 2008.
4 Interview with Beqir Ajazi on the TV programme *Opinion*, broadcast on TV Klan, October 2008.
5 Ibid.
6 Kokona, *Endur në tisin e kohes*.
7 Ermenji, *E diela debat* interview.
8 Ibid.
9 Ibid.

6. THE FOUNDING OF THE COMMUNIST PARTY

1 Interview with Beqir Ajazi on the TV programme *Opinion*, broadcast on TV Klan, October 2008.
2 Interview with Fadil Hoxha on the TV programme *Opinion*, broadcast on TV Klan, December 2000.
3 Interview with Kristo Frashëri on the TV programme *Opinion Plus*, broadcast on TV Klan, November 2007.
4 Ibid.
5 Enver Hoxha, 'Autokritikë në Plenumin e Beratit', Central State Archives.
6 Ajazi, *Opinion* interview.
7 Interview with Ramiz Alia on the TV programme *Opinion*, broadcast on TV Klan, October 2005.
8 Enver Hoxha, *Kur lindi Partia: kujtime* (Tirana: 8 Nëntori, 1981).
9 Ibid.
10 Todi Lubonja, *Nën peshën e dhunës: kujtime* (Tirana: Progresi, 1993).
11 Fadil Hoxha, *Opinion* interview.
12 Ibid.
13 Ibid.
14 Kristo Frashëri, *Opinion Plus* interview.
15 Enver Hoxha, 'Autokritikë në Plenumin e Beratit', Central State Archives.

7. A LEADER WITH AN IRON FIST

1 Interview with Kristo Frashëri on the TV programme *Opinion Plus*, broadcast on TV Klan, November 2007.
2 Enver Hoxha, 'Autokritikë në Plenumin e Beratit', Central State Archives.
3 Enver Hoxha, notes on the conference of Labinot, Central State Archives.
4 Kristo Frashëri, *Opinion Plus* interview.
5 Ibid.
6 Enver Hoxha, letter to Nako Spiru, March 1944, Central State Archives.

7   Enver Hoxha, order no. 46, 21 September 1944, Central State Archives.
8   Vedat Kokona, *Endur në tisin e kohes: kujtime* (Tirana: Botimet Kokona, 2005).
9   Josip Broz Tito, letter to Enver Hoxha, 22 September 1942, recorded in Vladimir Dedijer, *Marrëdhëniet jugosllavo–shqiptare 1939–1948* (Belgrade: Prosveta, 1949; repr. Tirana, 2005) [Albanian translation of Vladimir Dedijer, *Jugoslovensko–albanski odnosi (1939–1948). Na osnovu službenih dokumenata, pisama i drugog materijala* (Zagreb: Borba, 1949).]
10   Kristo Frashëri, *Historia e lëvizjes së majtë në Shqipëri dhe e themelimit të PKSH-së, 1878–1941* (Tirana: Akademia e Shkencave, 2006).
11   Ibid.
12   Enver Hoxha, letter to Anastas Plasari, 8 June 1943, Central State Archives.
13   Enver Hoxha, letter to Gogo Nushi, 7 October 1943, Central State Archives.
14   Nexhmije Xhuglini, letter to Enver Hoxha, 14 October 1943, Central State Archives.
15   Enver Hoxha, letter to Nako Spiru and Ymer Dishnica, 29 September 1943, Central State Archives.
16   Anastas Plasari, 'Takimet e mia me partite komuniste: kujtime historike' [manuscript, Plasari family archives].
17   Enver Hoxha, letter to Gogo Nushi, October 1943, Central State Archives.
18   Kristo Frashëri, *Opinion Plus* interview.
19   Surveillance report on Anastas Plasari, 27 February 1959, archives of the Ministry of the Interior.
20   Enver Hoxha, letter to Nako Spiru, 4 April 1944, Central State Archives.
21   Nexhmije Hoxha, *Jeta ime me Enverin: kujtime*, vol. 1 (Tirana: Lira, 1998).
22   Enver Hoxha, *Kur lindi Partia: kujtime* (Tirana: 8 Nëntori, 1981).
23   'Drita Kosturi: Qemal Stafa vrau veten', *Klan* [magazine], April 1998.
24   Ibid.
25   Enver Hoxha, 'Autokritikë'.
26   Ibid.

8. NATIONALISTS AND COMMUNISTS

1   Enver Hoxha, 'Autokritikë në Plenumin e Beratit', Central State Archives.
2   Telegram from British Major H. W. Tilman, *Zëri i popullit* [newspaper], 29 January 1944.
3   Minutes of the Mukja conference, 1 August 1943, Central State Archives.
4   Proclamation of the Committee for the Salvation of Albania, August 1943, Central State Archives.
5   Enver Hoxha, circular, 8 August 1943, Central State Archives.
6   Enver Hoxha, letter to Ymer Dishnica, 9 August 1943, Central State Archives.
7   Enver Hoxha, order for the National Liberation Army, 26 August 1943, Central State Archives.
8   Enver Hoxha, 'Autokritikë'.
9   Enver Hoxha, *Rreziku anglo-amerikan për Shqipërinë: kujtime nga Lufta Nacional-Çlirimtare* (Tirana: 8 Nëntori, 1982).

10 Bedri Koka in an interview with Afrim Imaj, 'Unë dëshmitari në pushkatimin e Liri Gegës', *Panorama* [newspaper], January 2011.

11 Interview with Abaz Ermenji on the TV programme *E diela debat*, broadcast on TVSH, June 1998.

12 Interview with Liri Belishova on the TV programme *Opinion*, broadcast on TV Klan, June 2004.

13 Interview with Hana Klissura on the TV programme *Opinion Plus*, broadcast on TV Klan, November 2007.

9. HEAD OF THE PROVISIONAL GOVERNMENT

1 Enver Hoxha, letter to Dušan Mugoša, May 1944, recorded in Vladimir Dedijer, *Marrëdhëniet jugosllavo–shqiptare 1939–1948* (Belgrade: Prosveta, 1949; repr. Tirana, 2005) [Albanian translation of Vladimir Dedijer, *Jugoslovensko–albanski odnosi (1939–1948). Na osnovu službenih dokumenata, pisama i drugog materijala* (Zagreb: Borba, 1949).]

2 Enver Hoxha, *Kur u hodhën themelet e Shqipërisë së re: kujtime dhe shënime historike* (Tirana: 8 Nëntori, 1984).

3 *Ylli çlirimtar* [newsletter], no. 1, 1946, Central State Archives.

4 Nako Spiru, discussion at the plenary meeting in Berat, November 1944, Central State Archives.

5 Enver Hoxha, order no. 45, 21 September 1944, Central State Archives.

6 Enver Hoxha, 'Bazi i Canes, Myslim Peza, Baba Faja Martaneshi', *Zëri i popullit* [newspaper], nos 11–12, February 1943.

7 Enver Hoxha, *Vepra 1: nëntor 1941–tetor 1943* (Tirana: 8 Nëntori, 1983), pp. 271–6.

8 Enver Hoxha, 'Bazi i Canes dhe Legaliteti, Helmës 1944', Central State Archives.

9 Xhelal Staravecka, leaflet no. 5, Balli Kombëtar.

10 Ibid.

11 Julian Amery, *Sons of the Eagle: A Study in Guerilla War* (London: Macmillan, 1948), p. 336.

12 Telegram of the Albanian mission to the United Nations, 10 January 1976, Central State Archives.

10. THE PLENARY MEETING IN BERAT — AN INTERLUDE

1 Mehmet Shehu, telegram to Enver Hoxha in Berat, 17 November 1944, Central State Archives.

2 Enver Hoxha, *Titistët* (Tirana: 8 Nëntori, 1982).

11. TIRANA AND THE WEDDING

1 Nexhmije Hoxha, *Jeta ime me Enverin: kujtime*, vol. 1 (Tirana: Lira, 1998).

2 Enver Hoxha, *Kur u hodhën themelet e Shqipërisë së re: kujtime dhe shënime historike* (Tirana: 8 Nëntori, 1984).

3 Nexhmije Hoxha, *Jeta ime me Enverin*, vol. 1.

4   Ibid.
5   Nexhmije Hoxha, interview, July 1995.
6   Interview with Liljana Hoxha on the TV programme *Opinion*, broadcast on TV Klan, April 2007.
7   Ibid.
8   Enver Hoxha, diary, 5 October 1981. Hoxha's diaries are in the Central State Archives.
9   Nexhmije Xhuglini, letter to Enver Hoxha, 14 October 1943, Central State Archives.
10   Nexhmije Hoxha, *Jeta ime me Enverin*, vol. 1.
11   Ibid.
12   Interview with Hana Klissura on the TV programme *Opinion Plus*, broadcast on TV Klan, November 2007.
13   Enver Hoxha, order no. 59, 28 September 1944, Central State Archives.
14   Bedri Spahiu, 'Bedri Spahiu revizionon Bedri Spahiun', *Republika* [newspaper], 6 June 1991.
15   Ibid.
16   Klissura, *Opinion Plus* interview.
17   Musine Kokalari, *Si lindi Partia Socialdemokrate. Artikuj, shrime, esse, kujtime*, ed. Platon Salim Kokalari (Tirana: Naim Frashëri, 2000).
18   Ibid.
19   Lazër Radi, 'Shënime për Musine Kokalarin, kujtime burgu dhe arkivi', *Aleanca* [newspaper], 1994.

12. A REIGN OF TERROR

1   Enver Hoxha, order no. 96 to General Dali Ndreu, 17 November 1944, Central State Archives.
2   Enver Hoxha, letter to Gogo Nushi, 7 October 1943, Central State Archives.
3   Enver Hoxha, order no. 44 to Colonel Mehmet Shehu, 10 November 1944, Central State Archives.
4   Muntaz Kokalari, letter to Makbule Vrioni, 8 November 1944, Central State Archives.
5   Kristo Themelko, *Tirana e përgjakur* (Tirana: n.p., 1996).
6   Enver Hoxha, *Rreziku anglo-amerikan për Shqipërinë: kujtime nga Lufta Nacional-Çlirimtare* (Tirana: 8 Nëntori, 1982).
7   Enver Hoxha, *Titistët* (Tirana: 8 Nëntori, 1982).
8   Gogo Nushi, discussion at the plenary meeting in Berat, 25 November 1944, Central State Archives.
9   Vaskë Koleci, report to Enver Hoxha, 20 January 1945, Central State Archives.
10   Ibid.
11   Enver Hoxha, telegram order to Mehmet Shehu, 1 February 1945, Central State Archives.
12   Enver Hoxha, telegram order to the Second Corps, 10 February 1945, Central State Archives.
13   Enver Hoxha, telegram order to the Military Tribunal in Shkodra, 10 February 1945, Central State Archives.
14   Enver Hoxha, 'Autokritikë në Plenumin e Beratit', Central State Archives.

15   Kastriot Dervishi, *E vërteta e fshehur e një procesi: gjyqi i Koçi Xoxes, lidhjet e tij me Enver Hoxhën* (Tirana: Shtëpia Botuese 55, 2009).
16   Interview with Pjetër Arbnori on the TV programme *Opinion*, broadcast on TV Klan, April 2000.
17   Ibid.
18   Todi Lubonja, *Nën peshën e dhunës: kujtime* (Tirana: Progresi, 1993).
19   Enver Hoxha, *Kur u hodhën themelet e Shqipërisë së re: kujtime dhe shënime historike* (Tirana: 8 Nëntori, 1984).
20   Ibid.
21   Dervishi, *E vërteta e fshehur e një procesi.*
22   Bedri Koka in an interview with Afrim Imaj, 'Unë dëshmitari në pushkatimin e Liri Gegës', *Panorama* [newspaper], January 2011.

13. DEPARTURE OF THE BRITISH AND THE AMERICANS

1   Enver Hoxha, *Rreziku anglo-amerikan për Shqipërinë: kujtime nga Lufta Nacional-Çlirimtare* (Tirana: 8 Nëntori, 1982).
2   Ibid.
3   Ibid.
4   Ibid.
5   *Paris Peace Conference 1946, Selected Documents* (Washington DC: US State Department, 1946).
6   Enver Hoxha, *Rreziku anglo-amerikan për Shqipërinë.*
7   Robert Papa, *Ngrica mes Uashingonit dhe Tiranës* (Tirana: n.p., 2006).

14. THE YUGOSLAVS: A MATTER OF LOVE AND HATE

1   Milovan Djilas, *Conversations with Stalin*, trans. Michael B. Petrovich (New York: Harcourt, Brace & World, 1962), p. 146.
2   Enver Hoxha, letter to Dušan Mugoša, April 1944, recorded in Vladimir Dedijer, *Marrëdhëniet jugosllavo–shqiptare 1939–1948* (Belgrade: Prosveta, 1949; repr. Tirana, 2005) [Albanian translation of Vladimir Dedijer, *Jugoslovensko–albanski odnosi (1939–1948). Na osnovu službenih dokumenata, pisama i drugog materijala* (Zagreb: Borba, 1949).]
3   Interview with Alfred Moisiu on the TV programme *Opinion*, broadcast on TV Klan, November 2002.
4   Interview with Fadil Hoxha on the TV programme *Opinion*, broadcast on TV Klan, December 2000.
5   Ibid.
6   Enver Hoxha, *Titistët* (Tirana: 8 Nëntori, 1982).
7   Ibid.
8   Enver Hoxha, discussion at the extraordinary plenary meeting of the Central Committee of the CPA, 18–20 December 1946, Central State Archives.
9   Kastriot Dervishi, *E vërteta e fshehur e një procesi: gjyqi i Koçi Xoxes, lidhjet e tij me Enver Hoxhën* (Tirana: Shtëpia Botuese 55, 2009).
10   Interview with Fadil Hoxha, conducted by the author.

11   Enver Hoxha, *Titistët*.

12   Interview with Liri Belishova on the TV programme *Opinion*, broadcast on TV Klan, June 2004.

13   Ibid.

14   Ibid.

15   Ibid.

16   Ibid.

17   Ibid.

18   Nako Spiru, letter to Tito on the career of Enver Hoxha, November or December 1944, recorded in Dedijer, *Marrëdhëniet jugosllavo–shqiptare 1939–1948*.

19   Kastriot Dervishi, *Historia e shtetit shqiptar, 1912–2005. Organizimi shtetëror, jeta politike, ngjarjet kryesore, të gjithë ligjvënësit, ministrat dhe kryetarët e shtetit shqiptar* (Tirana: Shtëpia Botuese 55, 2006).

20   Koçi Xoxe, farewell message to Enver Hoxha, 11 June 1949, Central State Archives.

21   'Vrasja e ushtarakëve', *Korrieri* [newspaper], March 2002.

22   Mehmet Shehu, farewell letter to Enver Hoxha, 17 December 1981, Central State Archives.

23   Bashkim Shehu, *Vjeshta e ankthit: esse*, introduction by Ismail Kadare (Tirana: Albin, 1994; repr. Prishtina: Buzuku, 1997).

15. STALIN AND THE SOVIETS

1   Enver Hoxha, *Me Stalinin: kujtime* (Tirana: 8 Nëntori, 1979).

2   Milovan Djilas, *Conversations with Stalin*, trans. Michael B. Petrovich (New York: Harcourt, Brace & World, 1962), p. 143.

3   Enver Hoxha, *Me Stalinin*.

4   Ibid.

5   Enver Hoxha, 'Marksizmëm–Leninizëm mëson se populli është krijues i historisë', *Zëri i popullit* [newspaper], 14 April 1956.

6   Ibid.

7   Ibid.

8   Mahmut Bakalli, memoirs [manuscript, Bakalli family archives].

9   Interview with Agim Popa, *Panorama* [newspaper], 2011.

10   Spartak Ngjela, *Përkulja dhe rënia e tiranisë shqiptare, 1957–2010: refleksione për një kohë* (Tirana: UET Press, 2011).

11   Kastriot Dervishi, *Plumba politikës: historitë e përgjakjes së politikanëve shqiptarë* (Tirana: Shtëpia Botuese 55, n.d. [2010]).

12   Interview with Ramiz Alia on the TV programme *Opinion*, broadcast on TV Klan, October 2005.

13   'Enver Hoxha, red boss', *Time*, December 1960.

14   Interview with Çlirim Balluku on the TV programme *Opinion*, broadcast on TV Klan, February 2004.

15   Discussion between the author and Fadil Hoxha.

16   Interview with Robert Frowick on the TV programme *Opinion*, broadcast on TV Klan, September 2000.

17 Todi Lubonja, *Nën peshën e dhunës: kujtime* (Tirana: Progresi, 1993).
18 Ibid.
19 Interview with Liri Belishova on the TV programme *Opinion*, broadcast on TV Klan, June 2004.
20 Ibid.
21 Ibid.
22 Kastriot Dervishi, *Kadri Hazbiu: krimet dhe vrasja* (Tirana: Shtëpia Botuese 55, 2011).
23 Ibid.

16. THE BLLOK

1 Bashkim Shehu, *Vjeshta e ankthit: esse*, introduction by Ismail Kadare (Tirana: Albin, 1994; repr. Prishtina: Buzuku, 1997).
2 Interview with Liljana Hoxha on the TV programme *Opinion*, broadcast on TV Klan, October 2010.
3 Shehu, *Vjeshta e ankthit*.
4 *Ditëlindja e Shokut Enver* [documentary], 16 October 1981, Central State Film Archives.
5 Enver Hoxha, speech on the decoration of Myslim Peza, *Zëri i popullit* [newspaper], 3 May 1979.
6 Liljana Hoxha, *Opinion* interview.
7 Ibid.
8 Film of meetings of the Central Committee, October 1982, Central State Archives.
9 Ibid.

17. ENVER HOXHA AND MOTHER TERESA

1 Granit Zela, 'Gonxhe Bojaxhiu, Madhështia e dashurisë', *Fjala* [newspaper], August 2004.
2 Ibid.
3 Ibid.
4 Ibid.
5 Vaskë Koleci, letter to Enver Hoxha, 30 January 1945, Central State Archives.
6 Enver Hoxha, telegram order to Mehmet Shehu, 5 February 1945, Central State Archives.
7 Gjon Sinishta, *The Fulfilled Promise: A Documentary Account of Religious Persecution in Albania* (Santa Clara, CA: n.p., 1976).
8 Office of the minister of the interior, Shkodra, report to Enver Hoxha, 11 March 1948, Central State Archives.
9 Zef Pllumi, *Rrno vetëm për me tregue. Libri i kujtimeve. Pjesa e parë 1944–1951* (Tirana: Hylli i dritës, 1995).
10 Bedri Spahiu, *Testamenti politik* (Tirana: Apollonia, 1994). See also Gjon Sinishta, *The Fulfilled Promise: A Documentary Account of Religious Persecution in Albania* (Santa Clara, CA: n.p., 1976), p. 53.
11 Sinishta, *The Fulfilled Promise*.

18. SPLIT PERSONALITY

1   Interview with Ismail Kadare on the TV programme *Opinion*, broadcast on TV Klan, October 1998.
2   Ibid.
3   Interview with Bashkim Shehu on the TV programme *Opinion*, broadcast on TV Klan, May 2004.
4   Conversation between the author and Ismail Kadare, 2011.
5   Conversation between the author and Aurel Plasari, 2011.
6   Ibid.
7   Ibid.
8   Interview with Kristo Frashëri on the TV programme *Opinion Plus*, broadcast on TV Klan, November 2007.
9   Enver Hoxha, *Kur u hodhën themelet e Shqipërisë së re: kujtime dhe shënime historike* (Tirana: 8 Nëntori, 1984).
10 Ibid.
11 Sejfi Vllamasi, *Ballafaqime politike në Shqipëri (1897–1942): kujtime dhe vlerësime historike* (Tirana: Marin Barleti, 1995).
12 Bashkim Shehu, *Opinion* interview.
13 Ibid.
14 Todi Lubonja, *Nën peshën e dhunës: kujtime* (Tirana: Progresi, 1993).
15 Vedat Kokona, *Endur në tisin e kohes: kujtime* (Tirana: Botimet Kokona, 2005).

19. THE MEDICAL TEAM

1   Interview with Isuf Kalo on the TV programme *Opinion*, broadcast on TV Klan, December 2009.
2   Ibid.
3   Paul Milliez, *Ce que je crois* (Paris: Grasset, 1986).
4   Kalo, *Opinion* interview.
5   Interview with Ylli Popa on the TV programme *Opinion*, broadcast on TV Klan, December 2007.
6   Interview with Isuf Kalo in *ONE* [periodical], 2009.
7   Popa, *Opinion* interview.
8   Diagnosis of Enver Hoxha, in French, October 1972, Central State Archives.
9   Popa, *Opinion* interview.
10 Ibid.
11 Ibid.
12 Interview with Isuf Kalo in *ONE* [periodical], 2009.
13 Kalo, *Opinion* interview.

20. THE GREAT PURGES

1   Todi Lubonja, *Nën peshën e dhunës: kujtime* (Tirana: Progresi, 1993).
2   Ibid.

3   Kastriot Dervishi, *Kadri Hazbiu: krimet dhe vrasja* (Tirana: Shtëpia Botuese 55, 2011).
4   Ibid.

21. DEMISE OF A PRIME MINISTER

1   Bashkim Shehu, *Vjeshta e ankthit: esse*, introduction by Ismail Kadare (Tirana: Albin, 1994; repr. Prishtina: Buzuku, 1997).
2   Ibid.
3   Author's interview with Isuf Kalo, 2011.
4   Arshi Pipa, *Albanian Stalinism: Ideo-Political Aspects*, East European Monographs 287 (New York: Columbia University Press, 1990).
5   Author's interview with Isuf Kalo, 2011.
6   Shehu, *Vjeshta e ankthit*.
7   *Ditëlindja e Shokut Enver* [documentary], 16 October 1981, Central State Film Archives.
8   Ibid.
9   Mehmet Shehu, farewell letter to Enver Hoxha, 17 December 1981, Central State Archives.
10   Ibid.
11   Interview with Liljana Hoxha on the TV programme *Opinion*, broadcast on TV Klan, April 2007.
12   Interview with Liljana Hoxha on the TV programme *Opinion*, broadcast on TV Klan, October 2010.
13   Author's interview with Fatos Lubonja, 2011.

22. THE FINAL PURGES

1   Interview with Ramiz Alia on the TV programme *E diela debat*, broadcast on TVSH, June 1998.
2   Author's interview with Isuf Kalo, 2011.
3   Bashkim Shehu, *Vjeshta e ankthit: esse*, introduction by Ismail Kadare (Tirana: Albin, 1994; repr. Prishtina: Buzuku, 1997).
4   Interview with Behgjet Pacolli on the TV programme *Opinion*, broadcast on TV Klan, March 2011.
5   Enver Hoxha, notes on Kadri Hazbiu, 14 January 1982, Central State Archives.
6   Film recording of the plenary meeting of the Central Committee, October 1982, on the TV programme *Opinion*, broadcast on TV Klan, February 2004.
7   Interview with Ramiz Alia on the TV programme *E diela debat*, broadcast on TVSH, June 1998.
8   Kastriot Dervishi, *Kadri Hazbiu: krimet dhe vrasja* (Tirana: Shtëpia Botuese 55, 2011).

23. THE YEARS OF SOLITUDE

1   Bashkim Shehu, *Anatomia e bibliotekës së një diktatori* (Barcelona: n.p., 2002).
2   Sulo Gradeci, *30 vjet pranë shokut Enver: kujtime* (Tirana: 8 Nëntori, 1988).

3 Interview with Max Strauss on the TV programme *Opinion*, broadcast on TV Klan, March 2007.

4 Interview with Liljana Hoxha on the TV programme *Opinion*, broadcast on TV Klan, April 2007.

5 Enver Hoxha, *Zëri i popullit* [newspaper], 30 November 1984.

6 Nexhmije Hoxha, *Jeta ime me Enverin: kujtime*, vol. 2 (Tirana: Neraida, 2001).

7 Film recording of the meeting of the Politburo, February 1985, on the TV programme *Opinion*, broadcast on TV Klan, February 2004.

8 Interview with Isuf Kalo in the periodical *ONE*, 2009.

24. DEATH AND WHAT REMAINED

1 Nexhmije Hoxha, *Jeta ime me Enverin: kujtime*, vol. 2 (Tirana: Neraida, 2001).

2 Interview with Ylli Popa on the TV programme *Opinion*, broadcast on TV Klan, December 2007.

3 Film recording of the meeting of the Politburo, 11 April 1985, on the TV programme *Opinion*, broadcast on TV Klan, February 2004.

4 Speech of Ramiz Alia, broadcast on Albanian radio and TV, 14 April 1985.

Bibliography

Ajazi, Beqir, *Nga shkaba me kurorë te drapëri me çekan: ne çetelë të kujtimit* (Tirana: Mokra, 2000), 478 pp.

———— *Kush ishte Enver Hoxha* (Tirana: Shtëpia Botuese 55, 2007), 132 pp.

Amery, Julian, *Sons of the Eagle: A Study in Guerilla War* (London: Macmillan, 1948), 354 pp.

———— *Bijtë e shqipës*, trans. Felatun Vila (Tirana: Lumo Skëndo, 2002), 386 pp.

Bakalli, Mahmut, memoirs [manuscript, Bakalli family archives].

Courtois, Stéphane, and Marc Lazar, *Histoire du Parti communiste français* (Paris: PUF, 2006), 480 pp.

Dedijer, Vladimir, *Jugoslovensko–albanski odnosi (1939–1948). Na osnovu službenih dokumenata, pisama i drugog materijala* (Zagreb: Borba, 1949), 225 pp.

———— *Marrëdhëniet jugosllavo–shqiptare 1939–1948* (Belgrade: Prosveta, 1949; repr. Tirana: Medaur, 2005).

Dervishi, Kastriot, *Historia e shtetit shqiptar, 1912–2005. Organizimi shtetëror, jeta politike, ngjarjet kryesore, të gjithë ligjvënësit, ministrat dhe kryetarët e shtetit shqiptar* (Tirana: Shtëpia Botuese 55, 2006), 954 pp.

———— *E vërteta e fshehur e një procesi: gjyqi i Koçi Xoxes, lidhjet e tij me Enver Hoxhën* (Tirana: Shtëpia Botuese 55, 2009), 275 pp.

———— *Plumba politikës: historitë e përgjakjes së politikanëve shqiptarë* (Tirana: Shtëpia Botuese 55, n.d. [2010]), 240 pp.

———— *Kadri Hazbiu: krimet dhe vrasja* (Tirana: Shtëpia Botuese 55, 2011).

Djilas, Milovan, *Conversations with Stalin*, trans. Michael B. Petrovich (New York: Harcourt, Brace & World, 1962), 214 pp.

Fischer, Bernd, *Balkan Strongmen: Dictators and Authoritarian Rulers of South Eastern Europe* (West Lafayette, IN: Purdue University Press, 2007), 494 pp.

Frashëri, Kristo, *Historia e lëvizjes së majtë në Shqipëri dhe e themelimit të PKSH-së, 1878–1941* (Tirana: Akademia e Shkencave, 2006), 471 pp.

Gradeci, Sulo, *30 vjet pranë shokut Enver: kujtime* (Tirana: 8 Nëntori, 1988), 424 pp.

Halliday, Jon, *The Artful Albanian: The Memoirs of Enver Hoxha* (London: Chatto & Windus, 1986), 394 pp.

Hoxha, Enver, *Fjalim i mbajtur me rastin e përvjetorit të pare të çlirimit të Tiranës me 17 nëntor 1945* (Tirana: Bashkimi, 1946), 15 pp.

———— *Klika e Titos, xhelat i popujve të Jugosllavisë dhe i minoritetit shqiptar të Kosovës e Metohisë: pjesë nga raporti në Kuvendin Popullor. Sesion i VII i zakonshëm, dt. 1. VI, 1949 mbi planin dy vjeçar të Shtetit* (Tirana: n.p., 1949), 121 pp.

———— *Fjala e mbajtur në mbledhjen solemne kushtuar 40 vjetorit të Revolucionit Socialist të Tetorit (2 nëntor 1957)* (Tirana: Ndërmarrja Shtetëtore e Botimeve, 1957), 39 pp.

———— *Hrushovi në gjunjë përpara Titos* (Tirana: 8 Nëntori, 1977).

———— *Konferenca e Pezës: ngjarje e madhe historike* (Tirana: 8 Nëntori, 1977), 43 pp.

———— *With Stalin: Memoirs* (Tirana: 8 Nëntori, 1978), 224 pp.

———— *Me Stalinin: kujtime* (Tirana: 8 Nëntori, 1979), 218 pp.

———— *Reflections on China*, 2 vols (Tirana: 8 Nëntori, 1979), 783 & 810 pp.

———— *Shënime për Kinën: nga ditari politik*, 2 vols (Tirana: 8 Nëntori, 1979), 760 & 790 pp.

———— *Eurocommunism Is Anti-Communism* (Tirana: 8 Nëntori, 1980), 291 pp.

———— *Eurokomunizmi është antikomunizëm* (Tirana: 8 Nëntori, 1980), 280 pp.

———— *Hrushovianët: kujtime* (Tirana: 8 Nëntori, 1980), 462 pp.

———— *Kur lindi Partia: kujtime* (Tirana: 8 Nëntori, 1981), 455 pp.

———— *The Anglo-American Threat to Albania: Memoirs* (Tirana: 8 Nëntori, 1982), 446 pp.

———— *Rreziku anglo-amerikan për Shqipërinë: kujtime nga Lufta Nacional-Çlirimtare* (Tirana: 8 Nëntori, 1982).

———— *Titistët* (Tirana: 8 Nëntori, 1982), 592 pp.

———— *The Titoites: Historical Notes* (Tirana: 8 Nëntori, 1982), 643 pp.

———— *Vite të vegjëlisë* (Tirana: 8 Nëntori, 1983).

———— *The Khrushchevites: Memoirs* (Tirana: 8 Nëntori, 1984), 492 pp.

———— *Kur u hodhën themelet e Shqipërisë së re: kujtime dhe shënime historike* (Tirana: 8 Nëntori, 1984), 536 pp.

———— *Laying the Foundations of a New Albania: Memoirs and Historical Notes* (Tirana: 8 Nëntori, 1984; repr. Toronto: Nat. Publ. Centre, 1985), 583 pp.

———— *Mes njerëzve të thjeshtë: kujtime* (Tirana: 8 Nëntori 1984), 322 pp.

———— *Dy popuj miq: pjesë nga ditari politik dhe dokumente të tjera për marrëdhëniet shqiptaro-greke, 1941–1984* (Tirana: 8 Nëntori, 1985), 436 pp.

———— *Two Friendly Peoples: Excerpts from the Political Diary and Other Documents on Albanian–Greek Relations, 1941–1944* (Tirana: 8 Nëntori, 1985), 455 pp.

———— *Vite të rinisë: kujtime* (Tirana: 8 Nëntori, 1988), 267 pp.

———— *Kosova është Shqipëri: nga ditari politik*, prepared by Ilir Hoxha, ed. Teuta Hoxha, preface by Ilir Hoxha, introduction by Nexhmije Hoxha (Tirana: Neraida, 1999), 296 pp.

———— *Një jetë për kombin: kujtime dhe shënime*, ed. Ilir Hoxha (Tirana: Neraida, 2008), 506 pp.

Hoxha, Ilir, *Babai im, Enver Hoxha: kujtime, letërkëmbim, publicistikë* (Tirana: Extra, 1998), 205 pp.

Hoxha, Nexhmije, *Jeta ime me Enverin: kujtime*, vol. 1 (Tirana: Lira, 1998), 400 pp.

———— *Jeta ime me Enverin: kujtime*, vol. 2 (Tirana: Neraida, 2001), 392 pp.

———— *Miqësi e tradhtuar: shënime historike dhe kujtime për marrëdhëniet midis Enver Hoxhës dhe Mehmet Shehut* (Tirana: n.p., 2004), 378 pp.

Jaubert, Alain, *Le commissariat aux archives: les photos qui falsifient l'histoire* (Paris: Barrault, 1986).

Kokalari, Musine, *Si lindi Partia Socialdemokrate. Artikuj, shrime, esse, kujtime*, ed. Platon Salim Kokalari (Tirana: Naim Frashëri, 2000), 128 pp.

Kokona, Vedat, *Endur në tisin e kohes: kujtime* (Tirana: Botimet Kokona, 2005), 288 pp.

Lazri, Sofokli, 'Raportet shqiptaro-gjermane', *Klan* [magazine].

Lubonja, Fatos, 'Blloku (pa nostalgji)', *Përpjekja* 24 (2007), pp. 11–31.

────── *The Second Sentence: Inside the Albanian Gulag*, trans. John Hodgson (London: I.B.Tauris, 2009), 224 pp.

Lubonja, Todi, *Nën peshën e dhunës: kujtime* (Tirana: Progresi, 1993), 298 pp.

Milliez, Paul, *Ce que je crois* (Paris: Grasset, 1986).

Ngjela, Spartak, *Përkulja dhe rënia e tiranisë shqiptare, 1957–2010: refleksione për një kohë* (Tirana: UET Press, 2011), 638 pp.

Papa, Robert, *Ngrica mes Uashingonit dhe Tiranës* (Tirana: n.p., 2006).

Pipa, Arshi, *Albanian Stalinism: Ideo-Political Aspects*, East European Monographs 287 (New York: Columbia University Press, 1990), 291 pp.

Plasari, Anastas, 'Takimet e mia me partite komuniste: kujtime historike' [manuscript, Plasari family archives].

Pllumi, Zef, *Rrno vetëm për me tregue. Libri i kujtimeve. Pjesa e parë 1944–1951* (Tirana: Hylli i dritës, 1995), 336 pp.

────── *Rrno vetëm për me tregue. Liria mes dy burgimeve. Pjesa e dytë, 1950–1967* (Tirana: Hylli i dritës, 1997).

────── *Live to Tell: A True Story of Religious Persecution in Communist Albania*, trans. K. Schank (Lincoln, NE: iUniverse, 2008), 296 pp.

Puto, Arben, *Nëpër analet e diplomacisë angleze: planet antishqiptare të Britanisë së Madhe gjatë Luftës së dytë Botërore në bazë të dokumenteve të Forein Ofisit të viteve 1939–1944* (Tirana: 8 Nëntori, 1980), 216 pp.

────── *From the Annals of British Diplomacy* (Tirana: 8 Nëntori, 1981).

Radi, Lazër, *Mirash Ivanaj, kujtimet e një ministry* (Tirana: Lilo, 1996).

────── *I pari gjyq special në Shipëri. 1 mars 1945–13 prill 1945* (Tirana: Reklama, 1997), 139 pp.

Shehu, Bashkim, *L'automne de la peur: récit*, trans. Isabelle Joudrain-Musa, introduction by Ismail Kadare (Paris: Fayard, 1993), 203 pp.

────── *Vjeshta e ankthit: esse*, introduction by Ismail Kadare (Tirana: Albin, 1994; repr. Prishtina: Buzuku, 1997), 174 pp.

────── *Rrëfim ndanë një varri të zbrazët: ëndërr autobiografike* (Tirana: Onufri, 1998; Prishtina: Buzuku, 1998), 129 pp.

────── *Anatomia e bibliotekës së një diktatori* (Barcelona: n.p., 2002).

Sinishta, Gjon, *The Fulfilled Promise: A Documentary Account of Religious Persecution in Albania* (Santa Clara, CA: n.p., 1976), 247 pp.

Spahiu, Bedri, *Testamenti politik* (Tirana: Apollonia, 1994), 136 pp.

Staravecka, Xhelal, *Torturë e terror: Traktet* (Tirana: n.p., 1944).

Themelko, Kristo, *Tirana e përgjakur* (Tirana: n.p., 1996).

Vllamasi, Sejfi, *Ballafaqime politike në Shqipëri (1897–1942): kujtime dhe vlerësime historike* (Tirana: Marin Barleti, 1995), 363 pp.

Index